Foundations in Psychology

Foundations in Psychology

Dr. R.M. Verma
Ex-Principal
Clinical & Neuropsychologist NHS,UK
&
Dr. (Mrs.) Shashilata Verma
Ex-Principal & Professor of Psychology,
Bihar University

COMMONWEALTH

Foundations in Psychology

Edition : **2026**

ISBN 81-7169-782-8

Published by :
COMMONWEALTH PUBLISHERS
4831/24, Prahlad Street,
Ansari Road, Darya Ganj,
New Delhi - 110002
Ph. : 23275511, 23257835
Fax : 91- 011- 23257835
e-mail : commonwealthbooks@gmail.com

Laser Typesetting by :
Rishu Computers
Delhi

Printed at :
Roshan Offset Printers
Delhi

Preface

Psychology as a science has come of age. It has made striking stride and tremendous advance leading to increasing popularity. The subject primarily interests college students, but is also used in professional courses.

The subject matter of Psychology is vast with interdependent areas of interest, relating to human behaviour. The scientific study of human behaviour, therefore, involves the understanding of happenings within the body of human beings, as well as the overt reactions made for survival and adjustment with the complex environment.

Human being is a biosocial entity which functions in relation to outside forces like any other living organism. In order to understand him properly his psycho-physiological processes need to be studied.

The present book is intended to deal selectively with the structures and functions of the nervous system, sensory processes, endocrine system, emotions, motivations and abilities in which biological components play a significant role and also extended to cover the psychological topics of perception, learning, remembering, forgetting, thinking, abilities, and personality.

Ram Mohan Verma
Shashilata Verma

Acknowledgement

Our acknowledgement to authors; Messer E. Hilgard, R. C. Atkinson, R. L. Atkinson, N. L. Munn, L. D. Fernald and P. S. Fernald from whose books some of the ideas and materials were borrowed and adapted.

We also acknowledge invaluable help of Ms. Smita Verma and Dr. Nadeem Mohsin in getting the book organized.

Ram Mohan Verma
Shashilata Verma

Contents

1 Psychology : Its Meaning and Nature

The science of psychology is one of the youngest in the family of science and has got a contentious background. In this vein it seems appropriate to trace briefly the historical forces that shaped the evolutionary growth of psychology as it is today. Initially psychology was described as a science of soul by the philosophers and because of the impossibility in establishing soul a subject matter of study, was replaced by the concept of mind. The study of mind was equated with the study of conscious mental experience and the method of investigating such an experience was adopted as introspection. This meaning of psychology was the brain-child of the traditional philosophers, particularly the British Empiricists from John Locke (1632–1704) onwards to John Mills (1773–1836) and his son Stuart Mills (1806–1873). These empiricists were dualists believing in separate entities of mind and body, but at the same time acknowledging the influence of one upon the other. The striking contribution of these empiricists was that all human knowledge could be gained through experience, through observation and thinking about those observations. A set of concepts was used by them to describe these contents of mind and the ways they were organized.

The contents of mind or the building blocks of knowledge, as they interpreted them, were, composed of sensations and images or ideas. Sensations were regarded as the bases for perception, emotions and other mental processes. Ideas and images were the re-experiencing of those previously experienced sensation. Sensations and images were, further, integrated by 'association'; one sensation could associate and recall another image of another previous sensation and so on. Association, according to them, were easily formed between ideas that occurred together or between those which were similar in form and in nature (See discussion under the chapter Learning) etc. Moreover, these associations could cause merger or change of the original components of ideas and create a different kind of idea or new ideas. In other words, ideas or mental states occurred and combined to change.

The views of the British empiricists and a German philosopher named Herbert (1776–1841) exerted immense influence at the time. Wilhelm Wundt (1831–1920) was greatly impressed by this philosophy and fathered the first psychological laboratory in the world in Leipzig in 1879. This event ushered in an era of scientific study of mental processes. Wundt and his students studied mental events by means of introspection. This method to study consciousness was adopted at Leipzig Laboratory, which gave rise to several important contributions in later times.

The theory and method of study developed at Leipzig were taken to the extreme by an Englishman, Titchener, who trained himself under the tutelage of Wundt. He established a chair at Cornell University in America and wielded great influence on psychologists of his time and led them to study and identify the elements that made up the mental experiences. The group of psychologists specialising in this interest was known as 'structuralist'. These structuralists analysed the mental processes into simple elements of sensations and images using introspection. They believed that images actually carried the meanings of words or phrases etc. They, however, took seriously any 'stimulus error' because it caused mistake in describing mental experiences in simple elements of sensation etc.

The researches of Wundt, Tichener and others were prolific and quite considerable materials of systematic investigation accrued. But these researches did not satisfy everyone. A group of psychologists at the university of Wurzburg in Germany led by Kulpe (1862-1913) opposed the structuralists' theory. The Wurzburg school highlighted the weaknesses of the introspective method and the nature of the subjects' thought content. They showed that some subjects had no sensory or imagined experiences when they lifted weights in the experiments to judge whether one was heavier that the other. The occurrence of imageless thought was recognized by them particularly when intelligent thinking was done. In planning and making decisions, they did not observe sensory related imagery type material, in the content of consciousness. The Wurzberg criticism though suffered from methodological inadequacy, dealt a blow to the existing introspectionism.

Introspectionism was also challenged by the other contemporary schools—Gestalt and Behaviourist. The Gestalt school of psychologists (See discussion under Perceiving) argued that perception could not be analysed into the elements of sensation. Further, they added that the whole perception was a phenomenon in itself and could not be treated as a sum total of parts. The gestaltists' emphasis on the organizational factor in perception was considerable and presented significant evidence to prove that organisation in perception has its own characteristics relatively independent of the physical stimulation.

The death blow to the structuralists' viewpoint came from the behaviourism of Watson (1878–1958). The behaviourists distinguished themselves from other groups of psychologists for two reasons :

(1) They were interested in animal as well as human behaviour, and

(2) They used objective methods of study, particularly controlled observation and experiment in making prediction of behaviour of the subjects. Introspectionism certainly could not provide explanation for how and why animals do what they do. The behaviourists considered 'how and why' as the primary prerequisites of science in order to make psychology a science they strictly and resolutely drew on the methodology of science. Furthermore, they asserted that there were consistent relationships between environmental conditions and animal and human training. The result of behaviourists' movement was found in a rapid advancement of psychological researches, which shaped psychology as a science of behaviours and responses of the organism.

Behaviourists' movement was influenced by the new development in philosophy too. In philosophical thought at the time there was a new approach known as 'logical positivism'.

This group of philosophers stated that statements are meaningful if they could be verified as being true or false. Accordingly, sensations and mental experiences of other people, if not verifiable, were meaningless. A distinction between subjective experience and observable behaviour of the individual was sharpened by the positivists' discourses.

The forces of behaviourists combined with others shook the foundations of psychology as a science of conscious experience and its method of introspection. The theory of mental structure in terms of sensations and images propounded by the structuralists was rejected completely. On the other hand, observable behaviour became the important variable for an objective study.

The development of behaviourism was not a natural consequence of the collapse of analytical introspection, rather it was a result of confluence of other scientific thoughts and practices prevalent at the time. Physics, Chemistry, Biology and physiology were growing and making an impact on psychology. The monumental contribution of the theory of evolution and researches in animal behaviour provided vital clues to the understanding of human behaviour and its adaptive role in the environment. The making of psychology as a science of behaviour and function of the organism to adjust with the environment, therefore, were echoed in the researches in those sciences.

The behaviourists, on the other hand, took the extreme view and tried to explain every human behaviour in terms of S-R (stimulus-response) relationship. The matter reached the stage that a classic Joke can be quoted to illustrate the ridiculous extremism; two behaviourists met in the street, first asked the second 'you are feeling fine today, how do I?' The argument is that we can explain human actions neither in terms of observable behaviour alone nor in simple mechanistic terms. Human beings are not machines and their experiences of pain, pleasure, tension, satisfaction and frustration etc. constitute the real stuff of life and should also be the subject matter of psychology.

Nevertheless, explanations of human behaviour in terms of changes in unobservable mental events are still acceptable. The good old introspection has not been rendered completely dead and obsolete. The use of imagery in learning and recall (mnemonic aids) is increasing. There has been a swing of the pendulum and interests in inner experience have also been revived. In the last few decades of this century, there has been a rise of phenomenological psychology, which cares more for the personal inner experience of the individual than for his outer reactions (See discussion under chapter Personality). In addition, the growth of cognitive psychology has further lent support to this emphasis of individual thinking, which happens internally. The engineering and computer science contributing to the information processing theory (see discussion in the chapter entitled 'Perception') made a perceptible dent in the body-structure of behaviourism by demonstrating the law of behaviour in cognitive terms without reducing it into S-R relationship. The research explosions in psychology of the past few decades, have certainly set people thinking again to include both, behaviour or responses and mental experiences within its fold. Psychology, therefore, can be defined as a science of behaviour processes, that are observable, and neuro physiological changes that happen within, as well as mental processes that can be inferred there from, *viz.* thinking, reasoning, dreaming etc. Thus psychologists' main concern is to study 'why people act as they do'.

2 Psychology : Its Subject-matter and Scope

With the tremendous advances in psychological researches, the subject matter and scope of psychology as a science have widened considerably. In this chapter the major areas of psychological studies will be dealt with. Generally students come across the term 'general psychology'. Strangely enough, this is not a specific branch of study, rather cuts across all the fields and various systems of psychology and unifies them under a discipline of scientific psychology. In other words, this is concerned with epistemology (the study of knowledge and knowing). The principles governing individuals' behaviour are established by means of investigating different kinds and conditions of organisms' reactions. Psychologists today work with other disciplines, like, biology, physical science, sociology etc. to achieve this end.

Experimental Psychology

Experimental psychology can be regarded as the scientific core of modern psychology. It employs systematic and controlled observations and laboratory experiments as methods of study. In olden days experimental psychology was associated with a very narrow field of study, but now a days experimental methods are used widely in pure as well as applied fields of psychological researches. However, the experimental psychologists are known to study sensitivity, attention, perception, motivation, emotion, learning, memory, thinking and problem-solving, reaction time, decision-making, environmental effects, sleep, fatigue, consciousness and dreams etc.

Animal Psychology or Comparative Psychology

Psychologists study animal behaviour in relation to one species from another in the animal kingdom as well as in relation to human being. The comparative picture is very helpful. Besides, the study of simple behaviour of animal provides significant clues for the understanding of complex behaviour of mankind. We know how Pavlov's discovery of 'conditioned reflex' in dogs originated the learning theory of behaviourists (for detailed discussion, refer to the chapter titled Learning). Using animals as subjects in the laboratory studies information regarding drives, needs, and emotions, drug effects etc. is gathered which relate to human responses.

Apart from the laboratory studies on animals, ethological studies by observational means have also contributed to our knowledge on character formation. The ethologists like Lorenz etc. have brought to light the events of natural behaviour.

A combination of experimental as well as ethological interests has brought out significant information in the area of social-emotional response of animals. The effect of mothering and its deprivation on the monkeys has been shown by Harlow. The maternal deprivation caused disturbing effect on the development of social, emotional and sexual behaviour of the animals.

Physiological Psychology

The physiological psychologists, attempt to find out the neuro-physiological bases of human behaviour. It explains the relationship of bodily changes with responses; for example, how do hormones influence sexual behaviour or what area controls our speech or what happens to the memory functions when the brain receives an injury etc.? The current level of research activities in physiological psychology is very high and has been caused by the spectacular advances in technology. The electronic devices, like, electronic microscope, microspectrophotometer etc. have made it possible to study the structure and functions of individual cells; how they connect, how they relay energy and interact with each other, etc.?

The advances in surgery have brought to light the localized functions of the brain-parts. Electrical stimulation of important areas in the brain controlling drives and emotions, such as, hunger, thirst and aggression, etc. has widened the horizon of knowledge of the individual's bio-physical functions. The growth in biochemistry too has contributed enormously to our understanding of human functions. The isolation of RNA and DNA has opened up new vistas for psychologists and studies in learning and memory with the use of those structural variables are underway. A whole range of interests from the brain functions to sleep, dream and consciousness has been lined up for the physiological psychologists to investigate.

Developmental Psychology

The nature of human growth and factors contributing to the human development are the subject matter of this area of Psychology. It spans the period from birth to old age. Some Psychologists study specific areas of development, such as motor development or cognitive or social and language development etc. Some specialize in the study of a particular stage of development, like, infancy or the effects of early experiences on the development of personality, or psychosexual development and so on.

Within the developmental framework, problems such as social attachment, sex-role identification, acceptance of values, mother-child separation, interaction and abilities etc. are studied these days. The focus is on how certain behaviours develop and why they appear when they do?

Social Psychology

Social psychologists study the individual's reactions towards others and others' influence on the individual. How a person's thoughts, feelings and behaviours are shaped and what purposes do they serve—is an important question for the social psychologists to answer. This covers, indeed, a vast area of human behaviour. The fundamentals are as to how an individual perceives himself and others? What impressions the other person forms about forms about him? Why does he like someone and gets fond of him? Why does he dislike some? How does he satisfy his physical and psychological motives? In other words, his personality, beliefs and attitudes, tastes and likings, communication, relationship with the group, society and culture, conflict and co-operation with other members and institutions in the society etc. are the problems of social psychological study.

Social psychology, however, focuses on the situational variables of behaviour as opposed to the developmental and biological factors. The researches in modern times have come up with the interesting pieces of information like, the 'primacy effects', a bias in selecting attributes from first impression of any other individual. We attach much weight to our initial first impression and care less for the latter information. However, if the time interval between the two sets of information, former and latter, gets longer, the 'recency effects' take pace. The recent information pushes the earlier information into the background.

Studies in social psychology also show how individuals' liking of other individuals is influenced. The factors like physical appearance, competence, similarity of people with one another, reciprocal liking and familiarity have been found to be important in shaping favourable reactions of the individual. The role of stereotype and attribution process have been found to be influencing individuals' and group's judgement. The experimental studies on conformity, obedience and compliance against one's wishes on the part of individuals, have revealed interesting results supporting the import of situational variables in social psychology.

Psychology of Personality/ Personology

The study of personality is concerned with a person as whole. Why a person is, what he is? Why he does, what he does? The students of personality are occupied with finding answer to these questions. The theory of personality has got to be comprehensive to tackle manifold issues and problems. It is not concerned with single unit of human function, such as, learning and memory.

Personality study overlaps into different areas of psychology, like developmental, physiological, social and clinical. However, one could study personality in its own right. The personality processes, traits, behavioural correlates, modes of adjustment etc. are some of the important features of personality study.

There are different approaches and viewpoints of personality study, such as, psychoanalytic approach, social learning approach, humanistic approach etc. Some of them have been examined in detail in the chapter entitled 'Personality'.

Psychopathology/ Abnormal Psychology

The study of abnormal behaviour of the individual, its causes and control fall within the ambit of psychopathology or abnormal psychology. The methods of study of this complex phenomenon range from the qualitative to the experimental ones. It also draws on the quantitative method depending upon the problem. Emotional and personality disorders, like neuroses–anxiety, depression, hysteria and obsession etc.; psychosis–schizophrenia, hypomania, manic-depressive etc., addiction, delinquency, sexual problems etc. are studied under this branch of psychology. The applied side of this branch of psychology will be dealt with under the heading Clinical Psychology.

Methodological Research

One of the branches of academic psychology is methodological research. Psychologists specialize in developing tools and apparatuses, methods of experimentation, and techniques of investigation into psychological phenomena. These methodologists concern themselves with the problems of research design, statistics and mathematics applicable to psychological studies, high speed computer designs etc. in collecting and treating data. Psychometricians constructing psychological tests come into this category as well.

Applied Psychology

We have talked about the academic aspects of psychology so far. Now we shall concentrate on the fields of application. The applied psychologists relate academic theories to practice and use the expertise in the service of mankind. When it is said that the applied psychologists use the findings of the academics, this does not imply that they are not concerned with the research in the field, rather they do engage themselves in the research aspect as well as service.

Clinical Psychology

Clinical psychologists are by far the largest in number amongst other practitioners of psychology. Their function is to provide means of understanding, describing and helping individuals with problem(s). In other words, helping the sufferer to help himself is the primary concern of a clinical psychologist. To achieve this end the clinical psychology services are organized under *(a)* Diagnostic investigation, *(b)* Therapeutic help *(c)* Research activities and (d) Organization and administration of the clinical service.

Diagnostic investigation includes assessment and appraisal of mental abilities, learning abilities, brain damage and neurological disorder; physical handicaps, like, visual and hearing disorders; mental handicaps, like, retardation and sub-normality; emotional and mental disorders, like, phobia, anxiety, depression, hysteria and schizophrenia, manic-depressive psychoses; sexual problems, marital difficulties, drug addiction, alcoholism, suicide, crime etc.

Therapeutic services provide help to individuals with problems. Current practices are concerned with psychotherapy of individual and groups of individuals—which include, psychoanalytic type therapy, behaviour therapy, cognitive therapy, gestalt therapy, rational emotive therapy, reality therapy, transactional analysis, primal therapy, and non-directive counselling, vocational guidance and rehabilitation of psychiatrically afflicted persons, etc. Hospital care and management, community therapy and family therapy are also some of the preoccupations of the clinical psychology service.

Research in clinical psychology is directed at the diagnostic and therapeutic methods and their improvement. In modern times clinical psychologists are involved in researching with medical problems, such as, effect of drug therapy and psychopharmacology along with psychiatry.

Organization of clinical psychology service has become a separate entity, which requires expertise particularly in the light of the expanding interest of the authorities in people's mental health and welfare. Planning and administering such services in the form of interdisciplinary approach have assumed great significance and psychologists equip themselves to meet this demand.

Educational Psychology

Psychology applied to education is another important area for practising psychologists. How to educate normal children to the best of their abilities, how to educate gifted children, how to help slow learners, what methods could be used to appraise students' potentials and abilities, how to improve teaching methods, skills, and processes, how to handle the education of emotionally disturbed children etc. are some of the problems where psychologists are required to apply the principles of psychology.

Educational Psychologists use psychological tests, as do all applied psychologists to assess mental abilities and scholastic attainments of students. They are not only diagnosticians, but also act as therapists. Some of them work in the child guidance clinics to help children with problems, some concentrate on remedial teaching.

There are establishments of school psychology service or educational and vocational guidance services where psychologists organize themselves to administer psychological service to students, children and adolescents. They have to work not only with problem children, but with their parents and guardians too. Like any other branch of applied psychology, research and organization of service is important to the educational psychologists.

Counselling Psychology

Counselling psychology shares some of the function of clinical as well as educational psychologists, but largely deals with the problems within the normal range. Ordinarily the counselling psychologists work with students in high schools, colleges and university and give them advice on problems of social adjustment and vocational and educational goal etc. They are also employed by the industrial and business institutions etc. to help adults and employees with their vocational problems. Furthermore, compiling and providing information about jobs and opportunities, helping clients with preparation and embarkation upon vocational plans etc. are also practised under counselling psychology. The use of psychological tests is not uncommon in this field.

Industrial Psychology

The psychologists work in the industry to help raise the production as well as the efficiency of workers. They are concerned with selection and recruitment of employees, right man for the right job, employees training and placement, job analysis and time and motion study etc. The study of working environment; conditions leading to increased production, problem of fatigue, accident prevention on work; attitudes of workers and management, group morale etc. constitute the area of study for the psychologists.

These psychologists use all kinds of techniques from psychological testing to interview and work with the top-level executives down to the middle management, the supervisors at the shop floor. Industrial psychologists do not form a highly organized professional group like clinical and educational groups, but function in a variety of organizations under different names within the same framework of applied psychology to improve the quality of work and workers' efficiency.

Personnel Psychology/ Occupational Psychology

Personnel psychologists are found in a variety of settings of business, government agencies, industry and military etc.

Their major functions are : Selection and recruitment of workers and employees, placement and training of the new and old recruits, evaluation of personnel for promotion and development of managerial talents. Occupational psychologists do the same job of bringing the workers and work together. So the purpose is the same *viz.* to fit the right man for the right job and avoid wastage of human resources. In occupational psychology, on the other hand, the focus is on the individual worker and the job has to be fitted to him, and not him to the job. The man is made to select the right job then to make a success of it.

Organizational Psychology

Organizational psychology spans the area of study relating to the values of human relations in an organizational setting. It covers studies of human relations as process of functioning of any organization, in relating to work-mates, peers, and managers in it. It includes interactions of each one with one another for achieving the objectives of the organization in which they are employed.

The organizational psychologist concerns himself with the diagnosis of structure and functioning of organizations—the effectiveness of structure, leadership and personality of individual, inter-group's and intra-group's behaviour patterns in the organizations. Thus, organizational development is a process to improve an organization's problem-solving abilities in order to achieve success. It may need to deal with problems like, co-operation of working units, sagging morale of workers, loss of profitability and customers' complaints, etc.

Engineering Psychology

Engineering psychology is the offshoot of the advanced technology and has developed after the World War II. It is also known as human engineering, ergonomics, human factors research etc. The aim of this branch of psychology is to study the man-machine system in the working milieu. Actually, it aims at fitting the job to the man. The engineering psychologists help design the equipment and machinery so as to ensure the best use of human energy. The risk of accidents and unnecessary extraneous strain and fatigue, which cause the loss of lives and production are minimized.

These psychologists often work with engineers in developing equipment and instruments. Factors like sensory and motor capacities are effectively investigated by the psychologists and fed to the engineers. Engineering psychologists have contributed significantly to the development of improved radar sets, sonar gear, tracking devices and typewriter keyboard etc . They have also been consulted on the working conditions of airline pilots in respect of the effects of fatigue and circadian rhythms on decision-making etc.

Consumer Psychology

The consumer psychology aims at studying consumer's buying behaviour. Research methods used in market research, public opinion survey and sales promotion etc. have become important theses days. They are all directed towards buying behaviour. Advertising campaigns that we come across are the outcome of such psychology. However, these techniques are used to educate people not only about the consumer products, but also about other programmes, like, health, education or any other government projécts.

Forensic Psychology

This branch of psychology is not given wide publicity. It is also known as legal psychology and practitioners of it are required to give expert testimony to the court of justice on the behaviour of the individual facing criminal proceedings. These forensic psychologists base their testimony on the use of information collected by means of psychological tests and other research methods. The court wants opinion on the defendant's intellectual and social emotional functioning and gives due consideration to such opinion at the time of giving its verdict in the case.

Space Psychology

Space psychology gained prominence in recent years because of the spectacular development in space technology. Psychologists in this field study problems of the individuals who go to outer space or the moon and so on. Some examples of the problem can be cited here; how the weightlessness in the outer space, for lack of gravity, can cause problems of the coordination of body movement? How body temperature will reach the point of boiling in the outer space due to low atmospheric pressure?

The common aim of these specialities is to develop better understanding of human behaviour with a view to developing skill in helping individuals to adjust with the changing world.

Environmental Psychology

In relation to engineering psychology a sub-speciality of environmental psychology has grown since 70's. It can be defined as the study of physical and social surroundings influencing human behaviour. In actual fact, it overlaps the area of traditional engineering psychology, as well as, parts of consumer, community and clinical psychology etc.

The environmental psychology can have two-way interaction a study :

(1) Study of effects of environmental variables on human behaviour, and

(2) Study of the effect of human behaviours on the environment.

The former includes investigation into factors like illumination affecting work, atmospheric conditions, weightlessness, sensory stimulation, *e.g.* noise, etc., social crowding, environmental stress etc. The latter, on the other hand, spans individual's behaviour, such as littering, causing fire to forest, wasting fuel-energy, polluting environment, etc.

The speciality is getting much attention these days because of its linkage with architecture, urban planning and biology etc.

3 Psychology : As A Science

Science means knowledge but knowledge acquired by any means is not scientific. For science, the knowledge must be attained by means of scientific methodology. Thus science leads to our understanding of phenomena by explaining them. When scientists understand the phenomenon they exercise control over it and make predictions about it. Psychology as a science attempts to fulfil these three aims of science, that is understanding, control and prediction, in respect of human behaviour.

In a scientific enquiry all the facts and conditions governing the event or phenomenon have got to be observed objectively. These observations and recordings are termed as data. The data have to be organized and classified in an orderly manner so that they could show a kind of relationship that the investigator is interested in. In psychology, we find data like intelligence test scores, reaction times, and learning curves etc. The data are always verifiable in science. Psychologists like any other scientist try to find commonalties in observations and follow the procedure of measurement to develop a system.

When the phenomenon is fully known and understood, scientists gain control over it and can manipulate it the way they want to. The control certainly facilitates predication. Scientists can say what would happen if similar or the same conditions occurred. This forecast of happening will be the result of the principle discovered in the working of the phenomenon. In scientific studies, the first step to organize investigation is to frame a hypothesis or a provisional assumption and to conduct inquiry in order to prove or disprove the hypothesis or a provisional assumption. Only when the hypothesis is verified that a generalization can be drawn after further investigations. Prediction will then follow suit. Psychologists employ statistical techniques to make prediction.

They predict aspects of human behaviour, which are governed by a particular principle. Human responses can be predicted to be similar under similar environmental conditions and so on.

Scientists have demonstrated the functions of control and prediction. In these days of space flights a space capsule can travel millions of miles, land and return with admirable accuracy. These stupendous successes of science need no exaggeration. However, these strides pre-eminently prove that there is orderliness or a governing principle behind natural function. Thus to discover the cause-effect relationship and orderliness is an article of faith for all scientists and scientific pursuits.

Method of Psychological Study

In a general framework of scientific methodology, we discuss here some of the methods of study employed by the psychologists. First, we must explain the term 'variable', which is commonly used in psychological researches. A variable is any element or factor, which, when measured or studied, yields different values, for example, intelligence, age, learning ability etc. These variables can be designated as stimulus variable and response variable. The two terms depict different characteristics. Stimulus variable is something which initiates, spurs or stimulates the organic activity, like, unit of energy—light and sound waves etc., originating in the external environment. On the other hand, there are stimulus variables, such as, secretion of hormones, level of oxygen etc., occurring within the body, that is, originating in the internal environment of the organism.

The response variable is the reaction caused by the stimulus. A wide variety of responses is observed and studied by psychologists these days. However, a distinction in the nature of response variable must be drawn here. There are two types of response variables overt and covert. Overt responses are expressed outside and occur externally. Covert reactions, on the other hand, occur internally. Physiological responses, like blood pressure, heart rate and body temperature etc. are the examples of covert responses. Stimulus as well as response variables, both, can be external and internal and both are the subject-matter of psychological study.

Psychologists use another terminology to describe these variables of study and call them 'independent' and 'dependent' variables. These terms are used particularly in the context of experimental study. The experimenter varies and manipulates independent variable to find its effect on the dependent variable. Independent variable is operated as an antecedent condition as it is independent of what the subject does, and dependent variable is its function.

Experimental Method

Experiments are generally conducted in a laboratory situation where special equipment is available and where conditions can be carefully controlled, varied and manipulated and precise measurements can be taken. However, experimental methods are not restricted to the laboratory study alone; these can be employed outside the laboratory, too. In other words, it is not a matter of location, but of logic. The experimental study has to follow a procedure and design, which exercises strict controls over factors and conditions that may influence or affect the dependent variable. This also includes examination of the role of the independent variable one at a time, in discovering the causal relationship between independent and dependent variables. Thus in designing an experimental study, one has to be careful about three groups of variables in studying the dependent variable :

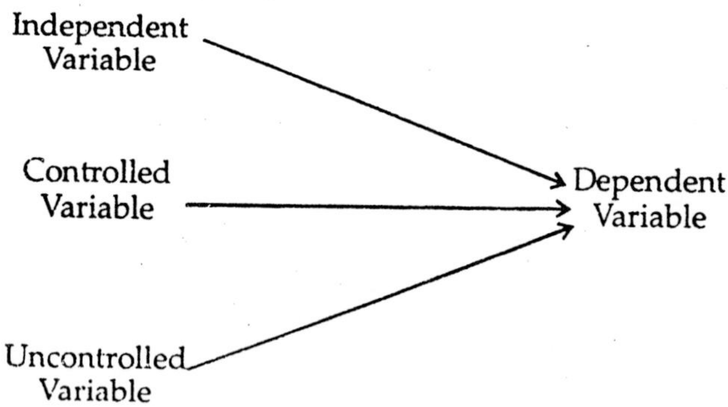

Independent variable can be varied and manipulated while keeping all other variables and conditions constant. Independent variable used in this way, is also called by some as experimental variable, and its manipulation shows whether or not its presence or absence causes the dependent variable or the effect. For example, in an experiment on learning non-sense syllable, the type of activity interpolated between learning the list and its recall is an independent variable, but the length of list, kind of contents in it, exposure time and method of presenting the material etc. are controlled variables and they are kept constant for individual and groups of subjects. Furthermore, subjects or groups of subjects on whom the experiment is carried out come under uncontrolled variables. These uncontrolled variables are allowed to vary roughly for the reason that they cannot be strictly controlled and would not seriously prejudice the result. The best way to deal with an uncontrolled variable is to test it as an independent variable or treat it by statistical means.

Generally in an experiment one independent variable is manipulated at one time to study its effect, although the design can be as complex as to include a whole range of independent variables. The use of advanced statistical techniques can make the employment of more than one independent variable possible. The experimenters have described, therefore, the use of two variables as bivalent and more than two, as multivalent and parametric experiments.

It is important to add that not all independent variables can be varied and manipulated. Some are organismic, such as, age, sex, or physiological condition, which can be matched or controlled through equation of equivalence. The group comparison is one of the techniques and will be explained later.

The dependent variable as a result of, or a function of, the independent variable can be more than one, too. In other words, there can be several responses to one stimulus. The experimental study has to take account of multiple responses as well and treat them accordingly.

We have talked about the control of conditions, known and unknown, which can influence the result or function. Now we shall mention about the method of controlling the subjects or groups of subjects in a psychological study. A matched-pair of individuals or group of individuals is commonly used method in such experiments. The psychologist matches individuals in respect of genetic characteristics, age, intelligence, learning ability, sex, etc. and forms two groups. Both the groups are subjected to the experimental study one as a controlled group and the other as experimental group. The independent variable is manipulated in the experimental group only and not in the controlled group. The functions of the two groups are compared in that context.

The study of psychological phenomenon on co-twins is extremely popular these days due to this factor of control, as they provide an excellent example of heredity control. In animal experiments, hereditary factors are controllable to a reasonable extent by way of in breeding and split-litter technique, but the same is impracticable with human subjects. Therefore, matched comparison method is favoured in human experiments.

When the individual matching procedure is not possible, the researcher turns to equivalent groups. For example, in the learning experiment referred earlier, all subjects who scored about the same could be divided into two or more comparable groups and the experimental variable could be manipulated with in the groups. The equivalent group can be organized on the basis of intelligence test scores and so on. For this purpose, the groups must be large enough to counterbalance the extreme characteristics of one group with the other.

However, in some individual and group studies, the pre- and post- test methodology of study is also adopted. This is very much used in the clinical field and with the drug treatment; the subject is tested prior to the introduction of the independent variable and then treated with it. And after the treatment is completed, the subject is again tested (post-tested) with the same measure. The change, if any, from the pre-test condition will be attributed to the independent variable, in this case a particular drug.

In many psychological experiments 'own control' method is used. It is similar to the one stated above. The same subjects are used in both, the controlled and experimental condition. This method eliminates the errors that the matched group subjects bring in. In such experiments two major conditions of the subject, which are caused by the progression of experiment need to be counteracted. Theses are *fatigue* and *practice* effects that creep in and affect the performance of the subject. If these two effects are not treated as independent variables, they need to be controlled or their effects neutralized. These conditions are the parts of systematic bias in the experiment. The value of control group is much appreciated when we consider these systematic biases in planning and designing psychological experiments. They have to be counter-balanced and neutralized to make the experiment meaningful.

In designing experiments of this kind, a sequence of events needs to be considered which can control or offset these effects of fatigue and practice. Generally **A B B A** design is adopted to offset those effects. For example, we have one condition **A** requiring special activity or the stimulus; therefore and another condition **B** requiring no such special activity or the stimulus, the sequence will be to have the condition **A** first, followed by a rest pause and then condition **B** . Again, after a rest pause, the condition **B will follow** first and condition **A** last with an equal interval in between – **A B B A**. The time interval between these conditions will be kept constant; otherwise time itself will act as an independent variable. Another way to get rid of the practice-effect particularly with the same individual is to randomize the presentation of stimulus variable. Further, the haphazard way of activity or the presentation of stimulus will break the expectation set and distribute the systematic bias.

The subject responds with his expectation and, therefore, does not give the correct reaction. The set unwittingly influences the subject's response. There are many studies available that establish the effects of response set on the part of subjects. The famous example of study with 'placebo' effect in drug treatment can be cited here. Two groups of patients were treated, one with the actual drug and the other group with the dummy drug. The results showed improvement in the conditions of both groups, treated and untreated, because the interested group was expecting good effect as well.

In addition to the above, systematic bias is caused by the experimenter bias effect, itself. This means that the bias of the experimenter influences the result of the experiment. In situations where dependent variable is some kind of subjective assessment, the experimenter bias gets the upper hand unknowingly. The ratings of success in treatment of mental patients have been found to be influenced by the attitude and expectation of the clinicians involved in the research. In order to control the experimenter bias 'double blind' method is advocated these days. This method proved very successful in evaluating the effectiveness of drug. For example, if a drug, whose efficacy has to be tested, is administered randomly mixed with the dummy drug to a group of patients and the experimenter researcher does not know which patient has been given which drug because it is given by a third party, the evaluation of the outcome by the experimenter will be bias free. In other words, experimenter effect will be neutralized.

Another kind of potential bias is the instructions, which are given by the experimenter in such studies. If the experimenter is favouring a certain kind of effect, he might unintentionally explain the task in a way that can give encouragement to the subject. Thus to ward off this unintentional queuing, the procedure of written and standard instructions are followed.

Experimental method fruitfully yields results if the controls are exercised and biases are eliminated and independent variable is precisely manipulated and measured. But, we know, there are many areas in the study of human behaviour and experiences where experimental methods are far from adequate. The results suffer from unnaturality and predictions become impossible.

Observation

Observation method is descriptive unlike experimental method. A careful observation was the first method of scientific enquiry and in some areas, like astronomy, it still is. The study in psychology originally started off with the observation of one's own consciousness and internal experience. The method of introspection discussed earlier was no different from the observation method that we are talking about now. The same, however, could not be very objective.

It is argued that experimentation is also a kind of controlled observation. The difference between the two is that the investigator does not intervene in the natural course of events when he makes his observation, whereas the experimenter does. The experimenter varies and manipulates events and things or aspects of the situation to discover the cause behind the effect.

Observations by themselves are of little use. The fundamental point about observation is that the facts gathered by this technique should make sense and help establish orderliness. Thus a systematic observation is needed under any conditions, naturalistic settings or laboratory conditions, which can lead to evolving principles and deducing conclusions about the functioning of a psychological or natural phenomenon. However, there has been a significant improvement in the technique of objectifying observation, such as, time sampling; observing and recording at definite time, for a definite period, with definite frequency, and definite piece of behaviour at one time, and so on. Furthermore, new gadgets and devices, like, filming, automatic recording etc. are in use these days to make the observation accurate.

The emphasis on naturalistic observation in psychology is important, the behaviour is studied as it occurs in the natural setting. The observer makes unbiased observation and records accurately the events or facts. In areas, like comparative psychology, developmental psychology and social psychology etc. the observational methods have been very successfully employed with valuable results.

Statistical Method

Scientific advancement has been extremely dependent on the development of mathematical sciences. Now-a-days the significance of quantitative relationship between variables of study has been pervading every branch of modern science, from biological to social and anthropological sciences. Statistics, one of the mathematical sciences, has made most impact of all, due to this reason, on these sciences. Francis Galton (1821-1911) introduced it in the field of psychology with his pioneering work on 'individual differences'.

In modern psychology, the use of complex statistical methods is inescapable and there is reason for that. When psychologists study human behaviour, they try to measure and quantify their observations. They also quantify the responses or reactions of the subjects. Because the data, observations and responses, have to be arranged and ordered to facilitate further treatment and understanding. The data in disarray are of no value. Thus they need to be summarized and presented in the quantitative form. Hence the reference to averages, means or modes etc. is much more conveying and communicating than a jumble of numbers.

Statistics in psychology serves a very important purpose. Statistics deals with the samples of behaviour as well as the samples of individuals. Since it is almost impossible to study every individual or every behaviour, psychologists have to be content with the representative samples in their studies. On the basis of sample study they make prediction about the population as a whole, as accurately as the statistical assumptions can permit.

The use of measurement in psychology is indispensable. Even in an experimental study, the statistical treatment of the findings shows the significance of independent variable to dependent variable. How much or in what degree the presence or absence of and independent variable causes the outcome, can be known only by means of measuring the variable and these quantitative results need to be treated statistically to show and establish relationships between independent and dependent variables or cause and effect.

Even when other means of data collection, *viz.*, observation or questionnaire, have been used, the statistical treatment of the data is unavoidable. Many functions and psychological phenomena are explained in terms of associations and relationships, so that one condition could explain the other. Correlation method, amongst other statistical methods, is used by psychologists to examine relationships. Besides, statistical methods to determine variability and differences etc. in the individuals' as well as groups' behaviour are frequently employed by psychologists.

Tests

Psychological testing is another kind of method used by researchers in psychology. Tests of intelligence, abilities, achievements, motor-perceptual skills, anxiety etc. are commonly known. Psychometricians, who specialize in this area, are always improving the old tools and constructing the new ones in order to fulfil the needs of psychological investigation. A test presents a uniform situation to individuals or groups of individuals to elicit specific kind of responses without involving an elaborate laboratory equipment (references to tests are given under personality & abilities). It can show individual's variations and differences in aspects of human behaviour.

A psychological test is meant to be objective, reliable and valid. It provides basis for comparing individual's reactions with its normative data. Tests are frequently used for understanding, preventing, diagnosing and treating behaviour disorders by clinical psychologists. They are employed by other applied psychologists, too. Although the use of psychological tests is widespread they suffer from limitations and need to be used carefully without over-generalizing the results.

Questionnaire

Questionnaires and inventories developed on the objective basis are also used under the banner of psychological tests. Personality tests or inventories in particular fall under this category. Although the assumptions, designing and principles of construction and standardization of these instruments are similar to the tests of abilities and attainments, they still fall short of the reliability and validity criterion of those tests. The reasons behind these shortcomings are the changing conditions and experiences of the person and the environment in which he reacts. However, they are not short of values and the information collected by means of them can be used in conjunction with other data for diagnostic and therapeutic purposes.

Survey Method

Psychologists use survey method to investigate and collect data about the issues of social and political import, consumers' interests and health care etc. They use questionnaire or interview to obtain responses or information. The area of investigation requires a careful planning of data collection. Samples of such surveys are of considerable importance and any predictions made on the basis of unrepresentative samples-study are not of much worth. Similarly, the handling and interpretation of data also need careful consideration as any other psychological research would need.

Case History

Case history is an important source of data about the individual. It helps the psychologist to develop understanding of the individual's problem in proper perspective. In a case history the relevant information about the person is collected from his early childhood in a longitudinal way. It is like preparing a biography of the person with the records of his past events and experiences. The reconstruction of the past is done retrospectively and, therefore, suffers from the limitations of inaccuracy and distortion of facts.

4 Biological Bases of Human Behaviour

Human beings are known to be at the top of the evolutionary process. They share a lot of physical endowments with the other organisms, but they have a lot more of their own, too. These additional physical and physiological structures of the human beings are very intricately complicated. We shall mention here in brief the basic structures and functions of the human organism, which make him behave so differently from other organisms. One cardinal feature of the structures is that they not only exist, but also change and develop in the process of living from birth to death.

Life starts with a single cell, smaller than the head of a pin. The cell is composed of cytoplasm with a nucleus in it. It is covered by a membrane. We know how a cell is born in the ovum (egg) of a mother when fertilized by the male sperm. This single cell divides and multiplies to make many more cells to grow into a human body. The entire human body structure is nothing but an arrangement of cells of different kinds.

The nucleus of the cell contains chemical materials organised in a complicated manner. These materials are called chromosomes. The chromosomes look like coloured bodies when stained on a slide and seen through the microscope. Male and female human beings have 22 and 23 pairs of chromosomes respectively, in their cell bodies. In addition, the male has two single chromosomes unpaired and make up the number of 46 chromosomes. The 23 pairs of female chromosomes are XX combination. The male, on the other hand, has an additional single X and single Y over the twenty-two pairs of Xs. In the process of fertilization if X chromosome of the male enters the female cell, the combination gets XX, responsible for the birth of a female human being. On the other hand, if Y gets into the cell, the combination becomes XY, causing the male sex of the new life.

These fourty-six chromosomes contain 'genes' responsible for characteristics of innumerable magnitude. These genes are inherited from the ancestors. Our being short or tall, black or white, having flat nose or pointed nose, curly hair or straight hair etc. are the products of our genes. Numerous physical, emotional and intellectual characteristics that we come across are the results of these genetic inheritances. These genes are like packets of chemicals strung along the chromosome. It is said that they look like beads on a thread. Now-a-days, one part of the gene is identified as deoxyribonucleic acid (DNA). It is an important scientific break-through and has in store many scientific revelations. These genes, however, interact with each other and with the cytoplasm in the cell resulting into different kinds, shapes and sizes of the cell. The change in the cell inevitably brings about the changes in their characteristics and functions; muscle cells, bone cells, nerve cells, skin cells etc. in the human body—all these are the consequences of the inter and intra-cellular interactions and arrangements. These interacting processes certainly emphasize the role of environment starting from the internal environment to the external one and exemplify the value of heredity and environment in human survival, development and adjustment.

Before we go on to discuss anything else it is important that we should point out about the birth of twins, because twins' study is a vital source of information to psychology and related sciences. Sometimes, instead of remaining as one and single cell organism, the cell forms two or more identical organisms giving rise to twins. If one ovum is formed into two, then we get identical twins. On the other hand, if two ova are present and fertilized separately, the fraternal twins are born. Now-a-days in experimental studies with fertility drugs, five to six ova have been fertilized at the same time in one mother's womb, producing the same number of babies.

A discussion on all the anatomical and physiological structures and functions of the human body will be less than helpful to psychology students at this stage. Therefore, we have singularly selected the nervous system for our discussion here, as the same has a profound significance in understanding and explaining complex human behaviour. The developed nervous system of the human organism is the finest creation of nature, which distinguishes man from the animal.

Like any other part of the human body, the nervous system is composed of nerve cells. The nerve cell is different from other body cells, because it is physiologically excitable and can communicate impulses to other nerve cells, as well as to other kind of body cells like, muscles and glands etc.

The basic unit of a nerve cell known also as a neuron has four parts; the cell body, the dendrites, the axons, and the synapse. The cell body receives inputs or impulses from the axons of another cell directly on its surface membrane or through the dendrites. Both bring the inputs to the cell body, which in turn sums the effect of the inputs. These inputs can be either excitatory or inhibitory.

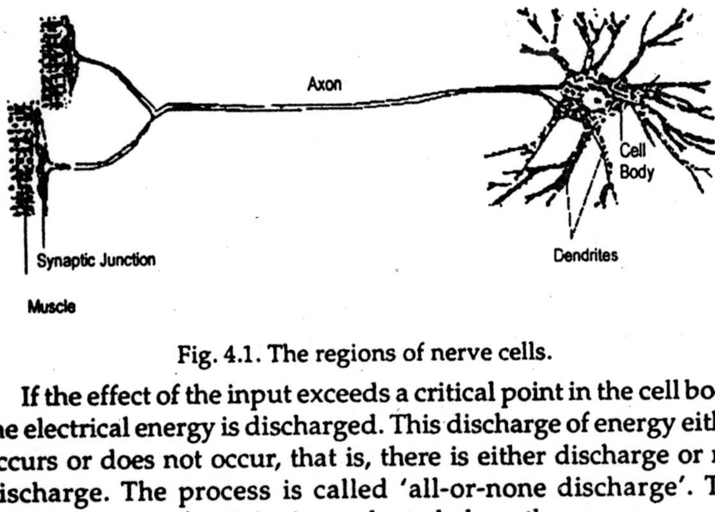

Fig. 4.1. The regions of nerve cells.

If the effect of the input exceeds a critical point in the cell body, the electrical energy is discharged. This discharge of energy either occurs or does not occur, that is, there is either discharge or no-discharge. The process is called 'all-or-none discharge'. The electrical wave of activity is conducted along the axon.

The axon is the output stage of the neuron and transmits the discharge from the cell body to the synaptic region. The synaptic junction, in turn, passes the neural impulse or message to another neuron of the system and so on. It may take it to the gland or muscle as well depending upon the nature of impulse.

The dendrites, as stated earlier, act as source of inputs to the cell body, too. The dendrites form a tree like structure with its network connecting the axons from other neurons as well as with the synapse in addition to the cell body. However, there is an important distinction in the conduction of electrical energy by the dendrites from the axons and that is, they follow decremental conduction and no all-or-none discharge. The decremental conduction means that further out the input from the dendrite, the smaller effect it will have on the electrical potential of the cell body.

The synaptic region is the spot where the inputs first reach and from there distribute in a diversified way. The nerve impulses acting upon the synaptic region release chemical substances in very small quantities. These substances are designated as transmitter substances. The gap between the synaptic region and the next neuron gets filled with these transmitter substances like, acetylcholine, noradrenaline and gamma aminobutric acid (GABA). The effect of the first group of chemicals/substances generates excitation and of the latter produces inhibition. These transmitter chemicals released by the synaptic regions are received by the specialized sites of dendrites and cell body of the next neuron.

The dendrites, cell body and axon can be described as electrical devices that discharge and transmit neural activity, which is electrical in nature. However, the transmission process is not a passive process as we find the copper wire in relation to the electric current. Rather it is an active process involving membranes, which act as pumps to counteract the passage of these substances.

The neuronal inputs are carried from one stage and system to another by the transmitter substances. Each successive neuron receives more than one source of input continuously, sometimes extremely large number of excitatory and inhibitory messages. It is estimated that a single cell in the brain has in the order of 104 synaptic inputs on to the surface of its cell body alone. The capacity of a nerve cell to combine a large number of inputs and messages, excitatory or inhibitory, justified it to be called an information processor.

Now we discuss the complexity of the nerve activity and system operation. The nervous system can be divided into two major parts : (1) Central Nervous System (CNS)—spinal cord, hind brain, mid brain, and fore brain, and (2) Peripheral Nervous System (PNS). The Peripheral Nervous System, again, forms two divisions : *(a)* Autonomic Nervous System (ANS), with para-sympathetic nervous system and sympathetic nervous system, and *(b)* Somatic Nervous System (SNS). The following diagram shows the divisions of the nervous system :

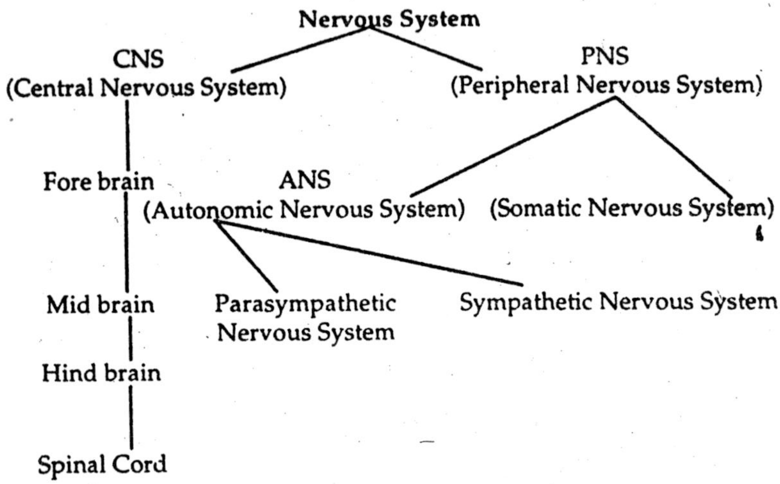

The division characterized here does not suggest that one system is independent of another. On the contrary, there is interdependence of each other, but their characteristic functions are distinguishable.

The Central Nervous System integrates and co-ordinates all the neural functions and includes spinal cord and brain. We have shown the hierarchical arrangement in our figure. The lower end, that is, the spinal cord is a large rope like segment of nerve tissues protected by the bony spinal vertebrae. The cord is a continuous channel through a string of vertebrae and the nerve fibers run from various parts of the body to and from the brain within this cord. This is a projection of the Central Nervous System and forms the backbone. At each vertebra there are two openings, one in the backside of the bone and one in the front through which the nerves pass. The back root is called dorsal root and the sensory nerves (afferent nerves) enter the spine through this, and the front one is the ventral root through which the motor nerves (efferent nerves) leave the spinal cord. The white matter of the spinal column is composed of the ascending and descending neurons. There is a link between the dorsal and ventral paths by a specialized group of nerve cells known as inter-neuron connection or association neuron. The inter-neuron brings the sensory and motor neurons together. The inter-neuron connection has a butterfly shape of gray matter, which is situated in the centre of vertebrae.

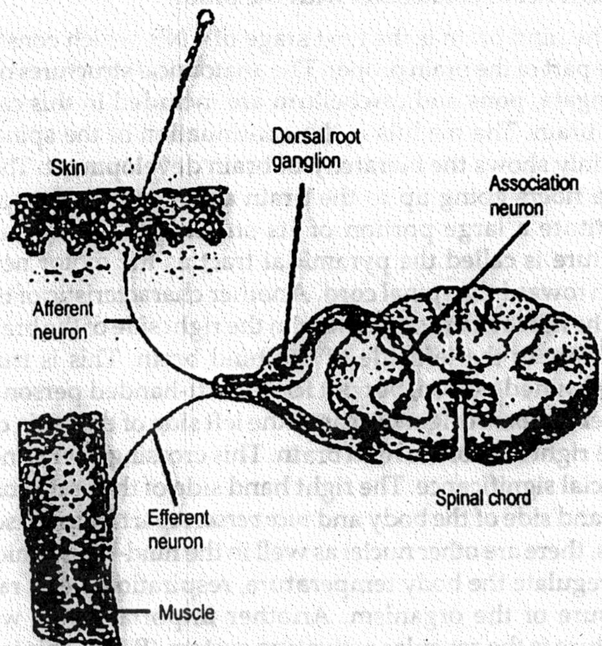

Fig. 4.2. Three neuron reflex arc.

The spinal cord is the basis to organize the behaviour of the organism. The simplest form of behaviour performed at the spinal level is a 'reflex'. For a reflex action the brain does not have to be involved. There is a reflex pathway for such simple activities. The sensory nerves carry the impulse through the dorsal root and the motor nerves take it out to the muscle or other part via-ventral root mediated by the inter-neurons. The arch is complete at the simple level. We find examples of reflexes like, blinking reflex or grasping reflex or knee-jerk reflex and so on in our lives. There are studies to show that some of the behaviours of animals can be performed through the spinal reactions alone even if the brain is disconnected with the spine. The experiment is described as 'spinal preparation' when the nerve pathways between the brain and spinal cord of the animal were severed and the animal still scratched when irritated, micturated and defecated and showed signs of sexual behaviour. Though the spinal cord mechanism can control and maintain behaviour patterns for a while, its function is generally in tune with the centrally coordinated behaviour through nerve connection with the brain.

The hind brain is the next stage of CNS, which constitutes the outer part of the brain proper. The anatomical structures of medula-oblongata, pons and cerebellum are included in this category of hind brain. The medula is the continuation of the spinal cord. It certainly shows the hierarchy of brain development. The sensory nerve fibers going up to the brain and down to the spinal cord constitute a large portion of its structures. The surface of the structure is called the pyramidal tract as the motor nerves pass down toward the spinal cord. Another characteristic of this part is that the nerve fibers originating in the right side of the brain crosses over here to the left side of the hind brain. This is true for the right-handed person, but not for the left-handed person in whom the nerve fibers originating into the left side of the brain cross over to the right side of the hind brain. This crossing over of nerves has a special significance. The right hand side of the brain controls the left hand side of the body and *vice versa*. Apart from sensory nerve fibers, there are other nuclei as well in the hind-brain which control and regulate the body temperature, respiration, heart rate, blood pressure of the organism. Another important part within the structure is the reticular activating system (RAS). This is a system of neural circuits that extends from the lower brain-stem up to the cerebrum traversing through some of the other central core structures. Many incoming and outgoing nerves pass through RAS either directly or nearby connecting it with the smaller branches of the main nerves. The RAS controls the state of arousal or awareness, from sleep to waking state and from diffuse awareness to the most alert attention. It is described as 'consciousness switch'. Lesions in this system produce permanent coma. Furthermore, the RAS plays an important role; when several messages enter the nervous system simultaneously, it decides which one is to be selected for transmission to the higher center and which one to be toned down or ignored.

The hind brain reticular formation has an influence on the spinal cord mechanisms too. It can facilitate or inhibit spinal reflexes and voluntary movements by its action on inter-neurons and alpha motor-neurons in the spinal cord. Thus stimulating the reticular formation while activating a reflex will lead to a faster rate of activity in that area.

The next structure in the hind brain is that pons, which means bridge. The bridge, therefore, contains nerve fibers that connect the two hemispheres of the cerebellum. The cerebellum is another structure of the hind brain and is situated above the dorsal surface of the hind brain. It co-ordinates muscular movements. The sensory information from the muscles, tendons and joints and from the sensitive structures of the inner ear which gives the idea of position of the body in relation to the force of gravity are received in this region of the hind brain. It uses extra-pyramidal system to send output to the brain as well as down to the spinal cord to control the alpha motors neurons. The pyramidal system mentioned earlier and extra pyramidal system have a complimentary function in controlling and co-ordinating motor activities.

Upwards to the hind brain is situated the mid brain. The mid brain chiefly concerns itself with the relay function by joining the hind brain to the fore brain. The reticular formation as well as the

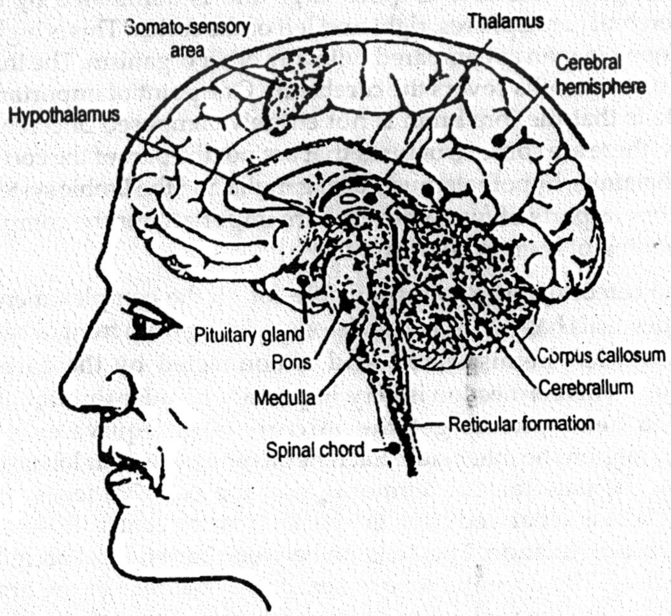

Fig. 4.3. Reticular formation in mid brain.

ascending and descending sensory and motor pathways are extended in this region as well. Like the hind brain, mid brain has specific role to play. There are neurons of special kind which have discrete functions. The reticular formation of mid brain influence the higher regions in the brain and is described as ascending reticular activating system (ARAS). However, there is a difference between the natures of the sensory systems and the reticular formation. In the classical sensory system the responses of the nerve cells are highly specific to some features of a stimulus modality. The reticular formation limits, on the other hand, are usually multi-model, that is, they may respond vigorously to more than one stimulus modality. For instance, it may respond to auditory, tactile and visual stimulations at the same time. Another distinction is that the reticular neurons get habituated by repeated stimulations and reactions wane, unlike other sensory systems where response is always aroused by the presentation of stimuli.

The fore brain is the recent of the three major brain divisions in order of evolution. This is the region, which is of great interest to psychologists. This area is quite large and is dominated by the two cerebral hemispheres, right and left of the cortex. This is highly developed in man as compared with any other organism. The thick layer of nerve cells covers the cerebrum. One point of importance to note is that the fore brain is not entirely composed of cerebral cortex, there are some structures that are not the part of the cortex, like, thalamus, hypothalamus, basal ganglia and the limbic system, but work as parts of fore brain and are important for the complex functioning of human behaviour.

The cerebral cortex is responsible for all the complex mental activities. This has two major divisions running from front to back, right and left hemispheres, and is connected by the corpus callosum. This connection is very important because through this the two hemispheres get the mirror-image equivalents of happenings on the other side. Each hemisphere has four lobes; the frontal, the parietal, the temporal, and the occipital lobes. The frontal lobe is separated from the parietal by the central fissure or the fissure of Rolando. The division between parietal and occipital is not clear. The occipital lobe is situated at the rear of the brain adjoining both the parietal and temporal lobes. The temporal lobe is marked at the side of the temples and is separated from the frontal lobe by the lateral fissure or fissure of Sylvia.

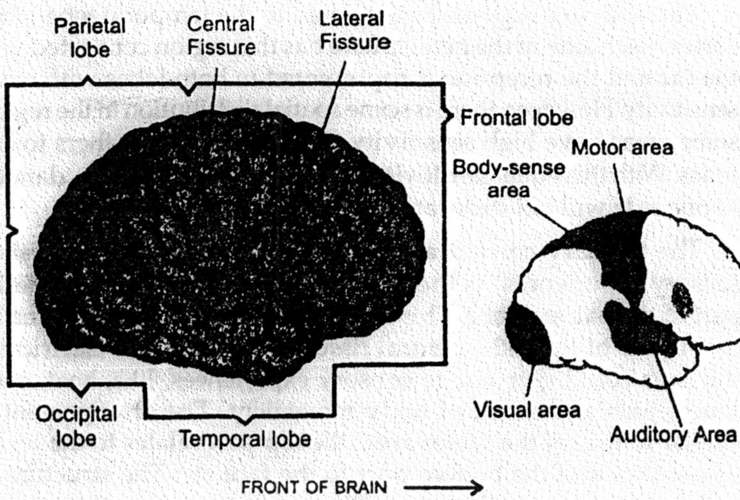

Fig. 4.4. Localization of function in the human cortex.

We can examine now the three types of major functions performed by the cerebral cortex : sensory, motor, and association functions. Some of the senses have specialized areas in the cortex. For example, the occipital lobes are the region for visual sensation. The striate area in particular in the visual cortex or occipital lobe receives impulses sent by each eye. The ability to differentiate visual details depends on the dispersal and distribution of impulses in the area. Some interesting studies with electrical stimulation in this part of the cortex reveal significant results showing that response from the visual cortex differs in an orderly way. Some cells respond to the horizontal light and others to vertical light. These experiments were done on cats and monkeys. The researchers argue that the visual sensory system is organised to perceive the aspects of form and movement and not to receive the points or waves of light (Hubel & Wiesel, 1965).

The research with electronic stimulation in the blind people's visual cortex gives further encouragement to the scientists to understand the electrodes was implanted in the visual cortex of the two blind subjects and after electric stimulation, those subjects experienced patterns of visual sensation (Dobelle and Others, 1974).

The auditory experience is related to the temporal lobe of the cortex. Each side of the hemisphere has this region connected with the ear and the reception is represented in both lobes with equal sensitivity. However, there is some spatial distribution in the region, some areas have high sensitivity to high tones and others to low tones. With this equal sensitivity to the two temporal lobes, damage to one side will not dislocate the hearing functions.

The primary cortical area for body feelings (somesthesis—sensory experiences) is the sensory area located on the anterior part of the parietal lobe. This is separated from the motor area by the fissure of Rolando (central fissure). If stimulated electrically, this area could give rise to sensory experiences, like, heat, cold, touch, pain and sense of body movement. The arrangement is similar to that of the motor area; the top part relates to the lower extremities and the bottom part to the face etc. The structure in both hemispheres is the same. Disease and injury in the sensory area can result into the process of sensory disturbance but a complete loss of sensation, strangely enough, is infrequent. Possibly, these senses do not have clearly established locations and are mediated at the sub-cortical levels of the brain.

Motor area is another part of the cortical structure that has been identified to be located in front of the central fissure. These parts are represented on both hemispheres of the brain. Electrical stimulation to this part produces movements. If the top part of it is stimulated, the movement of toes and extremities can occur.

Similarly, if the bottom part is stimulated, the movement of tongue and mouth etc. can be produced. In the event of damage or injury to this motor area, man develops paralysis of the limb. As stated earlier, the right-hand side movement is controlled by the motor area of left-hemisphere and the left-hand side movement by the right-hemisphere, so the paralysis of the limb will indicate the damage to the opposite area.

Language areas are generally organised along both the cerebral hemispheres except the speech, which is controlled by the left hemisphere alone. The speech area is localized above the lateral fissure in the frontal lobe. This area is also called as 'Broca's area' discovered by him a long time ago. Producing speech sound, involving tongue and jaws etc. is controlled by this area. Damage to this causes speech impairment. A near-by region to this in the

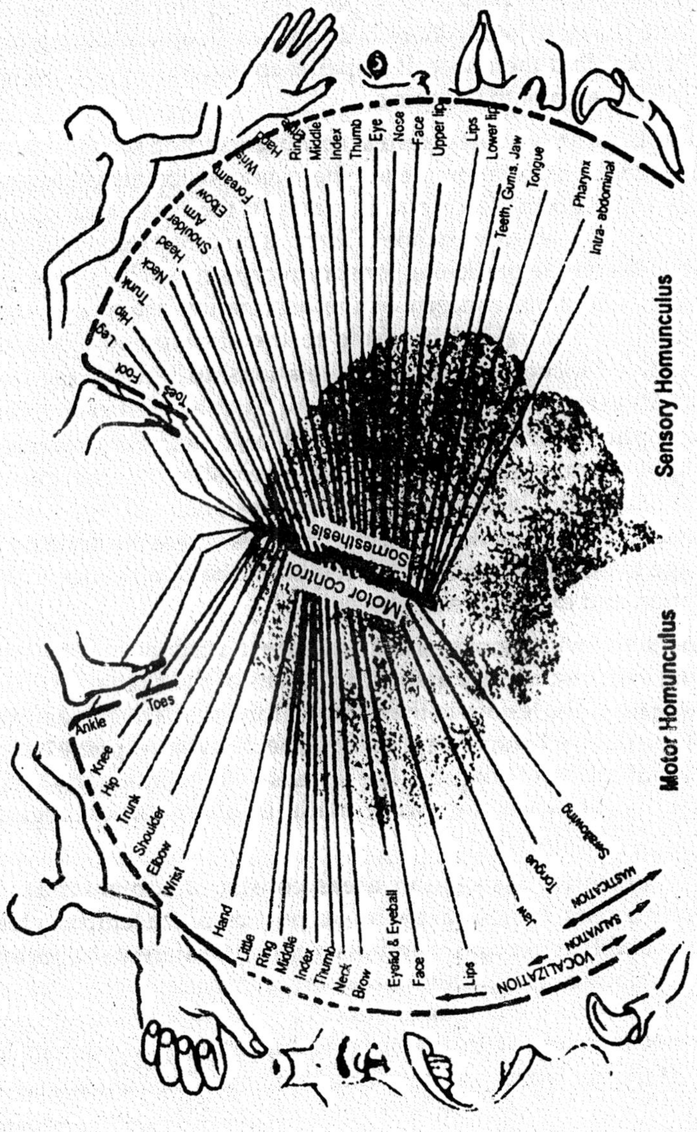

Fig. 4.5. Specialized sensory and motor areas. (Adapted from penfield and Rasmussen, 1950)

frontal area is involved in understanding speech, in writing words. Generally, spoken and written language abilities are located in the left cerebral hemisphere of most people, except for the left-handed in which the right hemisphere is dominant. People suffering from the 'stroke' find their speech impairment caused by the damage to the left—area of their brains.

The large area of the cerebral cortex excluding sensory-motor areas is called association areas. These association areas integrate inputs and information from all parts of the brain and include more than one sensory channel. There is no direct dependence of these areas on the particular sensory receptors, such as, eyes and ears etc. The main concern of the association areas is to store information and relate the same to the stimulation. Thus the associative function is to establish relationship between the store information and the stimulation present. Such a function is noticed in perception, learning, memory and thinking etc. For example, a red light might stimulate and arouse sensation of that kind in occipital area, but its meaning as a danger signal will be the result of the associative function. In some diseases where the disorder or damage to the associative tissues happens, the significance of that sensation and experience is not realized.

In a study with monkeys, the evidence to attribute the problem-solving behaviour to the association areas of the frontal lobe was investigated. The lesions in their frontal lobe affected their abilities to solve a delayed-response problem. The delayed-response deficit was significant and unique to the lesions in the frontal cortex, as it did not occur when they were made in other cortical regions (French & Harlow, 1962).

The posterior association areas consist of sub-areas along different senses. Lesions in the lower portion of the temporal lobe impairs ability to recognize and discriminate different shapes and forms (Pribram, 1969). Other areas around the temporal lobe are concerned with the language function. The tissue damage here does not interfere with the speech, but creates a problem for understanding words and recalling them etc. The disease known as 'dysphasia' is associated with the damage of this area. Since the motor function of speech is not destroyed, a person can utter words, with no significance.

Some investigation of the association areas in the temporal lobe has been very interesting. In a study, the electric stimulation of the area revived a child-hood scene unusually vividly and musical tune heard and forgotten long time ago. The memory could be turned on and off by manipulating that area (Penfield, 1969).

In this context it is appropriate to mention the experiments with the split-brain subjects. These studies were conducted on the subjects whose brain's two hemispheres had been separated by severing the connecting Corpus Callosium. These were the people who were the victims of accidents and brain-surgery was performed to save their lives. Studies on these subjects confirm how the left-hemisphere and the right hemisphere of the brain are involved in the specialized activities of verbal and motor functions. The left hemisphere receives no information about what the left hand is doing, because of you remember, the information goes to the right side of the brain. Similarly, the right half does not get the message of what the right hand is doing , because the information goes to the opposite side.

As referred to earlier, the forebrain is not entirely composed of cerebral hemispheres, it includes other structures as well. Within these layers of structures a few identifiable for specific functions deserve mention, such as, the thalamus and the hypothalamus, the basal ganglia and the limbic system.

The hypothalamus and the limbic system have been dealt with in the context of motivation and emotion later in this book. We shall state briefly the characteristics of the thalamus and the basal ganglia here. The thalamus lies deep in the cerebral hemispheres and is symmetrically arranged around the midline of the brain. All sensory modalities with the exception of olfactory system (sense of smell) pass through the specific nuclei in the thalamus. It plays an important role in the analysis and transmission of sensory information between the spinal cord and cerebral cortex. However, a number of thalamic nuclei do not have specific cortical projection, rather they project diffusely to the whole cortical area. Among them the reticular nucleus is one which receives the outputs from the reticular formation and then projects fibers to the widespread area of cortex.

The basal ganglia are a structure in the forebrain, which sits on the top of thalamus and connects the cerebellum and the motor area of the cerebrum. It has predominantly a motor function and affects movements of the body and its co-ordination.

All areas of the brain are not equipotential. Some functions are localized in the fairly circumscribed areas of speech; recognition of spoken words, and production of motor responses. Many different brain regions, on the other hand, are involved in the higher mental processes such as reasoning and problem solving. In addition, many functions are duplicated in more than one brain area. Consequently if one part is damaged, the other part takes over. Although there are many spectacular advances in knowing the brain functions, still very little is known.

The next part of the nervous system is the peripheral nervous system (PNS). As the name suggests this system includes all those nerve cells and fibers that are lying outside the central nervous system that is, spinal cord and brain. However, there is one exception with regard to the optic nerve, which is considered as a part of the central nervous system tract. The diagram shows two divisions of the PNS, somatic nervous system and autonomic nervous system. We shall deal with the somatic nervous system here. The autonomic nervous system is discussed under emotion. The somatic nervous system consists of all the nerves that convey commands from the brain or spinal cord to the muscles in the body and take the impulses from the receptors or sense organs to the brain and spinal cord. The fibers conducting these impulses to and from are sensory (afferent) and motor (efferent) nerve fibers. Some of these may be four feet long, for example, extending from the spinal cord to the toe. These afferent and efferent nerve fibers have been identified on the basis of their location along the brain and spinal cord and with reference to the body regions in which they emerge. There are forty-three pairs of nerves in this PNS, out of which twelve pairs are called cranial nerves because they connect directly with the cranium, a space in the brain known as cranial cavity. The rest of the thirty-one pairs are named spinal nerves. The table 4.1 will show the position and function of each of the cranial nerve.

The spinal nerves are arranged in a regular order along the spinal cord and classified as they emerge. The distribution of the spinal nerves is presented in the table 4:2.

The somatic division of the peripheral nervous system as

Table 4.1 : The Cranial Nerves

Name	*Origin*	*Afferent Intervention*	*Efferent Intervention*
1. Olfactory	Olfactory bulb	Muscosa of Nose	None
2. Optic	Diencephalon (upper end of brain stem	Retina of eye	None
3. Oculomotor	Midbrain	Eye muscles (except two)	Eye muscles (except two)
4. Trochlear	Mid brain	Superior oblique eye muscle	Superior oblique eye muscle
5. Trigeminal	Pons	Skin and deep tissues of head and face	Chewing muscle
6. Abducens	Pons	Lateral rectus Eye muscle	Lateral eye muscle
7. Facial	Medulla	Taste buds of anterior 2/3 of tongue	Facial muscle and salivary gland
8. Acoustic	Medulla	Inner ear and semicircular canals	None
9. Glossophary-negeal	Medulla	Throat, rear of tongue and taste buds on posterior 1/3 of tongue	Swallowing muscles and one salivary gland
10. Vagus	Medulla	Thoracic and abdominal viscera taste buds on epiglottis, skin and external ear	Muscles of heart other viscera, speech and swallowing
11. Hypoglossal	Medulla	Tongue muscles	Tongue Muscles

presented above provides inputs to and out puts from the brain by acting like a passive agent. In other words, the system just relays and transmits impulses and energies to the brain and back to the body, but does not control and integrate its functions. This is done by the central nervous system. The peripheral nervous system therefore, is the extension of the central nervous system and works for it.

Table 4.2 : Classification of the Spinal Nerves in Man

Name	*Pairs Included*	*Number*	*Location Along Spinal Cord*
1. Cervical	1 through 8	8	Neck
2. Thoracic	9 through 20	12	Chest
3. Lumber	21 through 25	5	Loin
4. Sacral	26 through 30	5	Sacrum
5. Coccygeal	31	1	Coccyx

Furthermore, although the autonomic nervous system (ANS) is dealt with under emotion, it seems necessary to relate its function with somatic nervous system and, thus, to put the two parts of the peripheral nervous system in perspective. The somatic nervous system mediates adjustments of the organism to the external environments, whereas the autonomic nervous system mediates adjustment within the internal environment of the organism. Accordingly, the somatic nervous system includes all those parts of the nervous system, central and peripheral, which transmit impulses from the receptor organs and on return delivers the motor impulses to the striated musculature of the limbs. On the other hand, the autonomic system includes all those parts of the central and peripheral nervous systems that innervate the cardiac muscles, smooth muscles of the intestine, urogenital tract, blood vessels and certain endocrine glands. As a matter of fact, both the systems influence each other.

Endocrine Systems

Before we conclude our discussion on the general biological bases of human behaviour, we would like to bring in a system, which, though not a part of the nervous system is considerably influenced by the functioning of the nervous system. In turn, it influences the nervous system as well. That referred to system is the system of endocrine glands, which has distinctive bio-chemical functions to perform and on whom depend man's physical, mental and emotional growth and maintenance of life.

The endocrine glands fulfill a maintenance function in the body by secreting chemicals known as 'hormones'. The endocrine glands mean ductless glands, so the hormones are directly secreted in the blood stream and circulated all over the body. These hormones are important to utilize food that is eaten, generate and conserve energy, and produce living tissues for the body. It maintains the metabolism that is the balance of functions of all systems in the human body. In view of these vital functions, one endocrinologist has said, "we are terribly at the mercy of our endocrine glands".

We shall outline briefly the salient features of the endocrine system now. The main glands of the endocrine orchestra are, the pituitary, thyroid, parathyroid, adrenal and gonads. The pituitary gland is the master gland of the endocrine orchestra as it stimulates and integrates all other glands' functions. All the endocrine glands act in tune with each other and dysfunction in one causes disruption in the other. The pituitary gland is a small structure situated at the base of the brain. It has anterior and posterior lobes. The details of hormonal secretion of these two lobes along with other glands are presented in the tabular form towards the end of this chapter. We shall pick out a few of the anterior pituitary secretions that are of vital significance. The growth hormone secreted by this gland is responsible for the growth and development of the body. If there is a hypo function (under-function) the individual will not grow and become a dwarf. On the other hand, if there is a hyper function (over-secretion), the growth will be that of a giant. Another important hormone secreted by the anterior lobe of the pituitary gland is the adreno-cortico-tropic hormone (ACTH), which stimulates the adrenal gland to function and to create several sources of life-maintaining chemicals. The pituitary also influences gonads (sex gland) functions.

Thyroid and parathyroid are other sets of glands in the endocrine system situated near the base of the neck, in front as well as behind, respectively. The effect of thyroxin, a hormone secreted by the thyroid gland is significant. It affects the general vigour of the person. Its under-functioning causes a disease known as 'cretinism', which reduces intelligence along with the body. The over functioning, on the other hand, produces tension and causes personality disturbance.

The adrenal gland or the supra-renal gland is another major member of the endocrine system. It is situated above the kidney in the body. There are two structures of this gland, inner and outer, called medulla and cortex, respectively. The adrenal medulla secretes adrenaline and noradrenaline, and the adrenal cortex secrets several steroids (chemical substances). The secretion from the former is needed to meet extra energies for the emergencies (under emotional arousal condition), and the latter provides for general physiological functions of living, vigour and strength. The under-activity of the adrenal gland can cause breakdown of the physiological functions and the over-activity can create other problems including premature growth.

The gonads are sex glands; in female they are called ovaries and in the male testes. The location of ovaries is in the pelvic region and testes in the testicles. The functions of sex glands have been discussed under motivation. They have special function but are still regulated by the pituitary and adrenal glands.

The hormones and their functions are summarized in the following table :

Table 4.3 : Principal Hormones and Their Major Functions

Gland	*Hormone*	*Major Functions*
1	2	3
1. Anterior Piututitary	1. Thyrotrophic (TTH)	Stimulates thyroid secretion.
	2. Adrenocortico-trophic (ACTH)	Stimulates secretion of some hormones of adrenal cortex.
	3. Lactogenic (Prolactin)	Stimulates milk secretion by memory glands.
	4. Leteinzing(LH)	Development of interstitial cells of testes and ovary, corpus luteum.
	5. Follicle-stimulating (FSH)	Development of spermatogenic tissue in male and follicle in female
	6. Growth (STH)	Stimulate growth.
2. Posterior Pituitary	1. Oxytocin	Excites nonstrained muscles especially of uterus, excites memory glands.

(Contd....)

1	2	3
	2. Vasopressin	Produces rise in blood pressure.
	3. Antidiuretic	Prevents loss of water through kidney.
3. Thyroid	Thyroxin	Influences metabolic rate.
4. Parathyroid	Parathormone	Maintains calcium and phosphorous balance in blood.
5. Islett Cells in Pancreas	Insulin	Necessary for the utilization of blood sugar.
6. Adrenal Cortex	Cortical Steroids	Increase carbohydrate metabolism, sodium retention and potassium loss; some androgenic and estrogenic effects.
7. Adrenal Medulla	Epinephrine (Adrenalin) Norepinephrine (Noradrenalin)	Increased sugar output by liver, stimulates most sympathetic nervous system end organs (differentially).
8. Ovary	Oestrogen	Produces female primary and secondary sex characteristics.
	Progesterone	Prepares uterus for implantation of embryo.
9. Testes	Androgen (Testosterone)	Sexual arousal: produces primary and secondary sex characteristics.

5 Sensory Processes

Sensory processes are extremely important for our knowing and doing anything in the environment. They involve the nervous system, already discussed, along with receptors and sense organs that receive and mediate the stimulations from the environment. There are multitudes of stimuli impinging on our sense organs and those are to be selected, received and processed for interpretation by the brain.

From the time of Aristotle five senses; vision, hearing, smell, taste and touch have been recognized. An addition of motor sense later made them six. But people are critical now-a-days about this view of sensitivity and think that the man possesses more than these sensitivities. However, some of these sensory capacities will be examined here. The sensitivity of an organism depends upon the structure of its receptors, which are connected with the sense organs. Every sense organ has minute receptors to receive and process special kind of stimulation such as, light, sound, chemical stimulation and other kinds of energy.

Sensitivity of the receptors varies from organism to organism. All animals attend to their environments, in their own ways and with special sensitivity. For example, dogs have sensitivity to receive sound frequencies of a higher range than other animals and man. Pigeons have a visual acuity of much greater degree than others. However, human beings have a wide range of sensitivity.

We begin with the visual sensation. This sensation is dependent upon the structure of the eye and connected optic nerve. The eye is sensitive to that part of electro-magnetic energy known as light, which travels through space. The energy forms variable waves in motion, from very short cosmic rays to long radio waves. All wavelengths of light are not perceptible to the human eyes; Man can receive light waves of certain range, from 380 (nn) nano-meters to about 780 (nn). Beyond this range, that is, lower than 380 nn and higher than 780nn, the sensitivity is out of bounds for a man. Furthermore, the distribution of light waves gives different colours to see. For example, if a white light is passed through a prism, a visual spectrum is produced as we see in the rainbow. The longer waves give the red and the shorter ones the violet on the spectrum.

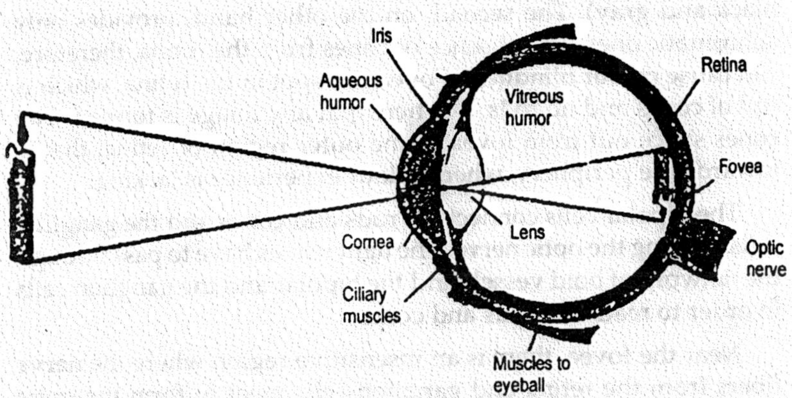

Fig. 5.1. A cross-section of the left human eye.

The light waves pass through the outer covering of the eye, known as 'cornea'. The cornea is tough, glossy and transparent. After it, the space is filled with viscous substance called 'acqueous humour' up to the lens. In other words, between cornea and lens, there is acqueous humour. The shape of the eye is maintained and transparency provided for the light to pass through because of this humour. The amount of light passing into the eye is controlled by the pupillary opening; the constriction of pupil helps adjustment to intense light and dilation to low light. This constriction and dilation of pupils is regulated by the autonomic nervous system.

The lens focuses the light on the retina. The retina is a photosensitive surface coated by the tough fibrous tissues known as choroid and sclerotic coats. The lens also adjusts curvature to focus on the distant object as well as nearby object reflexively according to the requirement. This accommodation process is affected by the ciliary muscle and the attached suspensory ligament. The retina, being the main instrument of photosensitive reaction is very important structurally in providing visual sensation. It is the inner lining at the back of the eye and is composed of three layers : (1) the rods and cones, (2) the bipolar cells, and (3) the ganglion cells. The rods and cones are the near layer of the three and are photo-sensitive cells. They convert light energy into impulses.

The cones are active in the daylight vision and the rods function under reduced illumination. The first provides both chromatic colours (red, green, blue etc.) as well as achromatic colours (white, black and gray). The second, on the other hand, provides only achromatic ones. The absence of cones from the retina, therefore, can cause colour blindness. Fovea is a spot in the retina, which is full of cones and no rods. It is here that any image is formed. The cones space out from fovea to the outer region of retina, that is towards the periphery, where colour experience is lacking.

The bipolar cells connect the rods and cones and the ganglion cells forming the optic nerve. The light waves have to pass through the network of bold vessels and the bipolar and the ganglion cells in order to reach the rods and cones.

Near the fovea, there is an insensitive region where the nerve fibers from the retina and ganglion cells meet to form the optic nerve. At this spot no visual experience occurs and, therefore, it is called a blind spot. Although there is a blind spot in our eye(s), we are not aware of it as it never comes in the way of our seeing. The optic nerves from each eye go to the visual cortex, occipital lobe where the interpretation of visual experience occurs. However one thing important to note is that unlike other sensory-motor arrangements the nerve fibers from the right eye go to the right cerebral hemisphere and from the left eye to the left cerebral hemisphere. Other fibers from the right eye go to the opposite hemisphere to the left and from the left to the right hemisphere crossing at optic chiasma. Thus due to this interconnection of fibers an injury into the occipital lobe of one hemisphere can cause blindness to both the eyes.

In the visual cortex the cells have different arrangements in relation to one another. A number of lateral geniculate cells with their centres lying in a straight line connect other cells. Consequently, the excitability of cells in the visual cortex is differential in nature. Some of these present a particular orientation.

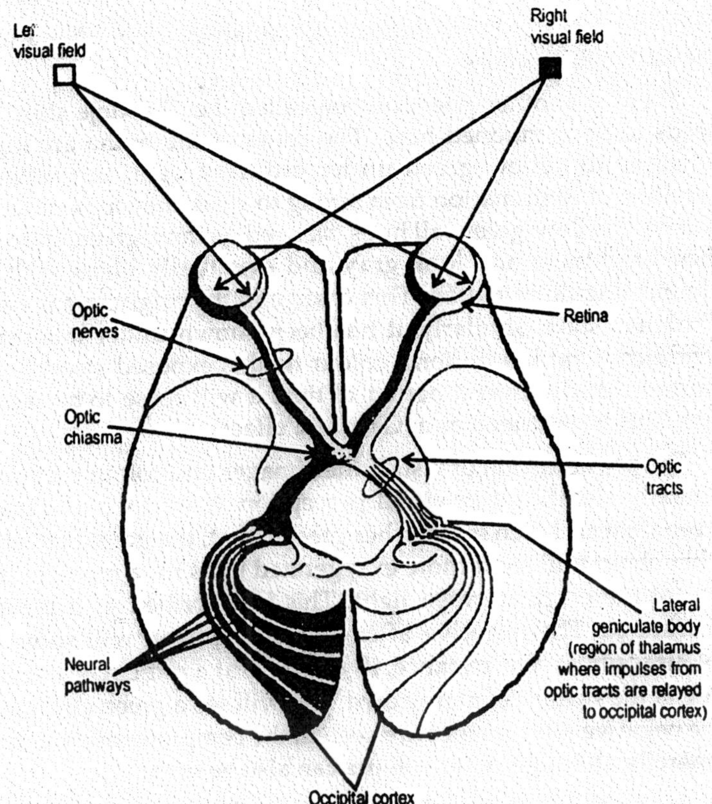

Fig. 5.2. Visual pathways.

The arrangements being hierarchical produce specific response at a particular level. Again different responses can be had at different levels where cells alone as well as in combination with others respond. Thus the visual system has many levels of operation and the stimulus requirements at each level become more and more specific.

There are some other phenomena in visual experience that do not appear very simple as a process of reception, transmission and interpretation of stimulation from the environment; for example, the phenomenon of dark-adaptation. When you enter the dark hall of a cinema, the transition from the light of the day to the inside darkness of the hall is such that the rods and cones of the retina do not operate effectively. Similarly, it is difficult to adapt quickly from the dim light to a bright light situation. Only after a while the adaptation occurs.

There is another phenomenon called the 'Purkinje shift' that needs to be mentioned here. The cones of the retina are highly sensitive to yellow-green under ordinary light, but with the variation of illumination from strong to weak they look different. Not only yellow-green, all hues, *viz.*, red, yellow, green, blue lose their brightness and look gray and eventually black with the diminishing illumination. This change in the brightness is called 'Purkinje' shift. Similarly, it has been shown under laboratory conditions that if a uniform colour field is exposed steadily and uninterruptedly over a period of time it will cease to be seen as that. This is described as a 'Ganzfeld effect'.

The phenomenon of visual after-images and colour contrast is similarly significant in visual perception. If we look at a bright green light and then see another green object, the greenness of the other object will seem more exaggerated to us for a moment than that of the original green light. This is described as a positive afterimage. The negative after-image, however, will show the colour contrast. For instance, if you stare at a red circle and then look at the surface of a gray card, you will see a green circle on it. The negative after images are seen in the complementary colours generally although other colours can also be seen.

In the field of visual sensation a phenomenon of colour blindness is also talked about. However, a complete colour-blindness, that is, a colour blind could see only black and white, and gray, is extremely rare. There is always a partial colour blindness in which red-green blindness is fairly common. Such colour-blind people can discriminate the blue-yellow and light-dark combinations. The yellow-blue blindness however is of rare incidence. This kind of deficiency affects 7 per cent of men and 1 percent of women.

Some Theories of Colour-vision

A theory of colour vision named after Young, an English physicist and Helmholtz, a German physiologist, postulates the relationships of cones with the wavelengths in determining colour vision. According to them, there are three types of cones, which respond to different wavelengths: red cones to long wavelengths, green cones to intermediate wavelengths, and blue to the short wave lengths. Yellow is assumed to be the result of simultaneous stimulation of the red and green cones. Furthermore, white is seen when all the three receptors, red, green, and blue are stimulated together. According to this theory, three colours are sufficient to produce all the colours of the spectrum. Some studies with the light absorption of individual cells in the vertebrate retina seem to support that there are three pigments segregated in each of the three types of cones (MacNichol, 1964).

The Young-Helmholtz theory, however, does not explain the facts of colour-blindness. If yellow is produced by the stimulation of red and green cones, then why does a red-green colour blind see a yellow colour?

Another theorist of colour vision was Hering. He also postulated three kinds of receptor cones, but in a different combination, red-green, yellow-blue and black-white. One responded to the degree of brightness (black-white) continuum, and the other two to red-green and blue-yellow. He based his theory on the psychological primaries and included yellow among them. He further hypothesized that each cone-receptor continuum worked in two ways : (*a*) by building up phase (anabolic), and (*b*) by tearing down phase (catabolic). The two phases cannot work at the same time, that is, cannot react both ways simultaneously in a receptor.

Both theories seem to have elements of truth in them. The micro-spectrophotometric studies measuring wavelengths of light passing through cones (MacNichol, 1964) are able to show the existence of three kinds of light sensitive pigments in the cones. However, the question is still unanswered whether there are blue, green and yellow or blue, green and red cones? On the whole, Hering's theory corroborates young Helmhotz theory of colour vision. It appears that the colour vision is a two-way process. The retina has cone-receptors, which respond to the lights of three different colours. When these responses are encoded for transmission through to the higher visual centres, they are done into a two-colour system with on-off signals.

The Auditory Sense

Like seeing, we have sensory experience of hearing. We hear

sound. Sound is an energy generated by the vibration of molecules in the environment. The sound waves, thus, are generated by vibrating bodies and transmitted through air. Unlike light, sound needs a medium to travel. When the sound waves reach the eardrums of the listener and stimulate the nerve fibers, the nerve impulses are produced and transmitted to the brain causing an auditory experience.

The sound wave has frequency. In other words, there are a number of vibrations in a sound wave. These frequencies are called pitch. The pitch can be very low to very high. All the sound frequencies, however, are not heard by the human ear. The human ear is attuned to receive frequencies from 20 to 20,000 cycles per second, but can process 2000 to 5000 cycles per second comfortably.

The loudness of a sound is the function of pressure activating the eardrum. In other words, it is the amplitude of the sound wave, its amount of compression and expansion. If the vibration is regulated and ordered, it becomes a tone; if not, becomes a noise. Noise is a combination of frequencies not in harmony. Finally, the complexity of vibration also differs from one vibrating body to another and thereby present different qualities of sound called timbre.

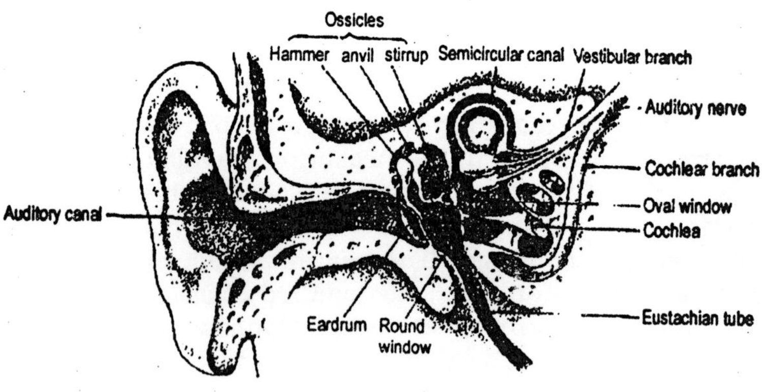

Fig. 5.3. The structure of the ear.

The characteristics of sound wave important to know are frequency and amplitude. All organisms cannot hear the same range of frequencies; variation in hearing is significant. Furthermore, it is seldom that we find pure tone. The frequencies always get multiplied and become overtone. Where two tones are sounded together, a third note is created on the basis of the difference between two frequencies. Besides, two tones may fuse and become consonant (pleasant) or do not fuse and become dissonant (unpleasant) note.

The anatomical structure of the ear consists of the outer ear, the middle ear and the inner ear. The outer ear provides auditory canal and the tympanic membrane, known as eardrum, which connects with the middle ear. The sound waves travel through the auditory canal to the eardrum. These waves rather strike at the eardrum and produce vibrations, which in turn activates the middle ear.

The middle ear acts as a transmitter. It modulates and amplifies the energy. It comprises three small bones; hammer, anvil, and stirrup. The hammer is attached firmly to the eardrum and stirrup to another membrane called oval window. The oval window relays the sounds to the cochlea, which is the auditory part of the inner ear. The vibration activates first the hammer and through it the anvil and stirrup. The tensor tympani is a muscle that adjusts hammer and the ear drum for different intensities—and prevents it from injury. The stirrup also has a muscle attached to it, which presses the oval window. Since the oval window is smaller in size compared with the tympanic membrane, the small movements of the eardrum are condensed in putting pressure on the oval window.

The inner ear has an important structure known as the cochlea (mentioned below). It is a canal filled with liquid and has got two divisions, vestibular (ascending) and tympanic (descending), separated by a bone and tissue. The cochlea has another smaller canal called cochlear canal, which contains auditory receptors, the organ of corti situated on the basilar membrane and the hair cells projected from it into the liquid of the cochlear canal. Pressure at the oval window creates motion into cochlear canal and receptors are activated, which in turn initiate nerve impulse. The organ of corti is connected with the auditory nerve; therefore, nerve impulses are processed from there to the temporal lobe via the thalamus in the brain. The auditory experience is the result of such a processing.

The auditory pathways are similar to the visual one in a manner that the nerve fibers from each ear go to the both temporal lobes, but similarity ends here as the damage to one temporal lobe does not produce complete deafness in either ear.

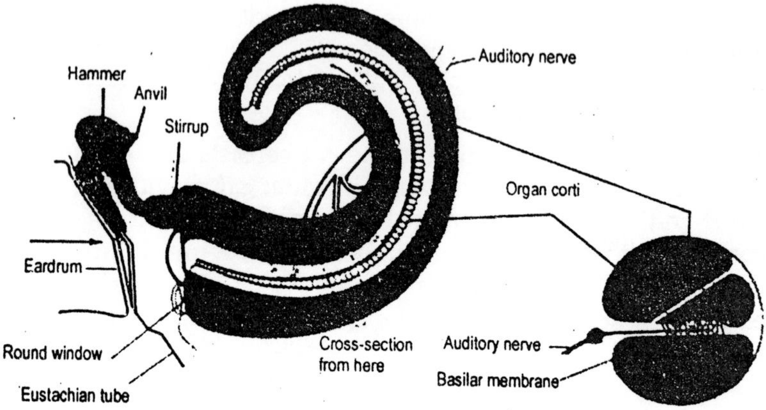

Fig. 5.4. Receptors for hearing.

Some Theories of Hearing

Helmholtz theory of hearing is described as place theory. According to this, each region of the basilar membrane is especially attuned to react to certain frequencies or pitch discrimination. The region is maximally displaced by the sound wave and the loudness depends on the total number of fibers as well as the king of fibers (high threshold fibers) being activated.

Experiments with guinea pigs with cut holes in the cochlea of those animals observed microscopically show that the function of basilar membrane in response to differential frequency tones was significant. It was also discovered that the high frequency tones displaced the narrow end (near oval window) of the basilar membrane in the highest degree, and the intermediate frequency caused the displacement at the other end of the membrane. The other finding of the low tone activation, however, is not consistent with this theory, because the low tones activated the entire membrane equally. Furthermore, it is believed that the impulses originating from different regions of the basilar membrane traveled up to different areas of auditory cortex and, therefore, the discrimination of pitch involves the degree of arousal of different localized spots in the cortex.

Another important theory of hearing is known as 'volley theory' or 'frequency theory' (Wever, 1949). This theory assumes that the cochlea acts as a microphone with the telephone wire of auditory nerve. The auditory nerve transmits impulses of different frequencies. The greater the frequency the higher the pitch. Studies have shown that the auditory nerve can transmit up to 4,000 cycles of frequencies per second, though no one nerve fiber alone can do more than 1,000 cycles per second. Here the volley theory assumes that the nerve fibers fire in groups and in turn a particular fiber group is discharged by one wave and not by the next. In other words, no single fiber responds to each stimulation. All respond in a synchronized way with the frequency of the sound wave. Some fibers in the group are more excitable that others and discharge accordingly. With the differences in excitability of the nerve fibers, there will be a spurt of impulses involving some of the fibers with every wave.

We need both, the place as well as the frequency theories, to explain hearing completely. The place of excitation of the basilar membrane and the frequency of nerve responses supplement each other in determining the message of a pitch and a tone.

Other Senses

Seeing and hearing play a very complex and significant role in our lives, but this does not mean that other senses like, smell and taste have no significance at all. On the other hand, the senses of smell and taste do have importance in our species, but have more relevance to the sub-human species. The fish or the dog etc. makes more use of these senses than the other ones. We shall mention the bases of these sensory experiences here.

Sense of smell is also termed as' Olfaction'. The olfactory sensation is mediated by the nasal cavity towards its upper end where lie the olfactory epithelium. The olfactory receptors are long thread-like structures leading from the olfactory bulbs into a small area at the extreme top of the nasal cavity. At the lower end small hair or cilia are embedded in the olfactory epithelium. The olfactory bulbs are situated just below the frontal lobes and connected with the olfactory cortex, which further extend inside of the temporal lobes, spreading to the nearby cerebral cortex. Smell processes itself, directly to the brain as compared with other senses. Only eddying currents reach the olfactory receptors.

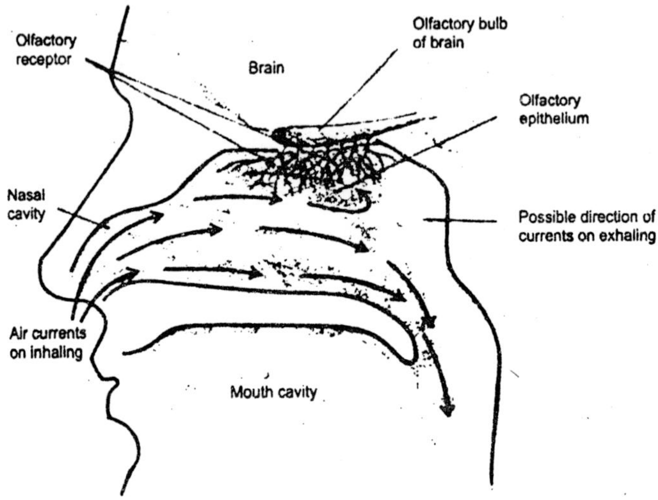

Fig 5.5. A cross-section of the nose.

A recent view assumes that we experience an odour when certain gas molecules provide stimulation to the olfactory receptors. This is known as stereo-chemical theory and explains the relationships between different shapes of molecules and shaped sockets in the receptors. Among other senses, olfaction shows rapid adaptation.

The receptors for the taste lie in the taste buds. They are situated on the tongue and are distributed along the edges of the tongue as well as back of the tongue more than elsewhere. A few are located in the pharynx and larynx. There are approximately ten thousand taste buds on an adult human tongue. They follow the system of reproducing and replenishing in seven days.

These taste-buds have specific receptivity; some respond to sugar, some to salt and acids, and so on. Apart from human beings, other animals differ in the receptivity of their taste-buds, too. For example, chickens show on reactions to sweet, whereas dogs and pigs do. The primary tastes are sweet, sour, salt and bitter. The rest are the fusion of these qualities in different proportion as well as a result of fusion with other sensory experiences. Sensitivity to

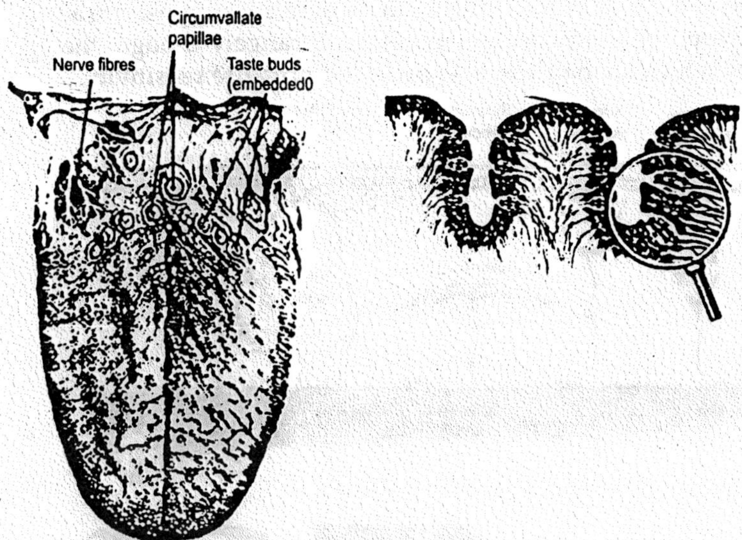

Fig. 5.6. Taste receptors.

sweet generally is the highest at the tip of the tongue; salt on the tip as well as on the sides of the tongue. The sour is experienced relatively more on the sides of the tongue than elsewhere and the bitter towards the back. The impulses go to the parietal lobe in the cortex to give gustatory experiences. The taste buds, however, decrease with the advancing age. The old people are sensitive to taste than children.

Cutaneous Sensitivity

The term 'Cutaneous sensitivity' refes to the sensitivities connected with the skin. For some time touch or pressure sensitivity was specifically denoted by the skin sense, but the scope has been enlarged now to include more cutaneous experiences, for example, itching, burning, roughness, smoothness, stickiness, wetness, vibration, pains, temperature etc. However, three major sensitivities of pain, pressure and temperature are recognised as primary ones and the rest are the combinations and differentiations of these.

The primary skin sensitivities depends on different spots in the skin. Although the precise mechanism underlying these receptors is in doubt these days, there is some known evidence about the occurrence of sensitivities of the skin. For example, nerve fibers at the base of hair follicles in the skin are supposed to act as receptors for touch or light pressure. Strangely though, the lip areas, which are hairless, also provided pressure sensitivity.

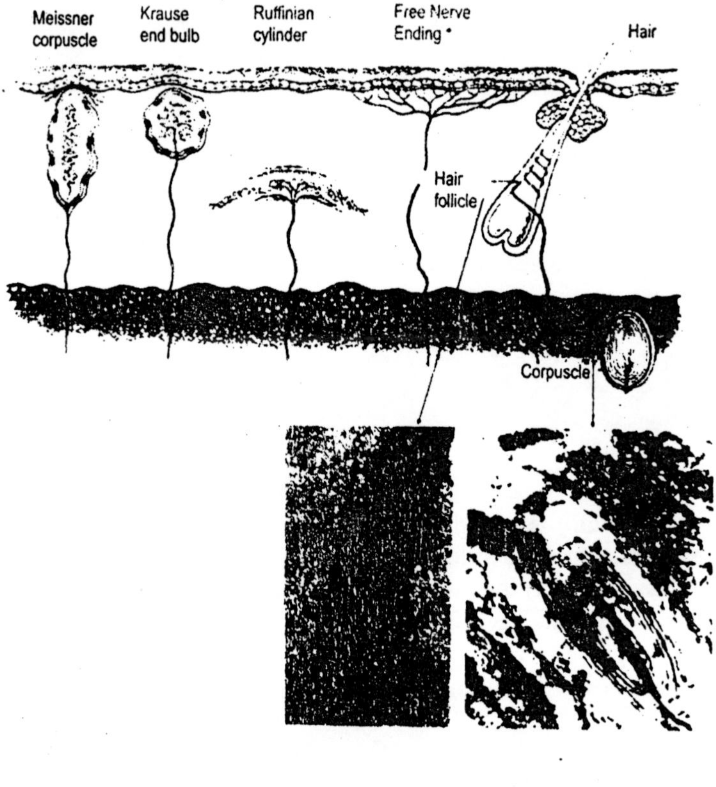

Fig. 5.7 :. A Cross-section of the skin.

Pain, on the other hand, is mostly associated with the free nerve endings located in the skin. It is spread all over the body but pain can also be activated through other receptors as well. If the other receptors are activated by the intense stimulation, the experience of pain will result. For example, a very loud noise or a boiling sherbet on the tongue can cause painful experience. The explanation is that for every sense modality, there is a threshold point beyond which the receptors cannot function normally and mediate pain.

The skin is sensitive to temperature in the same way, as it is to pressure and pain. The temperature receptors are again free nerve endings and the capillarics (blood vessels), which run over every part of the skin. Psychology students investigate temperature (cold and warm spots) by means of temperature cylinder. There are cold and warm spots on the skin, resulting in sensation of hot, because of the simultaneous stimulation of both, hot and cold. An interesting feature with the cold and warm spots on the skin found in the recent years is that cold spots have two thresholds; they respond to low temperature stimuli as well as to the high temperature stimuli, but not to the intermediate temperature stimuli.

Proprioception

Proprio literally means 'belonging to the self' and proprioception, therefore, implies sensitivity to various parts of the body. In other words, it involves sense of equilibrium and kinesthesis respectively. The awareness of body position in relation to gravity is equilibrium. When the body moves, the motion of the body provides the cues for relating it to the space and also one part of the body to another. The balance of the body, whether right side or left side, up or down, moving forward or backward, falling etc., are covered by the equilibriatory senses.

The sense organs for the equilibriatory experiences are located in the ear. In the inner ear as referred to earlier, there are two systems. One is directly related to the auditory system and the other to the non-auditory one. The equilibrium sense depends on the latter with a series of cavities in the inner ear extending from the cochlea. The non-auditory systems involve three semicircular canals and the vestibular sacs, which are all, filled with liquid. The three canals lie in three planes roughly perpendicular to the others and fluid within them moves when the head moves and exerts pressure on the hair cells, similar to those of the organ of corti. These hair cells are receptors of static sensitivity. Displacement of these hair cells by the movement of the fluid stimulates a non-auditory part, that is, the vestibular branch of the auditory nerve. Under ordinary conditions the semicircular canals and vestibules are stimulated simultaneously and impulses from both are co-ordinated in the cerebellum resulting into body balance.

Sense of active movements of body parts, *i. e.* muscles, tendons and joints etc, is described as kinesthesis or motor sense. There are nerve endings (receptors) in these body parts that give the sensation of feeling of position of movement like, the contraction or extension of muscle or the muscular tension to balance the posture etc. For example, when in applying extra force and adopting a posture to lift a heavy weight, the nerve impulses go to the brain providing information about the position of the limbs and from there impulses are sent back to the muscles, tendons and joints stimulating further activity. These activities draw on the feedback mechanism–motor activities act as stimuli for their own arousal and for the stimulation of other motor activities. The process becomes so automatic in many situations that activities and movements like walking, typing, knitting etc. can be performed without paying attention to muscle.

In the table below we summarize the aspects of all sensory experiences. (Adapted after Munn *et al.*, 1966)

Table 5.1

Type of Sensitivity	*Physical Stimulation*	*Sense Organs receptors*	*Area of Cerebral Cortex*	*Types of Sensation*
1	2	3	4	5
Visual	Light waves	Eyes: rodes and cones in retina	Occipital lobe	Hue, brightness, saturation
Auditory	Sound waves	Ears: hair cells in organ of Corti	Temporal lobe	Pitch, loudness, tone etc.
Olfactory	Gaseous substances	Nose hair cells in olfactory epithelium	Non mediated in lower brain centre	Smell
Gustatory	Soluble substance	Tongue: taste cells in taste buds	Parietal lobe	Salt, sour, sweet, bitter
Pressure	Stress on the skin	Skin : free nerve endings	Parietal lobe	Intensity

(Contd....)

1	2	3	4	5
Pain	Extreme stimulation	Any free nerve endings	Parietal lobe	Prick, pain, dull pain
Tempera-ture	Change in temperature of skin	Skin : Free nerve endings	Parietal lobe	Degree of warmth, cold
Equilib-rium	Position and change in rate of motion	Inner ear : hair cells of crista		Body position passive motion
Kines-thetic	Change in position of body parts	Muscles : Tendon and joints, nerve endings	Parietal lobe	Body movement

Inter-sensory Experiences

The sensory systems very much depend on each other and interact among themselves. The eyes, ears, and skin can register individual's own behaviour as well as the events in the environment. For one may be aware of ones head movements through kinesthesis as well as through hearing. Similarly, inter-relatedness of kinesthesis and vision has been demonstrated in typing activity (West, 1967). The integration of sensory systems and feedback from each other and the environment are the basis of all perceptual experiences, which will be dealt with later in the book.

Psycho-physical Method of Measuring Sensitivity

The sensitivity of different kinds and the nature and functions of receptors that are responsible for such sensitivities have been discussed. Now we shall mention about the stimuli and their perception in psychophysical terms, which have received attention of the psychologists for a considerable time. By psychophysical function the psychologists mean a relationship between a psychological variable (experiencing stimulus) and a physical variable (the intensity of stimulation).

Threshold

Psychologists use the term 'threshold' or 'limen' to denote the detection and discrimination of stimuli. These thresholds are of three kinds; absolute, terminal, and differential. The level of intensity at which the stimulus can be detected is described as the absolute threshold. In other words, the absolute threshold is the point at which the stimulation is perceived. For example, a sound or a spot of light must reach a measurable level before that can be heard or seen. The absolute threshold varies among individuals as well as within the same individual from time to time due to reasons of variation in physiological conditions, mood and sensitivity of the individual. Psychologists experiment with a number of trials rather than one trial, and determine statistically the absolute thresholds of sensitivities. Furthermore, it is not always a single intensity value of the stimulus, that is, below and above, which the subject detects it , rather a range of such values is taken into consideration in determining the threshold .

Following are the examples of some absolute thresholds :

Stimulus	*Threshold*
Light	A candle seen at 30 miles on a dark but clear night.
Sound	The tick of a watch under quiet conditions of 20 feet.
Taste	One teaspoon of sugar in 2 gallons of water.
Smell	One drop of perfume diffused into a 3-room Apartment.
Touch	The wing of a bee falling on your cheek from a distance of 1 cm.
	Taken from Galanter (1962).

Terminal threshold—The threshold that indicates the maximum intensity of stimulation beyond which the individual can not have sensitivity. For example, greater than 700 milimicrons of the electromagnetic wavelength produces no visual experience and so on. Moreover, intensities beyond the terminal threshold cause pain to the individuals.

Difference threshold—the perception of the smallest difference between two stimulations can be described as a difference threshold. This is the point of difference when two intensities become noticeable. For example, two tones, one louder than the other, must differ by some degree of intensities before they can be separated from one another. However, the perception of difference threshold depends on (1) the relative magnitude of the stimuli to be compared, (2) the sense stimulated, and (3) the manner in which the stimuli are compared.

Psycho-physiologists have been interested in measuring the change in physical energy necessary to bring about detection of a difference between two stimuli at least 50 per cent of the time. They have worked on this and come up with the concept of just noticeable difference (j.n.d.) mathematically. It may be explained as follows. Suppose there are three candles burning in a room and you add a fourth one, in this situation the increase in illumination will be clearly perceptible, as it will be significantly above the threshold. But if there are one hundred candles burning and you add another one, the increase in illumination may be just perceived. This perception at a minimal level is described as a just noticeable difference. It is quite possible that such a difference in illumination may not be perceived.

In the light of the above, psycho-physiologists talk about the ratio of change in stimulus intensity from the previous intensities, which facilitates discrimination. This ratio is expressed as 'Weber's law', named after a German physiologist who formulated it. Weber's law is stated mathematically as $\Delta S/S = k$. S is the standard stimulus intensity and ΔS is the change in S required to produce a j.n.d. in intensity. K is the constant ratio.

The Weber ratio K varies from one kind of sensitivity to another. For example, it is larger for visual brightness than for auditory pitch. Furthermore, the Weber ratio has also been found to vary with the extreme range of intensities, particularly at very low levels of stimulation. But it is fairly constant within an intermediate intensity range.

Weber's law was formulated for measuring threshold, but Fechner (1860) used it to develop scales for quantifying sensory experiences. By adding j.n.ds for successive trials, he formulated the principle of scaling psychological distances between two stimuli. The method is known as Weber Fechner law that gives a logarithmic equation of relationship between the sensory experience and the intensity of the physical variable. With modification the equation has been found extremely helpful in designing telephone appliances, tape-recorders etc. The designers find out how intense a signal should be in order to be perceived accurately under differing conditions.

6 Abilities

Biological bases, as discussed in preceding chapters, ultimately culminate in the generation of mental energy enabling mankind to adapt to the environment, in which he lives or survives. The functional aspect of this mechanism although native in potential is shaped considerably by the environmental forces. Various cognitive abilities the mankind develops are the optimal level of biological operation and will be examined here.

The term intelligence is widely known and psychologists are quickly associated with this name. In fact, the assessment and evaluation in psychology, on the whole, earned wide-spread recognition because of intelligence testing. The impact has been tremendous, so much so that even the unsophisticated people talk about the sophisticated term like IQ in common parlance.

Intelligence, although measured, has not got an agreed definition. However, in divergence there is a convergence to describe the construct of intelligence in terms of functions and operations. Thus, if some one learns a skill quicker than the other, one is considered more intelligent than the latter. Again, someone who does not learn a skill or learns slowly in relation to others is less intelligent than the one who does it quicker. Capability to learn, therefore, is identified by psychologists as intelligence.

Learning ability can be equated with the general adaptability of the organism to the environment. Human beings are far more adaptable than other animals and, therefore, are considered much more intelligent than them. In the process of adapting to a situation or environment, the individual finds ways to overcome problems. The problems can be simple and concrete or complex and abstract. While solving problems, however, the individual has to reason and use symbols. The reasoning enables the individual to perceive the relationship between cause and effect and to abstract element of relation between them. The same is used in making inference about the answers to the problem or problems. Of course, the individual draws on his past experience and previous learning in perceiving the relationship in the problem situation. Thus, the capacity to reason through to solve the problem constitutes learnability of the individual.

Some psychologists hold the view that intelligence is an all round cognitive ability and enters into most mental capacities and functions. Others, on the other hand, argue that it is a specific ability to perform specific kind of tasks. In the latter's views, there are intelligences rather than one intelligence. Accordingly, one who has got mechanical intelligence will do very well in that area, and the other who has academic intelligence, will succeed in school and college education, etc. The psychologists, who accept the all-round cognitive power or ability, postulate 'G', a general factor of intelligence. The originator of this theory was a British Psychologist, Charles Spearman (1927), who recognized that there was a general intellectual ability in addition to several special abilities, 'S', related to the specific kind of task (test). His theory evoked rigorous researches in the field and one of the most sensitive techniques of statistical analysis like, factor analysis, was employed to uncover the truth. The factor analysis, though a mathematical artifact, isolates independent units of mental abilities which can be measured reliably. Thurstone and Guilford in America and Burt and Thomson in the UK, are some of the famous names associated with this kind of approach.

Thurstone and Thurstone (1941) discovered multiple factors as opposed to Spearman's 'G' and named them primary mental abilities. These are, V—verbal ability; N—numerical ability; S—spatial relation; R—abstract reasoning; P—perceptual speed and accuracy; M—rote memory; W—word fluency. The description of these mental abilities are given below :

- Verbal ability – capability to comprehend verbal meaning and relationship of words and symbols.
- Numerical ability – capability to deal with numbers and figures, understand quantitative relationship, facility in calculation.

- Spatial relation – capability of perceiving relationship of object in space, visualize changes in space, of third dimension etc.
- Reasoning – capability to find out solution to a problem by abstracting principle etc.
- Memory – capability of remembering things and symbols by association.
- Perceptual speed and accuracy – capability to observe and mark detail with speed and correctness.
- Word fluency – capability to use words and language with great ease and facility.

Thurstone's multiple factor theory of intelligence puts forward the view that there are a number of broad factors of mental abilities enabling different kinds functions. These factored abilities constitute aptitudes relating to different areas of work, educational and vocational; for example, scholastic aptitude, mechanical aptitude, clerical aptitude, etc. Although initially Thurstone opposed the existence of a general 'G' factor in view of his first order factors or primary abilities, his subsequent researches did find a higher or second-order factor in 'R' reasoning, which correlated with all other abilities in significant degrees. Thus, 'R' comes very close to the 'G' of Spearman and supports the case for an all round general cognitive ability.

Studies in education lend strong support to the general factor of intelligence with the findings that performance in subjects by students varying widely in nature, such as; teaching skill, arithmetic, hygiene, education, psychology, speech training, singing, physical training, etc. are significantly positively correlated (Burt, 1939a). Consequently, a person who scores high on tests of one of the factors tends to score high also on tests of the other factors. But there is evidence to show that apart from a single factor found in common to most of the mental activities, there are sub-groups or broad group factors as well.

Factor-analytic studies have not stopped at this stage, but gone up to extract a specific unit of ability numbering 120 (Guilford, 1967). Anyway, the details of these factors will not be discussed here. We shall mention the general stand taken by Guilford in the context of abilities. He is a supporter of the pluralistic view of intelligence. He formulates a three-line approach to the problem : (*a*) mental operations, (*b*) products, and (*c*) the content of operations. He describes five types of mental operation - cognition, memory, evaluation, divergent thinking and convergent thinking. The product dimension, according to him, has a six-way classification, units, classes, relations, systems, transformations and implications. Furthermore, content has a four-way classification, figural, symbolic, semantic and behavioural. The figure AB1 will show the structure, which looks like a cube with three dimensions.

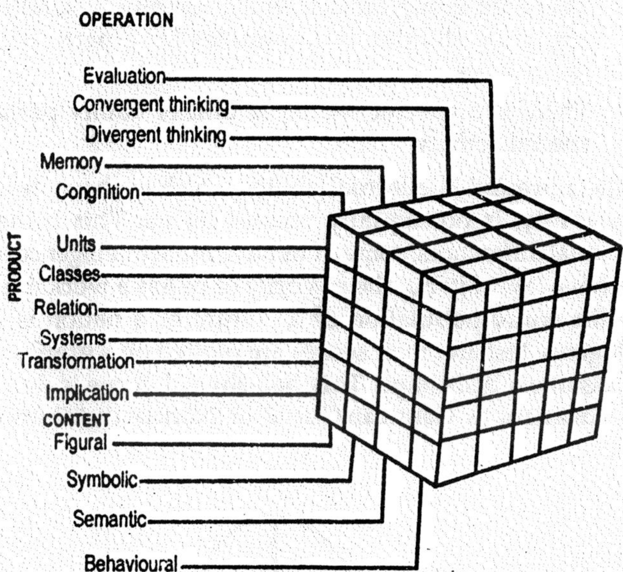

Fig. 6.1

These classifications, though have emerged out to intensive factor analyses, seem to be relatively inter-dependent in some areas. For example, memory operation will certainly involve symbolic content. The factored tests have been developed by Guilford and his colleagues, but still much evidence is needed to satisfy all psychologists. However, one of his dimensions of mental operations, convergent / divergent thinking, has received significant attention. Guilford describes convergent thinking as following precise rules to reach a solution, which is unique. Divergent thinking, on the other hand, is open-ended thinking using a new solution and not finding the conventional answer.

This divergent thinking is considered by him as a vital part of creativity and originality. Intelligence tests commonly used assess convergent thinking, but Guilford's divergent thinking tests do not assess that. Never-the-less, it has been found that his creative individuals score high on the IQ tests as well, although all the high scorers on the IQ tests do not turn out to be creative.

The following are the accepted views on abilities :

1. There is a general factor of cognitive ability known as general intelligence;
2. There are group factors which combine several factors to constitute abilities and aptitudes for a particular kind of job or work;
3. There is a specific factor or unit of ability pertaining to special activity.

The all-round intellectual ability, which we have described as adaptability, is not equally shared by us. This brings about individual differences, some of us have more intelligence and some of us have less of it; but the majority of us has a workable share of it. If the entire population of a culture or a nation is given an intelligence test and their scores are plotted on a graph, the curve will assume a bell-shape. This bell-shaped curve is described by the statisticians as 'Gaussian Curve' or 'Normal distribution curve'.

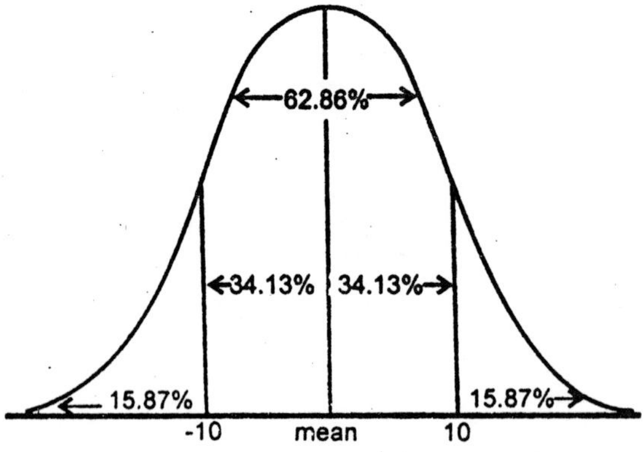

Fig. 6.2

The figure shows that 68.26 per cent of the tested population will fall in the middle, forming the average range (+1 and –1 standard deviations from the mean). Outside the average range, below and above, will be 15.87 per cent of the population each side. At the extreme end of the two sides, 2.2 per cent of the population will fall; on the minus side mental defectives and sub-normal and on the plus side intellectually very superior and gifted people. One of the popular classifications of IQs (W.A.I.S. IQs) demarcates 90 to 109 as average range, 100 being the mean IQ, 110 to 119 bright normal, 120 to 129 superior and 130+ very superior or gifted. On the other side, the IQs rated as below average, 80 to 89 (dull-normal), borderline 70 to 79 and mental defective or sub-normal 69 and below.

Some psychologists use the expression 'exceptional children' to indicate the upper and lower extremes of children's position on the intelligence scale for educational purposes. The special curriculum to suit the special needs of students is the cry of the day, as both extreme groups become problems for the educators. Education of the gifted requires special attention as much as the education of the mentally defectives. However, the first group does not become a liability on the society if special provision for education is not made, but the defective group becomes so. We shall mention, here, some of the characteristics of the mentally handicapped children often the society has to care for.

The intellectual handicap can be caused in the process of birth as well as through inheritance. When hereditary, the individual inherits a defective or under-developed brain along the family line which renders him less capable of learning any skill. Such people grow physically and chronologically, but not mentally. You hear psychologists and psychiatrists say that a particular person is 20 years old, but has got a mental age of 5.

The mentally handicapped people secure less than 70 IQs depending upon the level of deficiency. Now-a-days, in the USA and UK, the use of old terminologies describing the grades of mental handicap as idiot, imbecile, and moron has been discarded and replaced by the sub-normal–mild, moderate and severe/profound. This classification is based on the level of social competence, motor skills and independence of the individual suffering from the handicap.

The other group of low intelligence is characterized as a secondary deficiency as it is caused by injury to the brain and diseases. Some of the reasons accounted for are intoxication, poisoning, inadequate nutrition, thyroid dysfunction and other brain diseases, like, encephalitis, microcephalus, hydrocephalus, etc. The training and education of these handicapped and afflicted people need special techniques and special resources. Some of them can be helped to be independent and able to look after themselves and some can be helped to grow up to near normal level of behaviour in some respects, if not all, depending on the severity of their handicaps.

The intellectual ability grows with the chronological age of the individual; as the body grows, so grows the mind to a point. The growth of cognitive power stops and stabilizes whereas chronological age goes on. Psychologists have always shown interest in studying the relationship between the intellectual development and physical age. The rate and limit of the growth of intelligence are very much debated, but the consensus of opinion is that a no-growth point of intelligence reaches in the twenties for most individuals and then after it stabilizes. The analogy from the growth of physical stature can be drawn to illustrate this point; a person's height can reach a level and then stops growing, but expansion in the body muscle can be regulated due to exercise and control etc. Similarly, the intelligence can be sharpened and enlarged with experience and cultivation after the state of maximal growth. The gain in intellectual growth is faster in the childhood and early teens, but slows down later. Longitudinal studies with Wechsler tests for thirty-six years confirm the hypothesis of this rate of intellectual growth (Bayley, 1970).

Following the rate of growth and stabilization comes a point when the decline of intelligence sets in with certain age. Generally such a downward trend appears in the late sixties, depending on the physical and mental health of the individual. There are some examples, however, of a few individuals who do not show signs of deterioration even much later in their lives. Psychologists base their judgment about the decline of intellectual abilities in the individuals on their test performances. As we have argued earlier that intelligence is a combination of several abilities, all abilities do not decline at the same time and in the same degree with most people. Some do more than others at upper age levels. Wechsler

(1958) reported that vocabulary level remained pretty high with advancing age when ability to reason and ability to learn new skills showed declining tendency. The study of declining abilities has proved extremely helpful in diagnosing problems of brain-injury, brain-disease and pre-senile dementia.

Now it seems important to bring in the issue of the measure or test of intelligence. Intelligence was originally measured in terms of mental age (Binet and Simon); test items were included in a manner that if answered successfully, could be assigned scores in days, months and years of mental age. Alfred Binet (1905) pioneered this kind of intelligence test in France and since then several modifications, revisions and adaptations of his test have been done all over the world. One of the English versions known as Stanford-Binet scale is widely known. The last modification of the test goes with the name of Terman and Merril Test. Mental age is still in use for diagnostic purpose, but has given rise to the concept of IQ, which is in popular use.

The IQ stands for 'Intelligence Quotient' and is derived from the following : M.A / C.A x100. This is the ratio between physical age and mental age and same is multiplied by one hundred in order to avoid the fraction or decimal value of the dividend. The concept of IQ, of course, originated from mental age, but later users determine IQ without reference to mental age, rather relate performance on psychological tests of intelligence to physical age, scholastic achievement, etc. Earlier on, we mentioned a classification of IQs denoting different levels of functioning from sub-normal to very superior taken from the Wechsler Adult Intelligence Scale (WAIS), which is one of the examples where mental age is not used in computing the IQs. Wechsler has also developed intelligence scale for pre-primary and school children (WPPS) and Wechsler Intelligence Scale for Children (WISC). These tests though yield IQs, can give an estimate of mental age too. The number of psychological tests measuring intelligence of children, adolescents these days is quite large.

The prolific use of IQ measure in various walks of life from education to employment suggests that the role of intelligence is of paramount importance in our lives and the every effort should be made to develop this power of the individual in our society. In this context, it is appropriate to talk about the role of heredity and environment in the growth and development of intelligence. As usual, the nature-nurture controversy is extremely steep in this area. One extreme group emphasizes the hereditary factors in intelligence and argues that people are born with genetic blueprints in regard to their growth of intelligence. The support for inherited intelligence is drawn from the study of co-twins, who have identical heredity. The IQs of identical twins are highly correlated as. 9. The IQs of fraternal twins, on the other hand, do not show correlation coefficient of more than .55. Further, the case for inherited intelligence gets stronger when evidence from the study of co-twins reared apart under different environments is taken into account and the difference in their IQs is not found significant (Evienmeyer-Kimling & Jarvik, 1963).

The nurture group stresses the influence of environment on individuals' growth of intelligence. It is the environment, according to them, which plays an important part in this growth. The low IQ is the result of lack of opportunities and impoverished home conditions. The adverse environment and poor home conditions produce lower average IQs of children as compared with the national norm (Wheeler, 1942). The impact of home on the growth of intelligence has been supported by the findings that different children brought up under the better home environment (foster homes) showed high IQs. On the other hand, siblings reared together by the same parents present not very different intelligence scores (Skodak and Skeels, 1949; Erienmeyer-Kimling and Jarvik, 1963).

Studies showing the difference in IQs of rural and urban children as well as relationship between parents' socio-economic and professional status and their children's IQs (McMenar, 1942) indicate the role of environment in shaping intelligence. However, this does not tie all the loose ends; whether the socio-economic status and professional difference of the privileged parents were achieved due to their high IQs or not, is not answered by these studies.

The majority of psychologists accepts the view that intelligence or any other ability is the result of interaction between heredity and environment. Both are important and have their specific part to play in the development of intelligence. An individual is born with potential, and the same cannot develop without the favourable condition of environment. One without the other is inconceivable.

Besides, there are problems in studying the influence of one alone separately. The hereditarians cannot be sure of isolating genetic inheritance, as the genetic transmission may not be in the same form because of mutation of genes. These mutations alter the character of genes and thus transmission from parents to offspring may not remain the part of the original genetic endowment. Another important point worthy of note in this context is that the intra-uterine environment can bring about changes and cause defect (congenital defect), which may not have been inherited genetically.

Despite heredity-environment controversy, intelligence testing is in full swing everywhere. There are studies to associate IQ with different kinds of courses at schools, colleges and universities and occupations. One of the studies of occupations with the intelligence test scores (America General Classification Test) is given below :

Mean AGCT Scores and Range of Scores for Various Civilian Occupations

Occupation	*Mean Standard Score*	*Range of Scores*
Lawyer	127.6	96-157
Engineer	126.6	100-151
Teacher	122.8	76-155
Book Keeper	120.0	70-157
Radio Repairman	115.3	56-151
Salesman	115.1	60-153
Machinist	110.1	38-153
Mechanic	106.3	60-155
Plumber	102.7	356-139
General Painter	98.3	38-147
Truck Driver	96.2	16-149
Farmer	92.7	24-147
Miner	90.6	42-139

*(Taken from Harrell and Harrell, 1945) .

With the increasing use of intelligence measure, a large number of tests and tools have been developed and standardized. Attempts to update them and also to construct another ones are always going on. Two of the most widely used and famous tests, Binet and Wechsler, are referred to earlier in this chapter.

Before we go on to say something about other abilities, we must say that these intelligence tests can be presented into question-answer form involving language, known as verbal test, or in the form of concrete materials like blocks, cubes, designs, parts of machine etc. described as non-verbal performance test. In the latter, the problem has to be solved by handling materials or performing. These tests can be individual, requiring one individual to take the test one at a time. All tests must be reliable, measuring in a consistent way, and valid, purporting to measure what they intend to measure so that a prediction of behaviour or performance can be made. Further, tests must provide a standard of comparison or norm to show individual differences. These principles are cardinal in judging all psychological tests fall short of these objectives still and ideal tests are not available yet.

Next to intelligence we talk about abilities or aptitudes whose reference has already come earlier. Aptitude is defined as a trainability or educability of an individual for a skill. The nature of aptitude or ability is no different from the intelligence except it relates to a special area of education, work and vocation. In other words, it is narrower than intelligence. The rate and time of development of aptitude follows the same path as that of intelligence and the role of heredity and environment in its growth is no different either. Further, if all the individuals in a group are tested on an aptitude test and their scores are plotted graphically, the curve will be no different from the bell-shaped or normal distribution curve. Interestingly enough, if one normal individual is given tests of all the aptitudes, his performance on them will yield similar kind of distribution of scores.

As stated above, aptitudes show capabilities of specific area. Aptitude measures are used in the educational as well as vocational fields. The scholastic aptitude or scientific aptitude etc. we hear in describing educational potential of the individual student. In the vocational field we find greater use of the term aptitude to denote trainability of the individual for a skill and a job. The vocational significance concerns whole life of a person; his earning a living and making a success in it. It is also possible that one can have relatively high aptitude in a particular area of work without having a high IQ. For this reason, the relation of aptitude to vocation is considered primary. Popularly known aptitudes are, mechanical and engineering aptitude, clerical aptitude, musical aptitude, teaching aptitude, medical aptitude, literary aptitude, aptitude for graphic art, aptitude for flying etc. Psychologists and particularly psycho-metricians have developed tools and tests to appraise different kinds of aptitude. The endeavour is to assess the individual's promise and potential and make him aware of that. The vocational guidance counsellor and occupational psychologists are interested in evaluating the aptitudes and vocational fitness of a person to help him to recognize his abilities and realize the full development of the potential with proper opportunities. The employer, on the other hand, is concerned about aptitude testing because they want to select the right sort of person for the right sort of job, training, apprenticeship and promotion. Their effort is to minimize the waste of manpower resources and make the industry economic and profitable by picking the suitable person for the job.

Like others, the field of aptitude testing is not free from disagreement. One group of psychologists thinks that aptitude should be isolated in a pure cognitive ability form and be assessed likewise. This view concentrates on the factor approach, on a specific ability unit, and its combination in determining aptitude. The other group, on the other hand, takes a generalized view and advocates a pragmatic approach. According to the second group, aptitude is a function of cognitive and non-intellective personality variables together. For example, a medical aptitude test cannot predict one's success in the field of medical practice in terms of cognitive abilities alone. In addition, it has to consider information on one's other characteristics as well, like, the ability to get along with people, to have sympathetic understanding of others, motivation etc. The two together can make a person successful in medical practice.

The controversy between the purists and practitioners does not seem to be out of place. The purists take a strictly scientific view and want to establish the 'construct' and measure it reliably. The method and instrument of measurement receive particular attention of research in this kind of approach. The applied psychologists look at the situation a bit differently and concern themselves with the outcome and success of the individual on the job or training. Their pre-occupation with the prediction of success on the job is justifiable in the light of economic and manpower investment. Both approaches have points in their favour.

7 Attending

The biological bases and sensory processes discussed until now set the stage for the study of human beings' experiences and behaviour. In the following chapters we intend to examine the processes of perceptual and cognitive reaction of mankind. But before we go on to examine the aspects of perceiving and higher mental processes we must discuss a prelude to those processes known as attending.

Attention is difficult to define, but we know that when we want to perceive something clearly and correctly, we concentrate our attention on it. Attending, therefore, is a process that precedes perception. In other words, it is perceptive attitude, a readiness to perceive if we borrow the expression of Pieron (1929) and Paschal (1941), attention is a reaction of expectancy and exploration or anticipatory perceptual adjustment. However, a salient feature of difference between attention and perception can be noted as that all attending does not guarantee perception or perceptual experience. On the other hand, perception in the absence of attention is not practicable.

These days psychologists talk about 'orienting reflex' to describe attention and its correlates. In the laboratory experiments they have observed reactions of animals and human subjects alike to the problem of attention. In the process not only bodily movements occur, but other changes also take place, such as dilation of blood vessels in the head and constriction of blood vessel in the periphery, changes in electrical responses of the brain (EEG record), muscle tone, heart rate and respiration etc. On the whole, the attending process facilitates reception of stimulation as well as prepares the organism to react quickly. It is considered vital for survival. The neuro-physiological basis of attention has been discussed earlier in context of brain functions, particularly reticular formation and thalamus etc., and therefore, will not be dealt with here. However, as we have stated earlier, a sensorial perception draws on the strength of attention. Dysfunctions of attending process are the diagnostic features of physical and mental illnesses. The person under conditions of ill health becomes highly distractible and cannot hold attention for the time needed to find an answer to a problem. In some serious disorders the disturbance of attention can result into mental confusion and disorientation of time, place and events. In some of the functional psychoses attending process is the prime victim.

Attending is generally voluntary. While attending we receive stimuli of one kind or another and get information from the environment we have to be intentionally alert to look at or listen to or observe what we want to attend to in the environment. Furthermore, this attending is highly selective as we can't attend everything at one moment of time. At one given moment our sense organs are bombarded by a multitude of stimuli. Only a few out of those are attended to and the rest go into the background, which we are vaguely aware of.

Attending is tuned to the set, motivational process, interests and attitudes of the person. These are popularly called the internal determiners of attention. The selectivity of attention causes selective perception. The examples of selective attention and perception are dealt with under the chapter of perceiving. Further, it may be added that attending becomes habitual eventually and we do attend things without being aware of them.

The process of attending has received considerable attention from the psychologists who are interested in researching and using the information processing theory or signal detection theory to understand and explain human perception and cognition along with reactions. The nature of information processing theory has been examined and discussed in the context of perceiving and remembering later on. Nevertheless, it is important to point out here that its relevance to attention is basic, because the higher cognitive functions like perceiving and remembering etc. depend on the sensory input, storage and encoding of messages to be processed which are received at the level of attention.

Broadbent introduced the concept of 'filter mechanism to

explain selective attention. Filtering is a process of attending which selects stimuli for admission; the irrelevant messages or stimuli are rejected and the relevant ones taken in. This happens because we have a limited capacity for handling information at one time. Thus all input channels used for carrying any class of sensory messages have to operate within limits. The channels cannot be overloaded and consequently the selection of signals results into the rejection of others. Treisman also adds that attending process not only selects the relevant messages, rather attenuates (damps down) the irrelevant ones at the same time.

Attention cannot be absolute; because certain features of irrelevant messages are also noted while the relevant ones are attended to. One of the popular examples demonstrate this point is to show that even when you are in the midst of distractions or noises or loud music in a party, and some body at the distance calls out your name, you immediately hear it despite the distractions. This hearing of your name amongst irrelevant messages has been explained by Broadbent (1971) as a result of 'pigeon-holing' a kind of response set or bias in favour of hearing such words amidst irrelevant signals.

Outside the information theory psychologists also talk about attention span. Attending is scanning within limit. Any perceiving, registering or memorizing outside the span is not easy. Experiments with the tachistoscopic presentation of dots or numbers or letters provide evidence of the limit of this span of attention or apprehension. Sometimes practice helps the individual to widen his span. The number of digits has gone to eight from six due to practice in the span but rarely gone beyond that number. However, concentration of attention upon a small field of view exposed briefly may be improved significantly.

Another important characteristic of attention is that it fluctuates. In other words, we cannot hold attention upon a single aspect for an indefinite period. After a period, shorter in many cases, the direction of attention alters and it wanders spontaneously to something else. When a stimulus, light or sound, is presented at very low constant intensity for some length of time, the observer may report that it appears at one moment and disappears next. In other words, the threshold intensity fluctuates. This happens because of the disappearance of stimulus from the limen due to physiological processes

The fluctuation of attention can be demonstrated with the figure-ground phenomenon. How one figure stands out and the other goes to the background and the same alternate is a characteristic feature of reversible perspective or figure-ground phenomenon. The example of this fluctuating attention is discussed under 'perceiving'. However, this suggests that things and events that occur in the first place outside the central focus of attention, become focal afterwards in our perceptions and experiences. Some psychologists put forward the theory that there are different levels of attention; varying from the one in which the attention is concentrated and focussed upon the particular narrow aspect of the field to the lowest when there is marginal awareness or other part(s) of the field. With the involvement of the central nervous system the shifting attention is linked and organised selectively to give sustained meaning of perception. The attending process includes three kinds of peripheral adjustment : (1) adjustments of the sense organs, (2) general postural adjustment and (3) the attending individual's feelings of effort and tension. The individual adjusts sense organs in order to attend. He turns his eyes or ears towards the stimulus in the environment to scan or observe. Along with the sense organs the posture has also got to be adjusted to facilitate attentive process. He stoops down or leans forward to receive the stimulus. Besides, the attending individual feels muscle tension and related feelings when he is making such adjustments. All these lead to an increased clearness of the stimulus which is being attended to.

External Determiners of Attention

In the fore-going paragraphs we discussed the role of internal factors, in attending but did not mention the role of external factors. The external factors mean the stimuli in the environment. Some determinants of the factors are mentioned as follows.

The nature of stimuli, visual or auditory, is an important external determiner. The form of stimuli; whether it is visual, that is, a picture of an animal or a person or a product, or whether auditory, that is, a narration or singing etc. affects the attention. It has been found that pictures attract attention more than the words, particularly the pictures of human beings attract more attention than that of the inanimate objects; and similarly, the rhyming versions get more attention than the prose passages.

The location of visual stimulus matters in affecting attention as well. Anything in the front of eyes gets immediate attention. In other positions the upper left-hand position gets more attention than the lower right-hand portion.

Things that are novel (new) get quicker attention than those that are stereotyped and customary. Beside, the stimulus of contrast nature gets noticed quickly. Furthermore, something that is happening all the time, people pay no attention to, but if the same appears in a new or different form, or stops or becomes opposite to the existent one, the attention is drawn to it soon.

There are several factors like, intensity, size, colour, movement and repetition that affect our attention. In a way, all except the last bring about novelty of some kind. If the sound is too loud, or the size is unduly big or the colour of the stimulus is too bright, or the odour or pressure of pain is too intense, the attention will instantly be drawn towards the stimulating condition.

Moreover, the moving objects are more attention catching than the stationery ones. Humans and animals are quite sensitive to the moving objects in their visual fields. Many animals are safe as long as they keep still in the jungle, but as soon as they start moving, they become easy prey to the predators. The movement on their part attracts attention.

Repetition of the stimulus is another interesting factor that affects attention of the people. A stimulus that is repeated presents more chances of being attended to, as repetition increases our sensitivity to that stimulus. Advertisers capitalize on these techniques to promote the sale of their products. Attending process, which is fundamental to all cognitive processes, is influenced by the internal factors like, state of health, fatigue, interest in the task and motivation of the individual, as much as it is by the external determiners of the stimulus.

8 Perceiving

Perceiving is a basic cognitive process for knowing the environment we live in. Human existence in, and his adjustment with the environment are primarily dependent upon this process. A human being like many living organisms has to be familiar with his world around that is composed of physical and social stimuli and towards which he is expected to react and behave appropriately. He has to identify the object and matter, light and sound, heat and cold, events and persons, and multitudes of other stimuli that the world presents. The process of knowing and getting awareness of these things can be named as perceiving.

This process of perceiving is quite elaborate and involves the operation of several systems all at one time. This means that the process is not limited to sensory reactions, particularly not to single sense reaction, but is effected by a combination of sensory reactions and experiences, past and present, with several other factors like, needs, values and emotions of the perceiver, contributing simultaneously. A perception, therefore, is a complex reaction to a simple or complex stimulus. Let us take an easy example of an infant's perception of an apple. He will have to know the shape, size and colour and feel the smooth surface of the skin, smell, and, perhaps, eat to taste and above all remember the experience to really develop a complete perception of an apple.

In every perceptual experience and reaction the individual's neuro-physiological structures and functions play a part. The receptors and organisation for sensory experiences are discussed elsewhere. Here we will like to refer that any defect and disturbance in these neural functioning can cause perceptual distortion. As we know, perceiving is interpreting the neural impulses caused by the stimulation from the environment, the interpretation or giving meaning to those impulses or sensory information can easily go wrong because of these dysfunctions.

The phenomenon of perceptual distortion is also sometimes described as hallucination. Hallucination, however, can occur with or without sensory dysfunction as we find in some of the mental illness. This is sometimes confused with 'illusion' as in both, hallucination and illusion, we find the misinterpretation of impulses. Anyway, both are false perceptions but with a fundamental difference; in the former the experience occurs in the absence of the stimulus, whereas in the latter, the stimulus is always present. Apart from the mental disorders, hallucinatory experiences can be caused by sensory deprivations. Experimental studies with sensory deprivation support this conclusion, (Bexton, Heron and Scott, 1954; Heron, Doane and Scott, 1956; Vernon, McGill and Schiffmak, 1958; Soloman and Mendelson, 1962).

While we are on the subject of neurochemical functioning in our perceiving, it will be helpful to add that some interesting advance has been made in understanding the nature and function of the central nervous system by the use of microelectrodes in their experimental studies. It has been found that the visual cortex is the main structure in the brain where visual perception occurs. But the cells of this cortex react differently from the neurons of the retina and optic nerve. The implication is that the same stimulus which can stimulate the neurons of the retina may not stimulate the cells of the visual cortex. Microelectrodes implanted in the visual cortex of a cat for recording the neural activity showed that all visual forms projected did not stimulate cells in the cortex. These cells have been found to be highly specific in their responses to the stimuli. Further researches have shown that the organisation of these cortical cells form a hierarchical order, from simple to complex. A set of simple cells converges on a complex cell and a number of complex cells are linked to the hypercomplex cell and so on. The stimulus can be coded, therefore, at different levels in a hierarchical manner, higher centre using the information coded at the lower centres. Besides, a multitude of separate mechanisms is arranged in hierarchical order and operate in the same fashion in receiving the inputs from the lower ones, as do the others.

Close to the neurostructural contribution towards our perceptual experience and reaction there is a remarkable function of organisation in our perceptual process. This organising function is considered as a primitive and unlearned process. We use it to group or form patterns of stimuli we are exposed to, and see them as forms, shapes etc. In other words, these stimuli are not received as simple elements like sound waves and light waves etc. but as identifiable forms. Organising tendencies in perceiving have extensively been investigated by a group of German psychologists, called ' Gestalt Psychologist'. Gestalt in German means a ' form' or 'configuration' and the theorists, accordingly, emphasize the role of wholeness in determining perception. Our perception is not a summation of simple sensory experience; rather it is much more than compounded elements or parts. It is an experience of a whole or configuration of stimuli.

The Gestalt psychologists formulated some important principles of grouping and demonstrated the influence of stimulus organisation on perceptual organisation. If the stimuli are situated near each other or in close physical proximity, they will be perceived to belong together as one pattern. In our example, Figure 8.1 there are six vertical lines, but they can be perceived as three parallel lines as they exist close together in space. The principle of proximity can apply stimuli in time sequence as well.

Another principle of grouping is based on the similarity of stimuli; similar things look to belong together. The example of dots

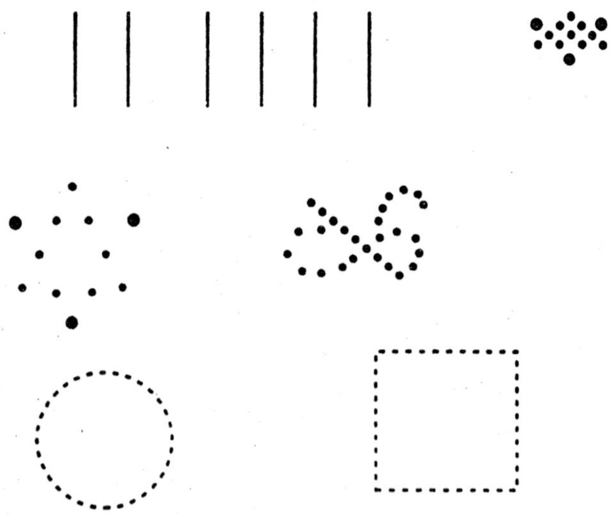

Fig. 8.1

and circles in Fig.8.1, shows that a triangle of dots has its apex at the top and another of circles at the bottom. We perceive two different triangles of dots and circles, dots grouping together on one hand and circles on the other. Sometimes, similarity may be imposed by the principle of good figure or symmetry.

In our example Fig. 8.1(c), a hexagon is easily perceived as a figure than two different figures of dots and circles.

The principle of continuity is another important grouping system. We see a stimulus, which forms a continuous pattern as a whole. If a line that starts out as a curve is seen continuing smoothly as a curve even if it is interceded. In our example, Fig.8.1(d), the dots can be perceived as a continuing curve or as a straight line even though they cross each other and have dots in common to both.

The above examples are drawn from the visual sense, but this principle of grouping applies in the area of other senses as well. In the field of hearing, a rhythm is formed because of the groupings of notes in time sequence and with the similarity of accents. Similarly a tactile perception in terms of grouping can be demonstrated as follows. Ask your friend to close his eyes. Map out the three points of equal distance on the back of his forearm. Touch with a pencil the two points on the forearm and delay slightly in touching the third point. After this, if you ask your friend to estimate the distance between the points, his answer most probably will be that the first two points were nearer to each other than the third.

Perceptual processes also tend to organise the sensory stimulation by filling in their gaps known as a principle of closure. This is a tendency to complete in perception what is incomplete in patterning in reality. The sensory experience of an object or thing is perceived as a whole even if there is a missing part in it. In our example, Fig.8.1(f), the gaps in the circle or square are not seen and they are taken as complete figure. Our retina in the eye has a blind spot with no sensitive cells, but we are not aware of its existence or its effect on the visual perception because binocular vision extends right across the spot and we have a complete experience.

Among the primitive tendencies of perceptual organisation, the phenomenon of figure-group is of striking significance. No field of view is perceived at one level, if there is anything in it. Some part of it organises to become figural and gets differentiated from the rest. It takes a form and distinguishes itself from the back-ground. The back-ground in turn becomes formless and goes behind the figure. In everyday life, we perceive innumerable things this way. Even while reading this text-book you will see the printed words on the back-ground of a page. The figure that stands out is readily perceived and attended to. The details of the figure become well-structured, bright and strong. In contrast, the ground falls back, gets unclear and quickly lost.

We separate objects or figures from the ground in our perception by following contour or outline. Contour is formed whenever a marked variation or difference occurs in the degree of brightness or colour of the back-ground. If we look at a piece of paper, which uniformly spreads whiteness from one end to another, it will not yield any perception of contour. But if on the same paper a marked and abrupt change of brightness is provided, we shall perceive as if there were two parts of the paper. This is perceiving a contour. Contours give shape and form to the objects and differentiate them

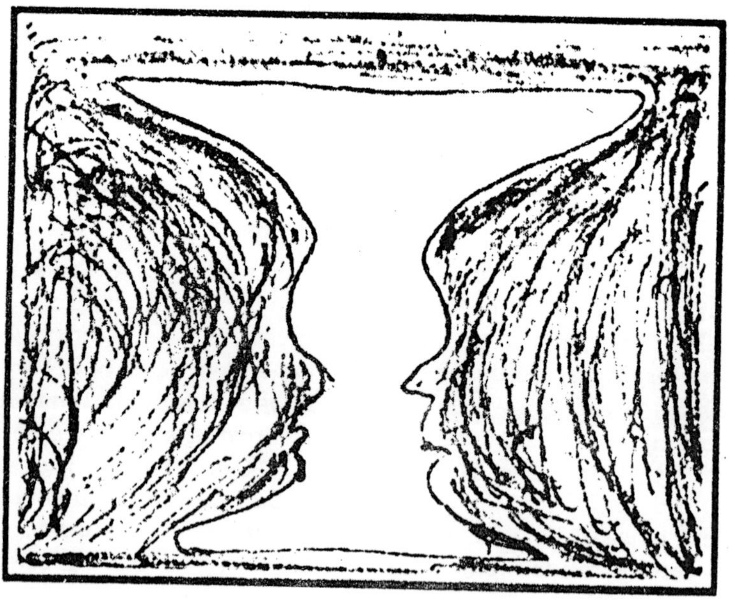

Fig. 8.2. Reversible figure ground.

from the background as well as from one another. Here one point is important to note that contours determine shape, they are not shape themselves. Further, in this context we find a reversible figure-ground phenomenon. Our Fig. 8.2, will show that only one figure stands out at one time and not both. We see either a vase (white one) or two profiles (dark ones) facing each other. If two parts are included in the visual field and have equal significance, there may be alternation of figure-ground between them. This aspect of reversible perspective has been referred to under 'Attention'.

Figure-ground experience is fundamental in our perception. Even people who were congenitally blind due to cataract reported figural experiences, that is, certain parts of the field standing out and making contours, after their operation and recovery of the sight. It has also been reported that in certain cases of brain-injury, the patient recovers colour vision gradually before any differentiated shapes can be perceived. Figural experiences need not necessarily be visual, they can happen with sound, touch, taste and smell as well.

Among primitive organisations of our perceptual process there is a unique feature of illusion. An illusion is commonly defined as false perception. When we experience an illusion, we perceive things, which do not correspond to the objective reality. It is a primitive organisation like the ones discussed earlier, but is far more complicated than groupings. As a matter of fact its origin is not very well understood. It also involves the working of the sense organs and nervous system, past experiences etc., in the same way as found in a perception. There are very many examples of visual illusion, but we shall mention here a very popular one. Muller-Lyer illusion (Fig. 8.3). In this we find an incorrect perception of the length of the vertical lines. Normally the vertical line. A looks smaller than that of 'B' although both lines are equal. Experiments with children old enough to indicate the nature of their experiences gave similar reports on this. Furthermore, chickens trained to discriminate the length when subjected to such an experiment reacted in similar way, as did humans. The findings certainly suggest that some animals react as if they see things the same way as we do.

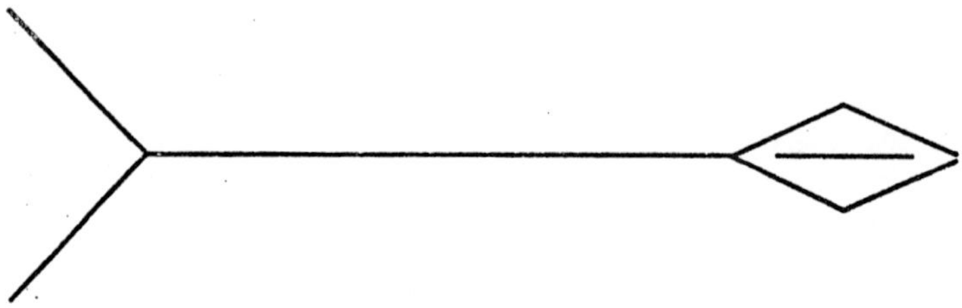

The Muller-Lyer Illusion

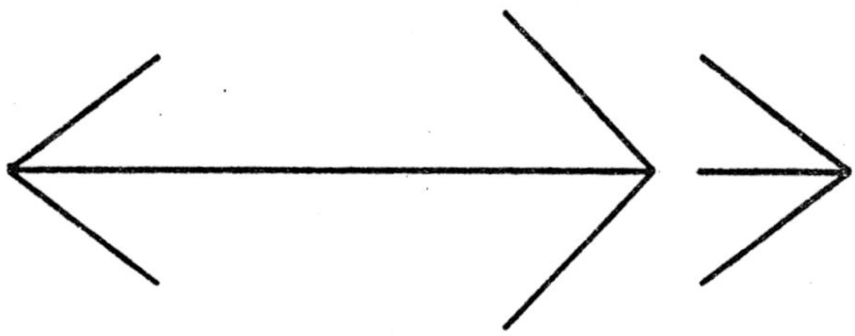

Fig 8.3

Which vertical line seems longer, A or B? Actually they are the same length.

The lack of one-to-one relation between the object we perceive and the way perceive it, is intriguing. Perhaps, the strong view expressed on this phenomenon is that we see things not as they are, but as we are. This statement, however, suggests the function of illusions in our lives. Perhaps, psychologically we experience illusions only. Now let us examine some of the important illusions which are taken as perception. We can start with the example of perceptual constancy to illustrate the point. We know that the mechanism of visual perception is very much dependent on the formation of retinal image of the object seen in the visual field. Further, we also know that the structure of the eye is like a camera, which for ns the image precisely the way, the latter does. The question is, then, why is the perceptual experience not true to the image formed on the retina? A 6ft tall man seen from a distance of 10 yards will not form the same image when he is seen from a distance of one thousand yards. Like in a camera a distant image will appear very short in height (size) in the viewer's eyes. However, the viewer will perceive the man of the same size and length even at a distance. Similarly, the shape of a familiar object to us will not appear changed if viewed from different angles or from above, although the retinal images formed under different conditions will definitely not be the same. It can be inferred, therefore, that the phenomenon of constancy in perception is not the result of sensory experiences, but determined by the psychological factors particularly of familiarity with the object or situation, which provide clues.

The constancy of colour and brightness, again, is governed by the same principle of perception. Objects endure in our experiences as we meet them too often. A well-known object is perceived as stable and unchanged even if viewed under varying illumination conditions. The popular example of coal and chalk is quoted here to explain the function. A piece of coal and a chalk seen under bright sunlight and away from the light under the shade will not cause different perceptions. In principle the coal piece should be perceived less black than the original appearance under the bright sun light and the chalk less white under the dismal illumination and *vice versa*. But do we notice variation in their brightness because of the change in their condition? The answer will be negative. Our perception has not changed by the varying wavelength of light reflected from them; rather the constancy of colour and brightness clues has affected our perception.

The constancy of colour, brightness, shape, size and location of objects draws on the perceptual cues as well as familiarity with the object. Experimental evidence has shown that the more information about the distance of the object is available, the more perceived size tends to be nearer the actual size of the object. As the distance cues are eliminated, there is a greater correspondence between the retinal image formed and size perceived. Again, this does not happen with the familiar object. The familiar object's size is estimated to its correct level in the absence of the depth and distance cues.

The size constancy for distant objects develops with experience and maturity. In an experiment with eight year olds and adults judging the size of objects at different distances ranging from 10ft to 100ft, it was found that both groups performed similarly close to size estimation at 10ft, but the children showed progressively less size constancy than the adults at the increasing distances. In other words, children's estimates were close to their retinal images.

The perception of depth by us is very complex. Our retina is a two-dimensional surface and enables us to perceive the third dimension. How this visualization in the space is achieved is said to be determined by the binocular cues to depth. There is experimental evidence to show that the two eyes together make a stereoscopic vision, they cooperate to give the experience of solidity and distance. The use of stereoscope by each eye will yield the difference in depth perception of the two eyes. Here is an example of retinal disparity. You shut your one eye and hold a pencil at the distance of one ft, right in front of your nose. Further, you line that pencil up with the opened eye against an edge of a wall or a door. Then close the opened eye and open the shut one looking at the pencil. You will notice that the pencil will look much removed from the aligned line and the edge of the wall. The two eyes relay independently the impulses as the nerve fibers from both the eyes start from different parts of the face, but merge and combine in the occipital lobe of the cerebral cortex where the visual experience takes place or perception is affected.

The binocular cues are essential for the perception of depth or distance but this does not negate the function of depth perception if, for some reasons, the two eyes cannot be used. The perception of depth can be affected by monocular cues as well, that is, cues received from one eye. Some of the monocular cues of depth perception are given here.

Interposition

If one object obstructs the view of another or super-imposes its position on the other, then the second object goes back to the distance and the strong first one looks nearer.

Size of the Image

If there are some objects of different sizes arranged in an order or row, the smaller size objects will be perceived in distance.

Linear and Aerial Perspective

Height or horizontal elevation on the same plane causes a perception of distance. If the same size things are presented on the same flat surface but at different heights. The higher one will look farther from the surface one.

In the situation of uneven, rocky or wavy surface, the texture of gradient creates the perception of distance. The grain looks finer when the distance increases.

Shadows

Light and shade help to define the contours of the object in third dimension, as we find in the picture painted by the artists : distant objects look hazy and blurred and dark areas as shadow away from the light.

Movement Cues

Movement of the object and the postural adjustment of the perceiver also contribute to the perception of distance. In judging distance a person will move his head back and forth and will get the kind of advantage that the retinal disparity would give in stereoscopic vision. Besides, the relative speed of moving objects provide cues for judging distance. Objects seen moving speedily by us are judged nearer than the ones, which move slowly.

Another illusion is found in the perception of motion when there is no motion. In sensory term, perception of movement is stimulation of sensory parts in succession, one after the other. When an image moves across the line of vision, it produces a pattern of stimulations of rods and cones happening in succession. The problem arises when sensory stimulation is not borne by the perceptual experience. It is possible to create successive stimulations without yielding the perception of movement. The sensory information has got to be organized to that effect by the higher brain.

The perception of real movement depends on kinesthetic information from visual as well as other senses. On receipt of the information the brain has to organize and decide about the reaction to a reference. In a visual movement it has to be judged which one is moving and which one is stationary in the context of visual field. However, our habituation with the use of reference, context and background in making perceptual reaction, always disposes us to succumb to illusions.

Let us take the perception of induced movement and not the real one. Such example we see is seeing the racing moon when framed in by the thin moving clouds. We see that the latter looks static, although the same is not true. It happens because the background or reference point starts moving and induces movement in the relatively stationary object.

The auto kinetic effect is another example of the illusion of motion. If we look into completely dark room at a single spot of light for a while it will appear that the light has started moving backward and forward, upward and downward and sometimes shooting off in one direction. This kind of perception is called auto-kinetic effect. It occurs because there is no reference point to which the light could be related in a completely dark room. The perception of apparent motion in the absence of actual movement can be seen in the projection of cinema or in the rotating lighting arrangement etc. This is called "Stroboscopic motion". Phi-phenomenon is another name of a simple form of stroboscopic motion popularly used in psychological laboratory. Here the motion is created by the presentation of still pictures in succession rapidly. We see all actions and movements in the film although they are no more than the presentation of separate still pictures.

In the fore-going discussion, although the emphasis was on the perception as an inter-sensory experience, most of the phenomena discussed were directly related to the visual perceptions. Here some of the features of auditory perception will be briefly illustrated. Auditory space perception is also dependent on cues. Like visual it can be monaural if only one ear is used or binaural when both ears. As far as the perception of distance is concerned, the monaural cues will do, but if further location of sound source is needed, the binaural cues will be absolutely necessary.

The monaural cues to the perception of distance are the loudness, complexity and volume of sound. Familiar objects when generating sound if heard less loudly, we infer that the object is away at a far distance. On the other hand, if the loudness increases, we think that the same is coming from a closer distance. Similarly, the distant sound does not make itself heard in all its complexities. A tune from a distance will be audible faintly; the complexities of its different notes will not be appreciated at all until it is heard from nearby. Again, along with the loudness, the volume of sound produced is another cue which helps determine the perception of distance. The short-distance sound will fill in more space than the long distance one; for example, a boom of a fired cannon will occupy more space near the source and drown every other sound in it, than the same boom heard from a long distance.

The binaural cues, though drawing on the afore said cues are very important in locating the direction of a sound. The localization of sound will be impossible, if both ears did not work differently. The time difference is one of the important factors, which influence the perception of sound in its location. The nearer ear to the source of sound receives the sound first and then the other ear, which is not nearer, gets the sound and this provides a cue of time difference. This is an important cue in locating the direction of the sound source. In the same context, the difference in intensity of the sound will be felt by the nearer ear. The greater the intensity of sound, the stronger the stimulation of the ear receiving it.

This strong stimulation makes a difference with the less intense stimulation received by the non-nearer ear. Intensity in this way provides a differential cue for the localization of the direction of sound. The other important binaural cue is related to the phase of the sound cycle activating both ears. The sound cycle may be different when they stimulate the two ears at the same time. This is called phase difference cues and is important when a tonal stimulus is involved. In a long wave cycle one ear may be stimulated by the condensation, crest of the wave, and the other by rarefaction, the trough or depression. However, with the short-cycle wave of high frequencies, the condition may be a bit different as one ear may be stimulated by the crest of one wave and the other ear by the crest of the other wave. Sometimes, it is difficult for some individuals to localize the sound direction on the basis of phase difference.

Generally the binaural cues of time, intensity and phase differences happen concurrently and facilitate locating unfamiliar and unseen sounds. The entire process of using these cues in auditory space perception is described as stereophonic hearing.

The perception of space can be summed up not as a simple sense reaction, rather an integration of cues from all senses; visual, auditory, tactile somasthetic, and kinesthetic. However in some animals, some of the senses may play more important parts than the others, as the value of olfaction and skin temperature in determining their perception of objects in some animals is well known. Human perception, none-the-less, has to rely on the combination of cues from all senses. This integration enables humans to handle the objects easily and freely without even looking at them every time. Besides, in the event of sensory handicap like blindness or deafness, the cues perceived by different senses turn out to be of enormous help. Experimental studies in making adjustment with the visually disturbed situation, the role of feedback from the muscles and motor parts of the nervous system has been recognized. The distortions created by wearing distorting lenses are compensated by active movements and explorations. The cues are gained from the muscles and postures used. It was found that the subjects wearing the same glasses, but were passive and immobilized being pushed around in the wheel-chair, could not adapt to the distorted visual field. The experiments carried out on kitten and infant monkeys presented similar results and supported the hypothesis that perceptual experience as well as behavioural experience, both culminate in providing visuo-motor co-ordination.

Furthermore, an important feature of perception is that the event is perceived, as pointed out, in the context of whole and against the back-ground of other events. The emphasis is on the relational determinants. One of the examples of the effect of the context in perception can be drawn from the experience of simultaneous colour contrast. If a small gray square is put at the centre of a coloured paper, which is large in size, the complement of the paper colour will be induced at the edges of the gray square. A red will produce green and so on. Simultaneous colour contrast will be seen. These induction-effects are caused by the context. Land (1959) has shown that many colours can be produced by super imposing two projected images on a screen.

The concept of adaptation level has been developed to quantify and provide a theory regarding contextual effect. The main theme is that the context sets a standard against which the events of perceptual objects are evaluated. Experimental studies in the field of sensory perception involving judgment of size of squares under different contextual conditions reveal that the bias is introduced in judgment due to these contexts. The back-ground of the large anchor resulted in a reduction of size estimate of the stimuli and small anchor increased the judged size of the stimuli (Helson, 1964). The concept of adaptation level is not only applicable to the area of sensory perception, but can also be extended to social perception. A mediocre student will give the impression of being dull amidst a class of bright students, but the same student will appear very good in a class of dimwits.

Figural after-effects are another phenomena, which strongly support the function of relational determinism. The idea was put forward by the Gestaltists. Experiments with the problem requiring the subject to fixate on the inspection object (I) for several minutes and then on the test object (T) presented at the same point of fixation and for the same length of time have shown that subjects report the displacement of this test-object relatively downward. The test object may also appear paler and farther back in the space in relation to another test object. There is an explanation available in terms of brain function for this type of perceptual function, but the Gestalt Psychologists explain it differently. According to them the events in one part of the perceptual field may affect perception in another part.

In the preceding paragraphs the structural and organizational tendencies in our perceptual experience and reaction have been discussed. Now we shall examine the psychological-functional part of the perceptual process, which is equally fundamental. We have always referred to familiarity and past experience in determining perception. These past experiences are results of learning. Learning helps us to perceive things, but also makes our perception selective. It is impossible to perceive everything that happens around us. We perceive those aspects of environment, which we find to give us satisfaction and reject those, which do not. In this process of selective reaction our mind shows remarkable capacity and efficiency. Let us take an example of looking for a friend in a big crowd at the railway station. We do not lose much time in searching our friend. We scan quickly and eliminate the unwanted information. We perceive our friend in the midst of so many faces.

Psychologists have demonstrated the function of mental set in selective perception. Set is a kind of general readiness to perceive and interpret the environment in a particular way. It can be created by internal as well as external factors. Among the internal factors; interests, emotions, attitudes and values, and needs are of striking significance. These variables are largely determined by our learning and past experiences. Even the biogenic needs of thirst, hunger and sex, which are unlearned, get influenced by our past experiences. In the light of our experiences we develop expectations, which set us to perceive aspects of environment selectively. Some of us perceive something which others do not and *vice versa*. In doing so, we avoid and overlook certain aspects of the environment that are not in consonance with our interests.

Perception, therefore, involves selection of relevant from the many irrelevant stimuli and gets them organized on the basis of stored knowledge. We perform such searching and scanning operations many times in one day. Let us take the example of looking up a number in the telephone directory of a person named Sinha whom we want to talk with for an important piece of information and who resides in Wellington Street. There may be hundreds of Sinhas printed in the directory on that street, but we do not lose much time in scanning down the person named 'Sinha' whom we really want. So many 'Sinhas' in the list, are passed on very quickly being irrelevant to our purpose as if they are not seen at all. Similarly, when we look for a friend at a big railway station where so many people are hurrying through, we find him quickly. The unfamiliar names in the telephone directory or unfamiliar faces in the crowd at the railway station must have been examined some way to enable elimination of the unwanted ones and selection of the needed one. The scanner, as a matter of fact, extracts information and passes on to different levels of perception from simple to the complex. It seems to be carried out, as referred to earlier by a vast number of independent mechanisms arranged in a hierarchy.

The personal values and attitudes of the perceiver towards the object are reflected in his perceptual reactions. Studies showed significant differences between rich and poor children in estimating sizes of the coin; the poor overestimated more than the wealthy. When sweet candy was treated as valued object, children judged the jars of candy heavier than the jars of sand of the same weight. These personal characteristics as organizing factors in our perceptual experiences and reactions have been demonstrated effectively. The physical needs of hunger have been found to determine the perception of food-related objects in vague drawings etc. In a study with the semi-starved people who demurred the World War II, interesting results were revealed; people showed markedly increased attention to cookbooks, recipes and pictures of foods.

The perception of social environment has been another area where individuals' personality has been found to play an important part. Religious beliefs and attitudes of the individual, pattern the way of their thinking and viewing things. Some of the social tensions and group conflicts that spark off are caused because the members of the respective groups interpret things differently due to these beliefs and attitudes. Social perceptions are very much group related; individuals' belongingness to a reference-group determines his perceptual reaction to a social and cultural situation or events.

Personal characteristics of an individual influence a good deal his perception of events as well. He perceives the situation in his own personal way with no intention of perceiving like others. He picks out things that suit him and ignores the other facts unknowingly. There are examples to show that how different witnesses to the same event give varying accounts of things happening, sometimes dramatically different, although they do not wish to lie or deceive. The distortions are imposed due to the personal hopes, fears and wishes of the perceiver.

Sets can be created by the external factors as well. Experimental studies with different instructional sets on individuals' performance under the laboratory conditions are reported. In these experiments the materials presented to be perceived are always vague and ambitious. Further, they are exposed or presented for a very brief time span so that the subjects do not get enough time to discern the details. One famous example is quoted here, in which the set was introduced by a definite set of instructions given by the experimenter. When ambiguous figures were exposed briefly like 0-0, and subjects instructed to expect a pair of glasses, they produced drawings like 0~0 and so on. In a similar experiment, the subjects were required to write down words shown on the screen. The exposure time was very short. The material exposed contained meaningful words as well as nonsense words. The same set of materials was presented to two groups of subjects, one expecting words connected with birds and animals and the other relating to travel. The results were very much expected; subjects expecting birds wrote 'parrot' for 'passport' and 'chick' for 'check', whereas those expecting travel, wrote 'passport' for the former and 'check' for the latter. Distortion in the nonsense words was also noted as an effect of set.

The influence of group pressure on individual's perception is another example of set created by external factors. The experimental study on 'autokinetic' effect (discussed earlier) was used in groups to estimate the length of light or distance travelled by the light and the judgment of the individual member of the group was found to be influenced by others' opinion. Even in a situation where the stimulus was an impersonal thing the perception of the individual was influenced by other members' estimation unwittingly.

Motivation learned or unlearned, influence of family, friends and groups colour our perception. Our emotional involvement with the objects, situations and persons constituting our world make our perception and judgment far from being objective. It is well known that we cannot convince people in argument who hold opposite views. When we are in love, we can't see faults in our sweetheart, whereas others, who are not involved, can.

The problem of perceiving has been tackled by another model and set of principles couched in the frame-work of communication theory. The physical communication sciences have given rise to communication theory, which is also known as information theory. This theory postulates systems of functional relationship among symbolic events and uses probabilistic terms to explain the phenomena. These models have been developed by psychologists working in the field of engineering and computer-sciences. Information theory has not provided answers to all problems of psychology, nor claims to do so, however, it has made positive advances in our understanding of human behaviour in several psychological areas. Further, this approach has come up with a powerful tool of statistical analysis. The basic unit of informational measurement is a' bit', a contraction of 'binary digit' used widely in distinguishing objects from amongst different classes.

As mentioned earlier, the theory depends on the use of systems. System may be defined as a group of components designed to fulfill a given set of objectives through their collective action. In any situation, if the system is used to transmit information from one unit to another, this will involve a communication and thereby be called communication system. The component, again, may differ from one system of communication to another, but some fundamental principles will govern them all. In a general communicating system five components are found; source, transmitter, channel, receiver and destination. A diagram of the system is presented in Figure 8.4.

Here the process is illustrated in the form of human communication, particularly vocal one. A person talks to another, so the first person acts as a source of information. When he says something to convey, he uses his transmitter (speech mechanism)

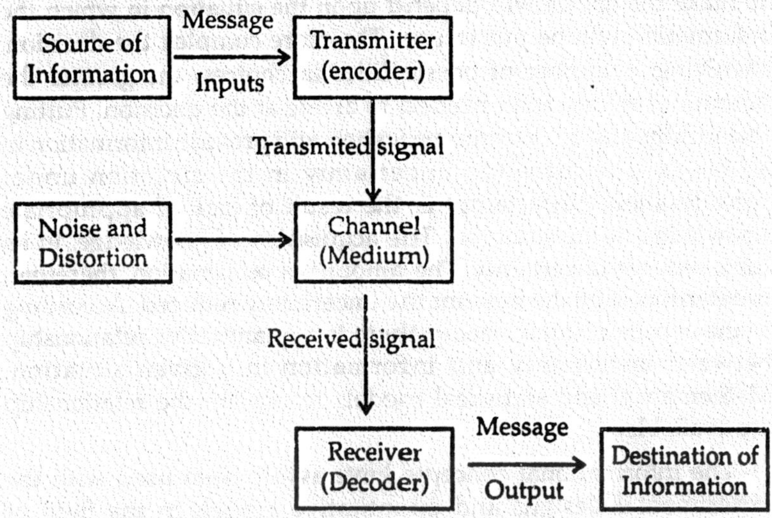

Fig. 8.4. Components of a general communication system.

and generates sound-waves of varying pattern, in other words, coded signals and transmit them. These transmitted signals are carried through the air—the communication channel. The channel connects the speaker's voice to the receiver in this case the listener's ears. The receiver (decoder) converts the signal into neural impulses and relay them (output) to the temporal lobe in the brain. The nervous system of the listener acts as a destination in this case. In this process of communication a message can be distorted and interfered with noise etc., and cause disruption in the passage of information and error can creep in.

In the information theory, the role of channel capacity should not be undervalued. The channel capacity is the upper-limit of the amount of information that can be transmitted in a system. With the increase in the inputs of information to the maximum capacity of the channel, the system does not work. In other words, when the stimulus uncertainty in a given situation gets unmanageably high, the communication does not take place.

The word 'information' figures in this communication theory too often, which means facts observed in the world. These can be acquired from people, objects and events. In making choice or reaching a decision in a given matter we seek information. The kind of information as well as the amount of information necessary to make the choice will depend upon the situation in which the information will be put to use. The more complex the decision, involving a number of possibilities in choices, the greater the amount of information needed to arrive at the decision. Putting technically, any act of communication will provide information in so far as it reduces the uncertainty in the situation under consideration. Uncertainty is the result of lack of appropriate knowledge in the situation. The acquisition of knowledge, in its turn, reduces uncertainty. The amount of information, therefore, is determined by the amount the uncertainty reduced. According to the communication theory there is a quantitative relationship between uncertainty and information in a given situation. Mathematical and statistical models to explain the relationship are available.

The informational concepts have avidly been used with the experimental designs and quantitative models in the field of perceptual recognition and discrimination. Here the significance of patterning and organization is emphasized. The stimuli are organized and patterned in terms of previously stored knowledge. The characteristics of the pattern are selected in at the loss of irrelevant details. By patterning salient features we categorize objects unambiguously. The researches in this area of pattern recognition have been drawn up from the domain of artificial intelligence and development of automation in computers. The programme fed in the computer to control pattern recognition is based on the functional specifications. The computer picks out the magnetic numbers or designs to identify the forms, shape, handwriting etc., as we do in our behaviour.

The fundamental step in recognizing pattern is to tackle the stimulus-equivalence. This is the phenomenon which is based on the hypothesis that a particular pattern or category is represented by a set of stimuli which differs from another. The stimuli form an equivalent class and can be differentiated from another class. In our example of Figure 8.5 Type-face A can be recognized even if A's are presented in unfamiliar ways. The process therefore, is explained as a template-matching behaviour. The stimulus is matched with some stored pattern for quality of fit. The process gets sophisticated from simple patterns to complex ones at the human level but does not become perfect. There are drawbacks in this pattern recognition; firstly, it cannot account for size invariance, where a pattern can be recognized even if it is of varying size. Secondly, its variation in perspective, that is, when the pattern is rotated or put upside-down, renders it unmatchable.

a **A** A A A *A* A A **A** **A** **AA**

Fig. : 8.5

Another model of pattern recognition is 'feature-extracting'. Here the stimulus is examined for the presence of various features and then on that basis assessment is made as to what set of features must imply in a particular category. A bank of feature detectors or 'computational demons' detects the presence of various features and passes the results to the next phase. The next phase is to receive the outputs of feature-detectors into the cognitive demon and make a re-synthesis of the features. There is one cognitive demon for every pattern and one input of detection at lower level can activate the output of cognitive demon in the same proportion. One advantage of this model is explained to emphasize that it has got less problems than stimulus equivalence. For example, if we detect the difference between rectangles and pentagons by counting the number of corners, we shall establish the correct pattern every time whatever the rotation of the figures.

The model can be used in the auditory as well as other fields. The feature detection is dependent on selective attention, which has been dealt with elsewhere. However, according to information theory, man can be seen not as a sensor but as a decision-maker on the basis of information he collects, filters, stores and evaluates.

9 Learning

In our discussion on perception we mentioned how do we learn to perceive? Here we want to say that this is also true that we perceive to learn. The psychological study of learning does not imply only the acquiring of skills, verbal or motor, or doing a whole lot of academic exercises, but it embraces our entire development, from motivation to perception, and from social and emotional behaviour to the full grown personality. We learn to be as we are. So our development as a person is a process of learning. We learn to be different from other animals and also from one another in our own kind. Suppose, what would happen if every thing we have learnt were erased by some technique without damaging the brain-cells and nervous system? We, certainly, would become a baby again, helpless and dependent, at the mercy of others. We would be aware of our environment, but would not be in a position to do anything. Even our biogenic needs of food and drink would not be satisfied, as we would not know how to meet them. Similarly, we would not worry about our success or failure, feeling of shame or guilt or fear.

In this wide context it is not very easy to define learning in the strictest sense of the term. Psychologists have debated this issue of definition and come up with varying emphasis, but there is unity in diversities that characterizes the nature of our learning process. Learning is regarded as a modification in behaviour resulting from experience and has a relatively lasting effect. Further, the change in behaviour should occur due to what happens in the environment or world around and also by our own doing in relation to that. The change should not be caused by factors other than learning itself. The behaviour modified by physical maturation happening automatically and naturally with the passage of time or caused by drug or injury or due to the effect of fatigue etc. will not count towards learning. In other words, the change in behaviour as a result of effort and experience caused mainly by external stimulation will be accepted as a learned behaviour. Further, it has also been argued that the change in behaviour should be meaningful and purposive and aim towards improvement. The change for change sake should not comprise the meaning of learning. But some observer points finger to this contention of improvement. They feel that we bring in value judgment in defining learning by this statement. Now we shall examine in detail how learning takes place.

The problem of learning preoccupied philosophers, particularly English, called 'associationists' and dates back to late eighteenth and early nineteenth centuries. These associationists postulated that learning involved association between processes in the brain representing stimulus events experienced by the person. This implied connection in time and place between events. It is like the occurrence of two events simultaneously or in succession. For example, lightening and thunder happen in close succession and can be taken to mean that light and sound are connected. Behaviourists borrowed this approach of philosophers to establish stimulus-response association and to reject the subjective introspectionism in psychological studies. Actually before the behaviourists could champion the cause of objectivity in psychology, psychologist like Thorndike has started experimenting with animals in establishing stimulus-response (S-R) association in learning.

Philosophers of the time employed ideas and images created by sensations to form associations, whereas psychologists used the concept to denote connection between two stimuli (S-S) or sensory experiences, as well as between stimulus and response (S-R). Although some psychologists believed that the association occurred between stimulus and stimulus and still do, the behaviourists rejected it on the ground that the same could not be studied objectively and strongly supported the theory of stimulus-response (S-R) association. In any association contiguity is of vital significance and the corresponding processes in the brain of the two experiences have got to be paired together. However, it cannot be ruled out that one stimulus may get associated with two different responses and one of the responses can interfere with the other. But generally the learner associates a stimulus event with a response and further makes a chain of associations facilitating automatic behaviour. The whole chain of associations can be responsible for the complex form of responses. In such an event the association takes place between stimulus-response and response produced stimulus-response and so on. The following example will illustrate the chaining :

S (starts process) → R1 → RS → R2 → RS →

Fig. 9.1

For example, while driving a car with a manual gear; first we press the clutch pedal then move the gearshift, which is a response produced stimulus, and then again release the clutch and press on the accelerator. It is hypothesized that chaining takes place in the nervous system and renders the learned behaviour in automatic sequence.

The value of motivation and reinforcement in experimental studies of learning must be emphasized here before we go on to discuss the theories and processes of learning. No experiment is possible with animal or human subject in the absence of these two.

The subjects are to be motivated by creating needs, biological or psychological, in them to perform activities. Hunger or thirst or praise or avoidance of pain drives the subject to act and these are to be satisfied with food or water or praise or escape from pain etc. In other words the activities performed by the subject to achieve these goals are to be reinforced. Reinforcement is widely used term with different emphasis in connotation. Originally, reward and punishment were used for reinforcement and were subsumed under the law of effect of Thorndike (1911). We shall discuss this law of effect when we mention Thorndike's trial and error process of learning. Here we must say that the concept of reinforcement has advantages over the concept of reward. The latter is always vested in the external agent or the experimenter and could not generate subject's activity as well as act as a modifier of the subject's behaviour by itself. Hence, the widespread use of positive or negative reinforcer in place of reward and punishment is found in the literature now-a-days.

The process of reinforcement has been explained in five ways in psychology. One among the five is the need reduction theory of

Hull (1943). According to him the physiological conditions or needs of the organism like hunger and thirst, and their satisfaction are the cruciai factors in forming association between stimulus and response. Closely related to this need-reduction is the drive-stimulus reduction theory of Miller and Dollard (1941). This theory broadens the need reduction to include a reduction in the intensity of stimulation arising from the need states. For example, the reduction in physical pain from the shock would be reinforcing the learning of association.

Guthrie presumes a third feature of reinforcement. He regards that reinforcer is an event that takes the learner out of the practice situation and, therefore, the last-made stimulus-response association is preserved. There is no interference by the other kind of association after the former association has been reinforced. He coins the phraseology of terminal-response theory to describe this phenomenon. Stimulus theory is the fourth kind of explanation of the effectiveness of reinforcement. The advocates of this theory hold that some stimuli are inherently reinforcing like sweet tastes etc. they argue that in talking about stimuli's inherent reinforcing quality, the effect to be produced should not display already learned effect. This view was put forth by several others and has found support in later researches of Pfaffman also (1964).

A fifth theory of Pirmack (1959) known as response-theory states that a weak response occurring at low rate if followed by stronger response in terms of rate and intensity, gets reinforced by the latter. The weaker response gets strengthened by the stronger one. For example, pressing the bar by rats increased from the low rate to high rate as the higher rate of pressing gave them more sugar-water to lick. Each of the five mechanisms has something to contribute to the concept of reinforcement. Sometimes one alone and at other times in combination can help reinforce associations and pave the way for learning.

Skinner (1953), on the other hand, disregarded the theoretical issue involved in reinforcement mechanism and draws on the empirical law of effect. He, along with others, believes that reinforcement can be any thing, which can make a response more likely. Reinforcements increase the frequency of responses. Any event or stimulus that increases the frequency should be called reinforcer. Further, reinforcer of one learning situation can also be used in another situation to increase the frequency of responses.

Obviously now, we can't talk about learning or stimulus-response association without bringing in the concept of reinforcement. It is therefore, of immense importance and will be used throughout the text in reference to the approaches of learning theory. We begin here with the Trial and Error theory of S-R association by Thorndike. Now-a-days, Trial and Error is treated as instrumental conditioning and should not surprise anyone who does not find the name mentioned in the modern text-book of psychology. He postulated that learning is a gradual process and depends on the strengthening of the stimulus-response bond. He experimented with animal subjects to demonstrate the phenomenon and observed his cats learning to press the lever to get out of the cage or his rats learning the correct pathway of the maze to get the food and so on. He found that his subject made many random attempts and fumbled before accidentally found or made the correct response. The correct response of the subject was always reinforced; food was made available or shock could be avoided. It was observed that with the repetition of trials the errors got eliminated and correct responses increased. Thorndike saw this stamping-in of the right response and stamping-out of the wrong ones as a basis to formulate his law of exercise and law of effect in trial and error learning. The first law implied repetition and practice and the second denoted reinforcement, *i.e.* reward or punishment.

In his subsequent pursuit he found considerable support for his law of effect, but not much for the law of exercise. Whatever the theoretical orientation, the law of effect finds an empirical justification in establishing the stimulus-response (S-R) connection and is used in the guise of reinforcement extensively.

The Trial and Error process of learning is ungrudgingly accepted by psychologists in acquiring motor and psycho-motor skills where practice is of paramount importance in achieving perfection. However, the theory of hit and miss method in learning faces severe criticisms. This approach cannot explain the problem-solving behaviour or perceptual learning of higher animals and humans. Further, this can also not justify single experience learning. Some psychologists argue that Thorndike's experimental conditions could not provide his subject with a whole view of the situation and, therefore, could not provide scope for the use of any other or higher mechanism of finding association in learning the path-way leading to the goal. On the contrary, some believe that trying out different schemes or plans to solve the problem in learning situation goes on mentally or covertly before the final correct response is expressed overtly by the subject.

In the S-R tradition of learning theory comes another well-known process of classical conditioning developed by a Russian physiologist, Pavlov (1927). His primary interest centred round gastric secretions and for the research in that area he was awarded the Nobel Prize. In an accidental way he stumbled on the Conditioned Reflex Theory. This theory later became the back-bone of the principles developed in explaining human learning and habit formation. Pavlov demonstrated his laboratory the procedure of conditioning a dog to salivate to the ringing of the bell. He inserted a tube in the dog's cheek to obtain salivary secretions. First he noted that the dog salivated not only when he saw the food, but also when he saw the bowl, the experimenter and heard the sound of the experimenter's foot-step. This observation led him to think that there may be happening some sort of association in the brain of the animal to respond to the stimulus and he started on the classical conditioning experiments.

In a classical conditioning procedure the important fact is to substitute a neutral stimulus in place of original stimulus, which elicited response. Pavlov showed that his dog could be conditioned

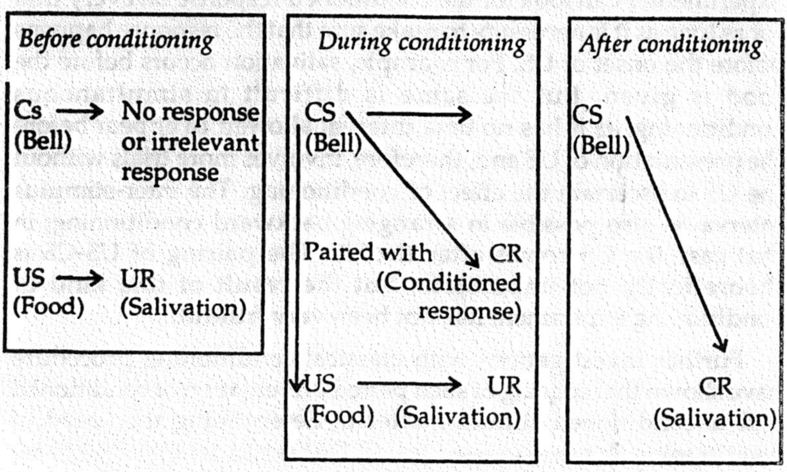

Fig. 9.2

to salivate in response to a sound of bell or flash of light or metronome beat. He presented the sound of the bell first followed by food that evoked salivary response. After repeated trials of sound followed by food, the sound itself could elicit salivation. The salivation became conditioned response to the conditioned stimulus of bell sound.

In the process of conditioning, a neutral stimulus (bell) called the conditioned stimulus CS is paired with the unconditioned stimulus US (food) for a number of times, which elicits unconditioned response UR (salivation). After conditioning, conditioned stimulus CS (bell) comes to evoke salivation, which becomes conditioned response CR in the absence of US.

With the use of this procedure we can have three variations in classical conditioning; simultaneous, delayed and trace. In simultaneous conditioning the CS begins a fraction of a second or so before the introduction of the US and continues along till the response occurs. In delayed conditioning, the CS is delayed a bit that is, presented several seconds before the US is given and continued through till the response happens. The trace conditioning, however, requires the CS to be presented and terminated or removed and interval allowed relatively longer than usual, before the presentation of the US. In this situation the subject responds to the neutral trace of the CS and conditioning is called trace-conditioning. In delayed and trace conditioning the experimenter can look for the conditioned response on every trial for as long as it is necessary to make sure that the response happens before the onset of US. For example, salivation occurs before the food is given. But the same is difficult in simultaneous conditioning, as it has no time interval allowed to appear before the presentation of US and, therefore, involves more trials without the US to ascertain the effect of conditioning. The inter-stimulus interval is also possible in arranging backward conditioning; in that case the CS comes after the US. The pairing of US-CS is theoretically not impossible, but the result of this kind of conditioning experiment has not been very fruitful.

Further investigations with classical conditioning procedure have shown that spacing of such paired presentation of conditioned and unconditioned stimuli matter in determining the speed of conditioning. It has also been found that when several CS-US are presented closely one after another, conditioning is slower as compared with the same number of CS-US units spaced apart. Another facet of classical conditioning needing reference here is the use of more than one conditioned stimulus at the same time, for example, using visual and auditory stimuli together. The results of such experiments indicate that a compound conditioned stimulus is no more effective than the single one used separately (Perlmuter, 1966).

It will not be out of place to mention here the other kind of experiment in classical conditioning before we go on to examine some other features of this learning process. Bekhterev another contemporary Russian neurologist pioneered the experiments in "reflexology" by means of conditioning procedure. He used electric shock rather than food used by Pavlov. In a way he started with negative reinforcer and presented a shock as US to the sheep's forelimb or hindlimb after the presentation of CS of light or sound in order to study sheep's limb flexion. The experimental hypothesis and procedure of classical conditioning remained unchanged and the flexion response to a previously neural stimulus of light and sound was established as the conditioned response. However, a significant difference from Pavlov's method was noted in Bekhtereuv. In experiment the test trial was not employed. In salivary conditioning, however Bekhterev's test trials of CS presentation without US were considered necessary to check whether or not the CS alone could produce that response. Bekhterev on the other hand, used the situation to foster "anticipatory" conditioned reaction. The subject anticipated the shock before the presentation of US and responded accordingly.

The classical conditioning method has been used with different kinds of responses on humans as well as animal subjects. Human conditioning with eye blinking reflexes, Galvanic skin responses, and heartbeat rates etc. have yielded valuable information about the process of acquiring skills and learning and our adaptive behaviour in the world, physical and social-psychological. Now we shall take a look at these features of conditioning process, which presented problems. The important one was the problem of extinction. If the conditioned response was not reinforced repeatedly and US was withdrawn in these trials after the presentation of CS, there occurred the eventual cessation of CR. This gradual weakening of the strength of the response turning into the stoppage of the response was described as a phenomenon of 'extinction'. For example, if the dog who was conditioned to salivate to the sound of bell when not given food every time it made conditioned response of salivation, gradually lost the learned response with unreinforced trials and finally stopped salivating. Moreover the experimentally extinguished response CR returned after a lapse of time spontaneously without going through the reconditioning process. This problem of spontaneous recovery of response was not that simple to explain. It was argued that even after extinction of the response some degree of association was retained between the CS and CR, which recovered the lost strength after a rest or no-trial period. Two possible factors were hypothesized to explain this phenomenon. One was interference; learning of new association (not respond the old way) interfered with the old one. The old and new associations competed with each other and in consequence the subject learned not to respond. The second factor was regarded as just 'inhibition' a tendency in the subject not to respond at all due to fatigue. So after the decay in built-up inhibition which dissipated with the passage of time, as well as, due to the slackening of interference between opposing associations which also happened with the lapse of time, the animal's learned response recovered spontaneously in the experimental situation. Even in some instances where the animals had to relearn to respond, the rate of re-conditioning was faster than the original conditioning.

Stimulus generalization is another interesting feature of classical conditioning. Pavlov established that if an animal was conditioned to salivate to the sound of a bell, it could be conditioned to other similar stimuli, like the sound of a buzzer or beat of a metronome. The subject responded to the similar stimuli or stimuli bearing some kind of resemblance with the original one. He postulated that the magnitude of response in such event was a function of the degree of similarity between the new and original stimuli. The stimulus generalization, according to him, was a result of effect of spread from one region of the brain to the other—a process of 'irradiation of excitation'.

Stimulus generalisation can extend over a wide field. For example, when a human subject's galvanic skin response is conditioned to the sound of a bell, it has been found to show changes even with the hearing of the word 'bell' and by seeing a bell. The work of a Russian psychologist Volkova demonstrated the effect of generalization in semantic conditioning with children. She established the salivary conditioning in some children by pronouncing Russian word for 'good'. The generalization was tested by pronouncing some sentences in the same language that indicated 'good' and others that did not. The differences in result were found to support the generalization hypothesis of conditioned response (1953).

A complement to the process of stimulus generalization is 'differential conditioning'. Whereas generalization is associated with the similarity in stimuli, discrimination is related to differences in them. In the way of classical conditioning, the subject may be conditioned or trained to differentiate between the two stimuli, to respond to one and not to the other. For example, a dog is conditioned to salivate when the stimulus bell is sounded. Here the food is given immediately after the dog has salivated. A little later when horn is sounded, the food does not follow. At first the dog will salivate to all sounds of that nature irrespective of their differences, but gradually by discrimination conditioning the salivation to sound other than the bell-sound will get extinguished. We find the example in our children learning the name "daddy". First the child uses the word for all men he sees, but by differential reinforcement and extinction the response is directed to a single appropriate stimulus, own daddy.

The second order or higher order conditioning is another important aspect of learning by conditioning procedure. When a dog learned to respond to a conditioned stimulus, the same conditioned stimulus CS could be used to reinforce a new form of conditioned response CR. It means that a CS could be used as a US or reinforcement to form association with another response. In principle, this second-order conditioning can be used for the third or higher level of association formation.

The subject is conditioned to salivate to the bell (CS_1) first, and then the sound of the bell is used as an unconditioned stimulus (US) in developing conditioning response to another conditioned stimulus (CS_2), the light.

The second-order conditioning though demonstrated by Pavlov in the frame-work of classical conditioning procedure, its full use and development were made under operant conditioning which will be discussed later.

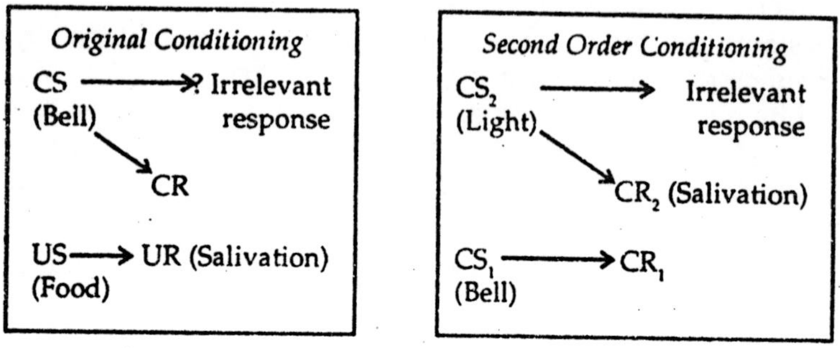

Fig. 9.3

The learning of skills and formation of habits are generally explained by means of Pavlovian conditioning principles. There are numerous studies to support this contention in the area of physiological reactions. For example, hunger pangs due to the gastro-intestinal mobility conditioned to time is very well known. The electric activity of the nervous system can be conditioned and many of our psychosomatic disorders are explained in this way as conditioned responses. Even many of our subjective feelings and emotional reactions of different shades and nuances fall under the category of conditioned reactions. The principle of generalization and higher-order conditioning, which employ symbolic associations, are behind these responses.

Today the conditioning procedure is used to determine the sensory capacities of infants, mentally handicapped, and animals to help them to improve their abilities. Treatment of behaviour problem of children with bed-wetting (enuresis) by means of classical conditioning technique has met with success in the majority of cases.

We shall discuss now another kind of conditioning procedure, which is equally important and famous as the classical one. This kind is called operant conditioning developed by Skinner (1953). Some learning theorists do not accept the name and class it as instrumental conditioning, but many do. However, despite dissension the term is in popular use. The proponent of operant conditioning emphasizes the fact that the "behaviour operates upon the environment to generate consequences". The consequences may be food, money, praise or escape from the shock etc. the fundamental difference from Pavlovian conditioning is focused by showing the absence of pairing between reinforcement and conditioned stimulus. In other words US does not follow the CS to evoke CR in the operant model. It is argued that when a dog is conditioned to salivate, it is difficult to say whether as the response has been learnt, as salivation is a natural response to food. The operant view is that the reinforcement is contingent upon certain responses only. The response may obtain something, which is needed, positive reinforcement, or may facilitate escape from the painful situation, negative reinforcement.

In classical conditioning procedure, an unconditioned stimulus, such as food or shock, is used to elicit a response first which will be conditioned later. On the contrary, under operant conditioning the response is not evoked by the experimentally controlled stimulus. The response is spontaneously emitted by the subject like pressing the lever to get the food. The emphasis, therefore, is on the voluntary response of the subject. Secondly, this voluntary response becomes instrumental in achieving the result is the point of emphasis in Skinnerian's.

Skinner's operant conditioning distinguishes two types of behaviour, respondent and operant. Respondent behaviour is directly under the control of a stimulus, but the relationship is not the same for the operant. Respondent behaviour is used in classical conditioning where a specific response to a specific stimulus is found. On the other hand, under operant behaviour the organism is considered to operate voluntarily in its surroundings. As a matter of fact, the respondent behaviour is identified by its effect. The paradigm of operant conditioning is given below :

Initiating Stimulus	Response	Reinforced Stimulus
S_1 ⟶	R ⟶	S_2
?	Bar-pressing	Food

Fig 9.4

A hungry rat was put in the Skinner box and was allowed to run around freely within tried a few times pressing the bar at varying intervals and got food. The rat learned to press the bar at a faster rate to satisfy its hunger.

A number of experiments were conducted using this operant conditioning technique like rats pressing the lever to turn the infra-red lamp when placed in the glass cylinder to maintain its normal body temperature, or pigeons trained to turn only when the sign 'Turn' was lighted and so on. Besides, there are many examples of learning effected by this conditioning process in human subjects. In every such learning, the learned response is reinforced by doing the act.

As referred to earlier and even in the preceding context of operant conditioning, the value of reinforcement in learning response is of paramount importance. In experimental studies of operant conditioning a plan to provide reinforcement is worked out which is called 'schedules of reinforcement' in psychological literature. The reinforcement cah be of two types, continuous and intermittent. Continuous reinforcement is that which is provided every time the appropriate behaviour is performed by the subject. This part is the acquisition phase of operant conditions, that is, when the learning is being affected. After a response has been learned, a partial reinforcement scheme is invariably employed which is called 'intermittent' reinforcement. The learned response is reinforced from time to time and not every time it is produced. In human sphere of everyday living situation we mostly get partial reinforcement for the correct responses we make and that too intermittently. However, before we discuss the issue of reinforcement further we must mention that sometimes a distinction is made between primary and secondary reinforcers.

From the need-reduction point of view, food, water or escape from pain etc. are called primary reinforcers. Because they reduce the innate needs of the organism and the subjects do not have to be trained to appreciate the value of the reinforcers. On the other hand, the secondary reinforcers are those, which effect the learning, but are not the reducers of physiological needs. The secondary stimuli after they have been paired with the primary ones act as secondary reinforces. For the sound of a metronome is not a reinforcer in itself to a rat, but when paired with food, assumes the value of a reinforcer. Another example we can give of a child who can know the value of a coin in buying sweets. As stated earlier, apart from serving as reinforcers for learning new responses, secondary reinforcers maintain learned behaviour in the absence of primary reinforcers. For example, a pigeon is trained to peck at lighted disc on the wall of the instrument and gets grain by doing so as reinforcer. Once the conditioned operant is established, the pigeon will go on pecking, even if it receives the grain occasionally.

The reinforcement schedules as referred to earlier, are of enormous significance in effecting learning. Particularly partial reinforcement is of great value because most of the organisms in actual life situations get that sort of reinforcement. Furthermore, the reinforcement schedule can be organised on the intermittent basis. It can be in the form of fixed ratio (FR) as well as fixed interval. In fixed ratio the reinforcement is provided after a fixed number of non-reinforced responses. If it occurs every 10 responses, the ratio of 10 to 1, is observed, that is, every response after the ten unreinforced ones is reinforced. Instead of having a ratio approach, we can introduce a Fixed Interval (FI) schedule. This will mean that the reinforcement will be given to the response made after a fixed time, *viz.*, after every one minute or five minutes. At a fixed interval schedule, no reinforcement will be provided until that fixed time has elapsed.

The same design as that of fixed ratio can be used for variable ratio (VR) and reinforcements can be provided after a specified number of non-reinforced responses, but with a difference in regard to the number of responses intervening between reinforcements. It varies from one reinforcement to the next. In other words, the rate of responding varies as the schedule of reinforcement varies. For example, a 20 to 1 variable ratio may be produced by requiring that the number of intervening responses be randomly selected from the numbers 0 to 40. A variable ratio schedule can be specified in terms of average number of responses needed for reinforcement. Variable intervals (VI), on the other hand, is another form of the reinforcement schedule which shows that reinforcement can occur after a specified period of time that varies from one reinforcement to another. In similar fashion as variable ratio schedule, a variable interval of, say one minute, can be generated setting the time period between reinforcements in a wide range of values from 0 to 120 seconds.

These four schedules of reinforcement come up with interesting results. On the first of the four, that is, fixed interval, the responding of the subject follows the time pattern. The rate increases with the reinforcing time getting nearer. On the variable interval, this does not happen and the rate of performance does not fluctuate heavily between reinforcements. Since the animal is not aware of the time when the interval will come to an end, it works at a steady rate.

In both ratio schedules, fixed and variable, the rates of responding are significantly higher. On ratio schedule the animal responds as if it knows that making certain number of responses will bring the result. However, there is always a burst of responses in terms of numbers.

Both the variable schedules, VR and VI produce resistance to extinction of responses and steady responding rates. Skinner used very many types of reinforcements schedule, but these four types are fairly representative of his approach.

Another differential feature of operant conditioning which is not to be found in the classical conditioning procedure is "shaping". The behaviour is shaped through the appropriate use of reinforcement. For example, if the experimenter wants the subject to respond in a certain manner, then he reinforces selected behaviour and continues reinforcing one and not reinforcing the other till it approximates the desired response. This process is also called the method of successive approximations. The essential feature of shaping is that the learner is guided to the finally desired response through the chain of simpler responses, one after another. Let us fit it into the shaping of a rat's behaviour in Skinner box. First, the hungry rat will be allowed to run about and familiarize itself with the box. Then, the rat will be given pellet from a piece of paper. This eating from the paper will be reinforced. After some time the rat will learn to eat quickly from the paper and be paper-trained. The next step will be to get the rat nearer the bar of the box whose operation we finally want it to learn. The rat will be watched and if it approaches the area where the bar is situated, the pellet will be released. However, if the rat goes to the other part of the box, away from the bar, no reinforcement is given. Every time the rat approaches the bar, gets the pellet. Now the pellet will be released very near the bar so that it might even put its paw on the bar while picking the pellet. Once the rat puts its paw on the bar greater quantity of pellets are released. The rat repeats this behaviour and gets reinforced and bar-pressing is learned through successive approximation or shaping. With the use of this method animals learn all sorts of tricks to perform as we see these exploits for our entertainment in circuses. The use has been very fruitful in training and modifying behaviour of patients in mental and sub-normal institutions as well.

The importance of reinforcement in strengthening behaviour is supported by the results of experiment with non-contingent reinforcement as well. By non-contingent reinforcement we mean the reinforcement given to the subject without being contingent upon a specific response. We cite example from Skinner's experiment when his hungry pigeons kept in different boxes apart and flashed lights at random intervals were followed by a reinforcement (food). The result was interesting. The birds tended to select and repeat what they were doing at the time reinforcement occurred. The frequency of those acts increased with the reinforcement and they happened very near the time of expected reinforcement.

We know the significance of secondary reinforcement in human learning much more than we can account for in animal learning. Money, a token of reinforcement, is a strong force in influencing and controlling human learning. Besides, the gestures shown by the trainer or words used or a smile or a pat on the back acts as secondary reinforcers quite effectively. But learning with operant conditioning is achieved only when reinforcement follows immediately after the required response has been made. The proximity between response and reinforcement is extremely important; the closer it is, the faster is the conditioning. The delay in reinforcement retards the process. However, once the response is established, the delay in reinforcement does not affect conditioning seriously. Another interesting point that has been noted is that where secondary reinforcers are in use, the delay in primary reinforcement does not dislocate the learning considerably.

After examining the establishment of responses one would like to know whether the learning affected by operant conditioning presents the feature of extinction, which was observed in the classical conditioning procedure. It has been reported that the role of extinction in operant conditioning is as influential as it is in classical conditioning. The learned response can be extinguished by withholding reinforcement. Although in the operant conditioning the rate of extinction will be variable depending on the strength of motivation and drive etc.; full withdrawal of reinforcement will eventually extinguish the learned response. Similarly, the spontaneous recovery of response is also noted in operant conditioning as in classical one.

The function of stimulus generalization is of similar importance in operant conditioning as in classical conditioning. For example, in one experiment a mute patient was conditioned to talk to the experimenter by means of shaping. Later the experimenter substituted a nurse and then another member of the hospital staff, the learned behaviour continued and was maintained by reinforcement. Besides, the feature of discrimination learning is, again, common in both kinds of learning processes, operant and classical.

Before we go any further we would like to mention a few words about the other two kinds of conditioning, which we come across in the literature. They are avoidance and escape conditioning treated as instrumental conditioning by psychologists. Procedurally there is not much difference amongst operant, avoidance, and escape conditioning, except that in the last two, punishment or pain is used as reinforcer. However, the cardinal feature of using behaviour as an instrument of achieving a goal is common to all. In operant conditioning this is achieved through rewarding the subject and in other by doing the opposite, that is, inflicting pain. Let us take the example of avoidance kind of instrumental conditioning. An animal is placed in a large cage where with the presentation of a buzzer sound, half of the cage gets electrically charged and renders the animal a nasty shock. After a while, the animal escapes the shock by jumping across a low barrier to the other half of the cage, which is not electrified. In subsequent trials the buzzer precedes the shock and the animal learns to avoid the shock by jumping to the safer half of the cage. The avoidance behaviour is, thus learned .

Avoidance learning is learning motivated by avoiding punishment/pain. Such punishments are widely used by the society to teach approved behaviour to individuals. However, there is evidence to suggest that in teaching new behaviour punishment can be ineffective. It may even cause neurotic disturbances. Some studies with punishment in extinguishing habits have shown negative results. Punishment temporarily depresses the rate of responding, but fails to diminish the total responses needed to bring about extinction. Extinction by non-reinforcing is usually regarded as a successful method of deconditioning. But some psychologists, as a result of studies with sophisticated organisms, suggest that if the punishment is too sever, it may completely suppress the habit in them. Others talk about conflict, fear and other undesirable reaction being engendered by the severity of punishment inflicted. In recent times there has been a strong support of the views amongst psychologist that the mild punishment might serve as a cue for judging something wrong and helping the person to do 'right'.

Enlargement of Conditioning

Learned behaviour becomes very complex. The process of learning a series of such behaviour is known as chained reaction and produces a behaviour chain. For example, you take the key out of your pocket, direct it to the lock of the door, fix it into the appropriate place in the lock, unlock it, open the door and enter through to reach your room of residence. There has been a series of action or behaviour involved in a particular sequence. These actions could not be done at random sequence to achieve the desired goal. In a behaviour-chain like this each response serves as stimulus for the next response in the chain and also each act as a reinforcer to another, of course of a secondary order. The successive cues in such sequence can be called response-produced cues for the stimuli. These cues can be internal as well as external. The internal cues are largely kinesthetic, such as turning the key within the lock etc. Verbal chains are also formed when we try to reproduce some poetry or talk etc.

Generally a response hierarchy is formed in many human learning situations and we learn more than one potential response to a given stimulus. These responses get organized in order of probability of occurrence. Thus in any complex behaviour there is not only a chain of relationships between various responses, but also a hierarchical order of responses is formed that can be used for a complex stimulus. In other words, a priority has to be decided in order to make the appropriate response from amongst alternatives. For instance, a student who is failing a course in his first year might try one of several responses; he might go to see the principal in the hope of being allowed to drop the course, he might go and see the Head of the subject and ask him to give him another set of papers for the examination; he might decide to leave the college and so on. He can pick out one of the several alternatives with high probabilities of reinforcing value in his circumstances. The most rewarding among the responses would be selected.

Many complex skills involve integration of simpler skills into successively higher ones. So in learning of a complex skill there is a synthesisation of simple and simpler acts at different levels or stages of complexity. For example in learning to ride a bicycle, one learns to balance the bicycle, steer it, and working the pedals. But after getting mastery over it one learns to balance, steer and pedal all at the same time automatically. They become integrated.

The theories of learning are variable. Some of the champions of learning theory talk about different kinds of learning rather than different processes of it. In fact all emphasize the relationships to be learned in different ways. Mowrer's (1951) two-factor theory of learning has been very widely quoted among others. He makes a distinction between the functions of the two conditioning processes, classical and instrumental. According to him, classical conditioning forms the basis for emotional-attitudinal response and instrumental conditioning enables the learning of problem-solving responses or "solution learning". In support of his theory his study of avoidance conditioning of guinea pigs is cited. In his experiment there were two groups of guinea pigs. One group was given electric shock shortly after the buzzer was sounded, and the other group was allowed time to avoid the shock by starting to run the moment they heard the sound. The buzzer became a conditioned stimulus for both the groups; both groups learned the meaning of the signal. But the difference in situation presented differential results. The subjects who received the shock regardless of their behaviour trembled, adopted rigid posture and showed signs of fear when they heard the buzzer sound; and the other group of subjects reacted by running and avoiding the shock at the sound of the buzzer and their running behaviour increased with the increase in trials. In this situation running was reinforced and punishment was avoided. Therefore the running could be described as operant or instrumental in avoiding pain and fostering learning to avoid. The argument put forward in support of Mowrer's theory is that although both groups initially showed fear responses, the second group learned to avoid the shock by voluntary running at the presentation of stimulus and constituted the example of solution learning. In other words, the meaning of signal (stimulus) is learned by classical conditioning and methods of coping with them are acquired through operant conditioning.

The S-R theory will remain incomplete if Hull is not brought into the picture. He was extremely influenced by the hypothetico-deductive method of science and tried to use it in psychology. The hypothetico-deductive method required setting up of postulates, general statements of process involved and to deduction of theorem out of these. The theorems have to be compared and verified by the results of the experiments. If the theorem is not verified or supported by the results, then it needs to be changed. The advantage of his system is that a large number of theorems can be deduced from a fewer postulates. Where the postulate is correct, it is expected that the theorem will predict the behaviour. His 'Principles of Behaviour' came out as an influential document in 1943. Later 'Behaviour System' (1952) suggested modifications of his postulates and brought the number down to seventeen with 133 theorems.

Hull propounded three kinds of variable. Two of these are in terms of input and output and are observable, for example, stimulus variation in intensity, degree of deprivation of the organism, number of trials with reinforcement come under input. And others, such as the amplitude, probability of occurrence or latency of responses are treated as output. The latency of a response is the interval between the response and the eliciting response. In addition, the third one Hull introduced is intervening variable like Tolman, (discussed under perceptual learning) linking stimulus and response, but with a difference. Hull's theory of learning has been in contrast with Tolman's in many ways. He used two stages of intervening variables. At the first stage the variables contributed to the performance. At the second they get combined in order to give an excitatory potential, which determined the tendency to respond. According to him, excitatory potential (SER) was responsible for speed, strength and resistance to the extinction of responding. The excitatory potential (SER) was again caused by Drive (D) and habit strength (SHR).

He considered drive as tension created by a deficit or deprivation of something the body needs and lasts for a short period. It would activate the organism. It could happen due to painful stimulation as well. Drive needed reduction of tension and caused learning. Drive-reduction therefore became the reinforcer. These drive reducing fostered habit formation. When a particular response to given stimulus led to drive reduction, the habit strength (SHR) linking the stimulus and response was strengthened. For example, if a hungry rat pressed a lever and obtained food, the drive reduction produced by eating the food would strengthen the habit of pressing the lever. Hull offered estimates of how drive and habit strength would build up to produce (SER), that is, excitatory potentials. He postulated that D (drive) and SHR (habit strength) multiply together to produce $S^{E}R$., $S^{E}R=S^{H}R^{X}D$.

Hull used a concept of reactive inhibition (IR). This denoted that a response could not be repeated later. Reactive inhibition could be equated with the state of fatigue. It was described as a negative drive, which dissipated with time and in the absence of a response. If it is a drive, it could lead to learning not to respond. What was learned was conditioned inhibition (SIR). Ordinarily IR and SIR built up less slowly than SHR. However, when the drive was not reduced by response, the built-up of inhibition would exceed the combination of SHR and D and the organism would not respond. According to Hull extinction was caused by inhibition.

In Hull's system, the strength of relationship between S and R depends on reinforcement. Some S-R theorists do not accept this, particularly Guthrie, who maintains that learning can be accounted for only in terms of continuity, stimulus-response occurring together without proposing the intervening event to strengthen the association. Besides, the drive reaction equation with reinforcement does not come out unscathed when instances of learning occurring in the absence of recognizable deprivation or states of need are observed. Further, single trial learning is not explained by Hull either. Hull's system has generated a large volume of experimental studies in this area and led to the refinement of designs and models of investigation. His theory is more scientific and mathematical than any and does not come hi and dri as the pragmatists would like it to be. Besides, several of his laws of prediction have not held up in others' investigation.

Perceptual Learning

Learning occurs also without the exercise of stimulus-response association. The change in response or behaviour can take place because the learner perceives the situation to respond in a particular way. Even with species lower than humans some responses are the results of cognition, that is, due to change in their perception of the situation. Cognitive theorists talk about such learning as the development of cognition in contrast to the formation of S-R bonds. However cognitive process is a comprehensive term, which includes more than just perceiving, rather it includes conceiving, judging, remembering and reasoning as well. Thus, these theorists argue that even the formation of simple habit involves perception and recognition.

Cognitive theorists unlike others point out the inadequacy of S-R theory and criticize Skinner's operant conditioning on the ground that it minimizes or ignores the contribution of the organism in learning responses. Learning responses, according to them, do not come automatically by simple presentation of stimuli to the subject; rather the subject learns the meaning of the stimuli or attaches signs to them mentally and reacts to them in those terms.

Perceptual learning is of two major sorts : (1) association model, in which perception of association between stimulus and stimulus (S-S) is organized, and (2) insightful learning model, in which the perceptual field is reorganized in solving the model problem. The S-S association requires pairing of two stimuli so that the presentation of one arouses the image, idea or some process in the mind of the learner when the other is not present. This mental picture of the learner is described as 'Cognitive map' and is used to explain the learning of spatial relationship of objects.

The insightful learning, on the other hand, does not accept any kind of association formation between stimulus-stimulus or stimulus-response. The association is rejected on the ground that it implies a mechanical connection. It is the insight, which occurs relatively suddenly, and gets the perception of the whole situation re-organized for learning in this model.

We shall examine first the stimulus-stimulus association theory which, although drew on association, changed the perspective of behaviourism into purposive behaviourism. Tolman (1932) was the leader of this approach who shared with Watson's objectivity and the measurement of behaviour as crux of behaviourism, none-the-less, shifted his emphasis to purposiveness. He propounded that the learner does not only respond to stimuli, but also strives towards goals. Stimuli guide towards the goal and determine what means can be used to attend it. The behaviour, therefore, can be predicted if the goal being sought is known along with stimuli. Tolman introduced the concept of intervening variable to link stimulus and response, S-O-R, stimulus—organisms' state,—. and response. It intervenes between the independent variable manipulated by the experimenter and the dependent variable, behaviour, which is served.

Tolman hypothesized that the intervening variable can be of two kinds, cognition and demand. The two work together to produce results. A cognition is formed as a result of experience with certain stimuli. For example, a way of making responses in reaching the reward, the path that leads to the goal or things going together to constitute a particular situation. Demand, on the other hand, is created by needs within the organism, like, deprivation of food or water etc. These needs seek to determine the goal to be achieved. In fulfilling the demand, cognition provides the means to reach the goal. Hence, learning does not imply acquiring a set of bodily movements by means of S-R association, it is much more than that.

The sign-learning theorists headed by Tolman believed that this type of learning involved latent learning based on cognitive map. The rats learn the route(s) to the goal rather than a pattern of movements. The mental picture of the routes to the goal is a part of the cognitive-map. Experiments with two groups of hungry rats are quoted here to illustrate the point. When the hungry rats (group 1) ran the maze without getting the reward (food), no improvement occurred in time or error scores. But when the reward was introduced after tenth trial, performance soon increased to the level of the other group (group 2) of rats who were continually rewarded. This sudden improvement is explained as the result of latent learning (Tolman, 1949). The animals had acquired the information regarding the maze running but did not take advantage of it. The cognitive map hypothesis is supported by several experimental studies. It was observed that relevant information was acquired by the subject but not utilized in overt responses until appropriate incentives were introduced.

The sign learning theorists have found support for their thesis from the example of 'place learning'—in experiments with animals.

The rat is guided to learn the location of particular goal rather than given a series of movements to reach the goal. The results show that when the subject learns the location of reward (food), it is able to reach the goal by different routes even by routes not explored before. The experiments in place learning make the cognitive-map hypothesis tenable (Munn *et al.*, 1969).

Transposition experiments throw further light on the working of the cognitive theory. Transposition is a discrimination learning situation but at a level higher than conditioning. Here the subject is required to discriminate the relationships between two stimuli and not their absolute shapes or sizes or not concerned with responding to a specific stimulus. A typical experiment in this area will illustrate the point. The subject is trained to differentiate between two gray circles C_1 and C_2. The response to lighter one C_2 is positively reinforced. After this training has been established, the experimenter tests the subject for transposition. Another lighter gray circle C_3 which is lighter than the second one, is presented with the original gray circle and the subject chooses the third lighter gray circle to respond. The subjects, rats or chickens, make the responses on the basis of comparison of stimuli. The transposition experiments strengthen the cognitive view of learning in opposition to the S-R theory as learning in these conditions result from the appreciation of relationships between the stimuli. However, the critics of sign learning say that transposition experiments do not appear very much different from the examples of stimulus generalization and second order conditioning of S-R association.

Perceptual learning in terms of S-S, stimulus-stimulus association has been shown in blocked-response experiments. One such example is demonstrated with the use of a drug named bulbocapnine hydrochloride, which produces a cataleptic or stuporous state for sometime. In this state no movement occurs. However, the drug wears off in time. Conditioning sessions are conducted while the subject is under drug influence. In the training period no movement is allowed, but the subject is exposed to see the light and shock pairings during the session. After 5 days of the conditioning trials,when the actual tests came the result has been positive in supporting the promotion of association between light and shock. Furthermore, some experiments have been done with severing the motor nerves of the animal, which could not allow it to make any movement response at all. The procedure of pairing two stimuli has been the same. The results after restoration of nerve section produce supporting evidence of S-S association (Beck & Doty, 1957).

The changed response experiments are another means of demonstrating the phenomenon of S-S association or cognitive map. For example, a task is learned with one set of responses and then something is done to prevent the utilisation of learned responses. After that new responses are learned. Now if the subject still shows the original or first learned responses after the new learning, it can be argued that the original learning happened due to S-S association and not S-R association, as we find no interference in the past learned responses with the learning of the changed responses. One experiment with rats in this area is mentioned. Rats were first trained to swim through the maze. Then the water was covered by a floor and the rats were required to run through the maze. The rats made no error in running through the maze after they had learned to swim through.

Now we shall take up the other form of cognitive learning popularly known as insightful learning. This insight theory was expounded by the Gestalt psychologists who deduced their principle from the study of problem-solving behaviour of the animals. Learning a maze or learning relationships among stimuli are situation of problem-solving responses. The situation can vary from simple to complex in scale and from animal to human learning, but the underlying principle of problem solving remains the same in all. Kohler (1925) and his colleagues were the first to pioneer the theory of insight into the domain of learning relationship. His subjects particularly chimpanzees, appeared to grasp the inner relationship between problem and solution. This perceiving of inner relation he described as insight which, according to him, became the basis of learning responses. His typical experiments is cited here.

Sultan, his famous chimpanzee subject, cannot reach the fruit, which is outside his reach. He sees one short stick, which is available there, but a large one is deposited outside the bars of his cage at a distance of two meters and cannot be grasped by hand. The placing of the large stick is such that it cam be pulled within reach by using the small stick. Sultan makes attempts to reach the fruit with the small stick, but in vain. After sometime, he tries another method to reach the fruit by using a wire from the netting of his cage with no success. Then he looks around and outside and suddenly picks up the little stick once more and goes up to the cage bars directly opposite to the large stick. He scratches the large one towards himself with the small one and eventually gets hold of it. Next thing he does is that he uses it in securing the fruit.

Kohler postulated that having a sudden solution to the problem in sight was a function of 'insight' or cognitive learning. The subject observed the relation between relevant aspects of the situation and suddenly 'got the idea' or 'saw the point' or as gestalt psychologists would put it, got the 'flash' of answer. This process is also described by them as 'Aha experience'.

In our day-to-day living there are numerous situations, which require problem-solving behaviour of some sort, ranging from simple to difficult ones. A well motivated organism other than human also tries to reach a goal-object and when finds the way blocked or presented with 'detour', gets its way through or by-passes the barrier. This finding the way-out is akin to problem-solving behaviour. In these experiments with animals, detours have generally been used and animals' reactions to detour have been studied.

The problem-solving behaviour in learning has been investigated extensively like other principles of learning. Most animals make direct approach and fail like Thorndike's cat and rat. In the higher organism like monkey and chimpanzee, the trial and error approach assumes a higher dimension and the subject of the experiment gets the idea of circumventing the barrier. In searching process it suddenly sees the significant aspects of the situation or problem and finds the solution. The fore-going argument does not answer unequivocally the question of getting sudden insight for some psychologists. They believe that the process is a successively improved trial and error. According to them a full play of the operation could not be demonstrated in Thorndike's experimental situation because of the limited view of the experimental conditions open to the subjects and also because the mental capacity of the subjects employed in such studies were not very high either. However, at the higher-lever-animals and humans, the process of trial and error learning is utilised significantly. Human subjects do make trial and error approach in solving problems. They try at random with hit and miss, turn one knob or the other and so on before doing the correct thing. Further, it is also possible for the human subject to solve the problem entirely by studying the situation silently with no overt action or movement. The result is that the subject can do it in one go. He has fully worked out the answer by trying and rejecting the incorrect ones mentally and the final act is a result of internal trial and error. This may be described as vicarious trial and error (VTE) process.

Insight depends on appropriate past experience. It also becomes easy when the essentials for solution are arranged so that relationships can be perceived conveniently. A chimpanzee solves the stick-problem because he sees the larger stick on the same side of the cage where the banana is located. It would not have been that easy though, had the stick been kept on the other side of the cage concealed from the sight and also away from the food. Human beings, on the other hand, have advantage over these higher animals and they can do their own arranging of the problem mentally. They can manipulate the mental images of the problems and answers. Sometimes they do the arranging and re-arranging of the problem without being aware of this.

However, one salient feature of this insightful solution is that it is repeatable with ease. It does not have to be gradual and graduated like trial-error solution. Once the chimpanzee has been successful in using the stick to secure the banana, he reaches out for that every time afterwards. Besides, there is a masked 'transfer effect' in this sort of learning. It is unlike a specific S-R sequence. On the contrary, a cognitive relationship between means and ends is understood by the subject who uses the learning for further solution of similar problems. Even the means or tools to achieve the goal can be substituted by the subject as a result of the understanding of relationship.

Some psychologists argue that insight learning is no more than a transfer of previously learned habits with new arrangement of the situation. The transfer of previous experience can result in the appearance of sudden solution to the problem. Harlow (1949) with his experimental studies of children and monkeys demonstrated the function of improvement in learning and transfer effect as a phenomenon of sudden solution. The experiment involved the solution of a large number of problems on the same subject. Among the problems, some were old, some were newer, and some were required to be answered in the reverse order to the given response cue. The last one is known as discrimination-reversal learning. The following conclusions were drawn : (1) the amount by which a subject can profit from a single experience can increase tremendously through learning; (2) inter-problem improvement is a transfer effect from one to another problem. This transfer is caused by learning set or learning to learn.

Our discussion has included the formation of basic habits and behaviour patterns through trial and error, classical and operant conditioning, and the learning of new response patterns involving observation, past experience and thinking or perceptual reorganization. Besides, an interdependence of different approaches and understanding of relationships among stimuli or parts of the stimuli or problem situations have been examined. Above all we also learn to learn has been highlighted.

10 Conditions and Techniques Affecting Verbal Learning

We have examined so far the processes and principles involved in learning with special reference to learning relatively simpler skills. In our account we have predominantly included the results of animal experimentation. However, this does not mean that those principles discovered are applicable to animals learning only. The same can be extended to human learning as much as it can be to animals. But this much is true that learning at human level is of complex nature and requires greater skill than animals' in solving problems. Besides, human learning is largely dominated by verbal learning.

At the outset we must bring in the concept of individual differences if we talk about human learning. As we know, no two persons are identical (except co-twins) and variation in individuals' learning capacity is significantly marked. Among the variabilities, the intelligence of the individual considered to be one of the most important factors to determine the level and rate of his verbal learning. There is evidence to show that the I.Q, score is positively correlated with learning. The higher the I.Q. of a person, the faster is the rate of his learning.

Further, verbal learning abilities are related to the chronological age of the learner. An infant or child cannot be hastened to learn things, if it is not mentally mature to take things in. The mental maturity is a function of physical age. The level of skill to be learned, therefore, must be suited to the level of maturity of the individual.

It is of crucial importance to consider the role or motivation in learning. There can be no learning if the learner is not motivated to learn. The subject will not try or make any effort to learn due to lack of motivation. However some examples are also available to show that incidental learning, that is, learning without intent, is possible. But such learning falls short of the intentional learning and happens under special conditions. Besides, it is hard to say that such learning could not be 'latent learning' with motivation of some kind not known on the surface.

Learner's sophistication and previous knowledge can affect his learning too. The previous learning will facilitate the acquisition of a skill at rapid and faster rate. This point will be discussed at length under 'Transfer of Training'. Here we need to mention that it is a variable that affects the learning of a skill.

In the back-ground of afore-said conditions of learning, we can discuss the nature and characteristics of verbal learning. Much of human learning is verbal and consists of forming associations between words. Words form the basis of ideas and all our knowledge and scientific experiments. Even quantitative reasoning depends on the use of words and symbols of that sort. Psychologists have been interested in investigating verbal learning from the time studies with principles of conditioning began. Ebbinghaus (1913) originated the study of verbal learning strictly in the behaviourist's tradition, that is, emphasising objectivity and explaining learning as a function of association. Like conditioning theorists he also rejected the method of subjective report and introspection. However, one significant distinction between the animal learning and verbal learning theories worthy of note is that in the latter empirical generalization of the experimental results was highlighted and in the former the formulation of theories was emphasized. In verbal learning experiments we use different methods of presenting materials as well as different kinds of materials ranging from very highly meaningful words or stories to the meaningless non-sense syllables. In early experiment non-sense syllables were mostly used. It does not mean to say that they are not in use today. The material is prepared with three-letter combination; three consonants like ZQJ.XFG, etc. or two consc ants joined by one vowel, *viz.* CUṢ, MUV etc. The rationale behind the use of non-sense syllables is that they are relatively free from association value or meanings and make the evaluation objective.

Eddinghous used serial anticipation and paired-associate learning methods to study this problem of verbal learning. He constructed a list of non-sense syllables to be used in serial anticipation method and presented them one at a time for a fixed period of exposure through the window of a revolving memory drum. The syllables were unfamiliar to the subject. The subject was asked to anticipate the syllable that had to follow on the basis of what he had seen. For example, if the list consisted of CEF, DAX,VUG, etc. the subject would be shown CEF and asked to anticipate DAX. After an interval, possibly 2 seconds, DAX would appear in the window of the drum, and the subject would be required to anticipate VUG. This procedure will be followed throughout the experiment. In the experiment the subject would certainly be told whether or not his guess or anticipation was correct. If not, he will see for himself the following syllable. With some experiments a cue for anticipating the syllable could also be offered by the experimenter. The item anticipated would serve as stimulus and response, both. The list would be presented repeatedly till the subject would reach the criterion of learning, one or the error-free reproductions.

In paired-associate learning the subject would be shown a list of paired words, such as CAT-LAWN, TABLE-WINDOW etc. These words would not necessarily be meaningfully paired, further, it would not be limited to paired words; non-sense syllables, numbers, or any other kind of symbols could be paired as well. In the experiment the first word of the pair would be presented, and the subject would be required to recall the second word of the pair. Here again, the first word would act as a stimulus to the second pair, which would serve as response. The correctness or incorrectness of recall could be confirmed depending on the experimenter's plan. In order to offset the effect of serial position of the response words, the paired words could be presented in random order from the list.

As we have seen, the afore said experimental designs are developed to support the general behaviourist approach of S-R association in learning. However, a theoretical issue is raised in this context as to whether the strengthening of association between stimulus and response is a function of trials of learning and increases with each trial or the association between the two are formed on a single trial basis and is unaffected by its repetition. Both views are prevalent. The first one is known as incremental or continuity theory and the second one is described as one-trial or non-continuity or all-or-none theory.

The incremental theorist like Hull (1943) explains that association between S-R is strengthened on each and every trial of the experiment, but the correct response will not be made until the associative strength crosses the 'Threshold Value'. After the threshold has been reached, the association is strong enough to manifest itself and to be maintained at the correct level with succeeding trials. According to the one-trial theory, on the other hand, the association between stimulus-response is either formed or not formed. If formed, it is formed fully. There is no gradual strengthening of connection, bit by bit, in this all-and-none approach. For instance, if a subject is given a pair of ZAK-XOF to learn and he does it on the fifth trial, his failure to learn on preceding four trials has not contributed to the association formation on the fifth. The fifth trial is really very important from one-trial learning point of view (Estes, 1960). The association has been formed and fully formed on this fifth trial alone. There has been no carry over from the preceding trials.

For most of us both theories hold good; some material particularly meaningless ones may be learned in incremental way and others, that is, meaningful materials, by one-trial or all-and-none formula.

The materials of learning can be arranged along two continua; rote-meaningful and reception-discovery. On rote-meaningful continuum the material can range from mere memorisation without understanding the acquisition of knowledge with full appreciation of facts. Learning by reception-discovery continuum, on the other hand, can be distinguished from the rote-meaningful dimension in terms of the manner of presentation of the task. For example, the subject is given the material in final form for reception or incorporation in the learning and the subject has to find out (discover) for himself the main content or missing material to learn it completely (Bruner, 1961). It may be suggested that the discovery is not an end in itself, the discovered material has got to be received and stored eventually (Ausubel, 1966a).

The reception learning and discovery learning, both, can be rote or meaningful. Meaningful reception subsumes or provides a general frame of concept. It becomes more inclusive to bring under it smaller units or materials. Meaningful reception is described as a sub-sumption process by which the less inclusive is encompassed in a bigger a general whole. In plain words, new materials are integrated under a generalised concept or frame of reference already learned. Some psychologists believe that sub-sumption enhances learning as well as remembering. In many experiments an advance organiser is employed to facilitate sub-sumption process. The advance organiser provides cues and information to receive the new material and to judge whether or not the same is similar to the knowledge acquired by the learner. In a study with advance organiser in two groups of students, one with and the other without the organiser, the difference has been significant in learning a scientific text. The advance organiser group scored higher than the other. (Ausubel and Fitzgerald, 1962)

The meaningful reception learning is very much the task of the day in education, none-the-less, the rote-reception learning has its advantages, too. It has been found that alphabet learning, learning of tables and exercise, foreign language idioms and other drills of that sort etc. are better served by rote-memorisation.

Reception and discovery learning methods, although dealt under two captions, overlap each other. The discovery learning may involve direction based on previous reception. Besides, research evidence to support the independence and superiority of either over the other is not clear cut.

Now we shall mention some of the techniques to optimise learning which psychologists have been advocating. One of the methods popularly talked about is 'massed versus distributed' practice. Within massed practice the learner works continually on a task till he learns it completely. On the contrary, under distributed practice, the learning time is spaced and distributed over shorter periods of practice punctuated by rest. The investigation into this hypothesis of massed vs. distributed practice in learning has come up with interesting results. The distributed practice method has been found to yield better results than massed practice. The explanation is that since prolonged activity in continuous practice produce fatigue and offset the effectiveness of effort, the short work unit keeps the learner's motivation at a high level (McGeoh & Iron, 1952). It is further argued that the neural processes aroused by the activity are preserved at the end of distributed work practice and consolidate easily, and the effect of reactive inhibition, making the subject resist to respond in the situation of prolonged learning activity becomes ineffective.

Sometimes a person's performance on a memory task shows a significant improvement after an interval in which there has been no practice. This phenomenon is described by psychologists as 'reminiscence'. The interference or inhibition by incorrect association disappears in this period of rest and correct ones are consolidated paving the way for higher start in learning after the rest. For many motor skills and verbal habits, the distributed learning is preferable.

However, one obvious advantage of massed learning is noticed in economy of time to gain a skill. If there is a time constraint, as it is found in many situations, the spacing of practice is not possible. Under these conditions, massed learning is the only choice. Besides, for some individuals who are slow in tuning up to learning, that is, take time to warm up to receiving a skill properly, the distributed learning will be of no great help. They will lose time in spaced practice. Each interval will cost time in terms of warming up. Further, it has been supported by studies that in tasks involving problem-solving or inductive thinking and some other verbal materials, the massed learning method is superior to the distributed one (Cook, 1934; Underwood 1961).

Another method of improving verbal learning often referred to is recitation vs. reading. Memorisation of materials by reciting and plain reading has been investigated (Gates, 1917) and the outcome has suggested the supremacy of reciting over reading method. Similarly whole vs. part learning has been another topic of investigation in the area of improving learning. The controversy does not seem to resolve in this area, however. The thinking behind part learning is that with this technique the learning in smaller units is quicker and, therefore, reinforcing due to its success. The whole learning method has its own support of generalisation from either as the findings are mostly task specific or can not be applied to different tasks.

Transfer of Training

Transfer of training is one of the most valued problems of learning psychology and has received considerable attention. The evidence of emphasis on this aspect of learning is overwhelming and the school and college curricula bear the implicit faith of the educators that what is learned in these academic situations, can be successfully applied outside in general life; in other words, transfer of training will occur.

The transfer phenomenon can be of two kinds : (1) positive transfer, and (2) negative transfer. The positive transfer indicates that what we learn to do in one situation can be applied to another. Positive transfer, therefore, helps the learning of a new task because of familiarity and experience with the old one. The effect of the positive transfer is referred to as 'facilitation' process. Further, the positive transfer effects may be of two sorts : general transfer effect and specific transfer effect. The general transfer includes acquisition of generalised habit or skili, and specific transfer effect, on the other hand, refers to specific similarity of relation between the stimuli or between the responses in the learning situation.

Let us examine the experimental design of investigating transfer effect. Two matched groups of subjects, experimental and control are employed in this experiment. The experimental group is given Task 1 first, and then Task 2, in that order. The control group is given no task for the period the experimental group is trying Task 1, and later given Task 2 alone.

Table 10.1

Group	*Task*	*Task*
Experiemental	1	2
Control	—	2

To prove the hypothesis of transfer effect, the learning of Task 2 should be better or faster in the experimental group.

One important disadvantage of this methodology is that the experimental group has an edge over the control group and, therefore, does not augur a fair comparison. This edge is described by investigators as an advantage of getting 'warmed up' or as having a 'set' favourable to performance of the task for the experimental group. This also includes subjects' familiarization with the apparatus. In order to off-set this effect in experiment, the study design can be planned in table 10.2.

This pre-test and post-test design is also described as before-and-after tests procedure and is in use with comparing treatment effects for the two groups.

Table 10.2

Group	*Pretest*	*Task*	*Post test*
Experimental	BX	A	B
Control	BX	—	B

Within the framework of positive transfer effect, specific transfer effect in verbal learning has been researched with. In such studies all the subjects learn one list of paired-associates, and after that the experimental group learns a list which has some features common to the first list. The control group, on the other hand, learns a list, which has no common element with the first list and has unrelated words. The difference between the two groups' performance provides the measure of specific transfer.

Opposite to the positive transfer is the negative transfer, which implies that the technique learned in one task or skill cannot be used for learning another. Further, the negative transfer hinders rather than helps learning in a new situation. In our aforesaid experimental designs the study of negative transfer will show a reduced performance of the experimental group. We find the example of negative transfer as habit interference in doing anything new in our lives.

Theoretical explanation for the occurrence of these transfer effects can be subsumed under two headings : (1) identical element view point and (2) generalisation view-point. Under the first, it is shown that transfer occurs when the contents and techniques used in performing the two tasks are similar. For example, a person who has learned to play the card game of one kind learns quickly to play the card games of another kind, because he knows the contents and some rules that are similar to the first one. The transfer of learning under these conditions will fall under the identical element category.

The generalisation view-point, on the other hand, stresses the cognitive element and not the characteristics and contents of the task-situation to be learned. This view-point emphasises the understanding of principles involved in doing the work or learning the skill. Once the principle is learned in handling the task, the same will be used in another similar situation. The generalisation view-point explains the use of principle in problem solving behaviour. The best-known example is of two groups taught to hit the under-water target with dart. One of the two was taught the principle of refraction during training, while the other was not. Later, when a changed situation was presented to the two groups, the group trained with understanding of refraction principle did very much better than the other, which had no such knowledge of the principle.

Positive transfer effect results when there is similarity in stimuli or responses. It has also been noted particularly in verbal learning that some positive transfer effect is found when stimuli are dissimilar and response is the same. However, in situations where responses are very dissimilar or opposite to one another, the negative transfer occurs.

Experimental studies in transfer effect have been evaluated and a reasonable account of those studies is presented by Osgood (1949). He has given the salient features of the transfer effect as : *(a)* learning to make identical response to new stimulus results in positive transfer; *(b)* learning to make new dissimilar or opposite response to similar or identical stimulus result in negative transfer; *(c)* the amount of transfer is a function of stimulus similarity and *(d)* whether transfer is going to be positive or negative will depend upon response similarity.

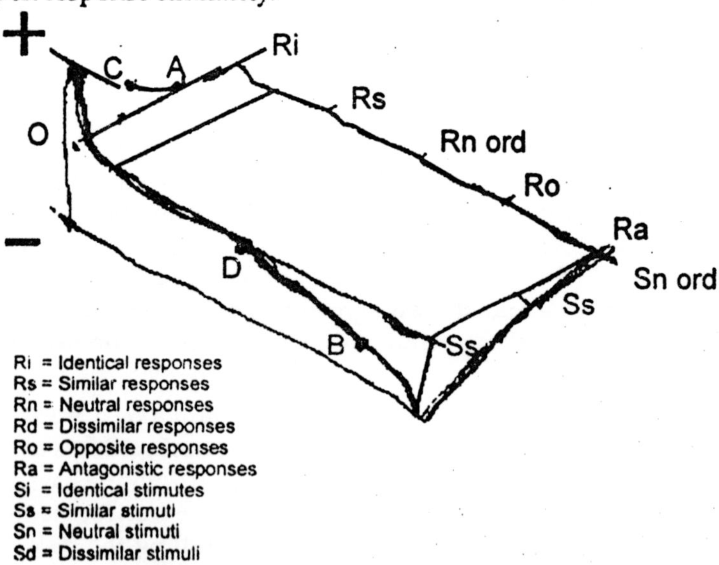

Fig. 10.1. Modified after Osgood (1949).

Further, Osgood has devised a transfer surface as presented in Figure 10.1, which can be used to summaries previous work and predict future results. Though in some studies his transfer surface has not fully been confirmed, in others it has found complete confirmation.

The findings of transfer effect investigation have shaken the beliefs of traditional educationalists in tracing formal mental faculties. The concept of formal mental discipline which emphasised studying subjects like Latin and Greek etc. to train the mind to learn any academic subject does not hold good and is discarded in modern times. The emphasis is strongly placed these days on the positive transfer of elements and principles learned from the school curriculum to the working of everyday life. For this reason, school problems are made as realistic as possible to the life situation.

All the methods of optimising learning referred to above draw heavily on the feed-back of information. By feed-back of information is meant the knowledge of results in one's performance. Experimental studies are strongly suggestive of the striking influence of the knowledge of results in acquiring skills. The knowledge of results increases the subject's motivation in performing the task and any success or near success in performance reinforces the response or performance. A chain of reinforcements through repetition of correct responses improves the learning considerably towards perfection. Besides, the feed-back gives the information about inadequacy or error in incorrect responses and leads towards making improvement. One of the examples from studies on knowledge of results is quoted here to illustrate the point. Two groups of subjects were given training in hitting the target. One group was given the knowledge of its accuracy in performance every time and the other group was kept in the dark and not given such information. As expected, the result of the experiment showed a significant difference in performance and learning between the two groups. The group with knowledge of results improved rapidly and considerably in its performance in contrast with the other group (Elwell and Grindley, 1938).

While talking about the conditions of improving learning it seems relevant to say something about an important problem that school and college students are faced with. This problem is related to their academic study. It is true that a well-motivated student finds the subject of the study interesting, but there are others who do not find it that way. Even those who are interested in it did not do well, because their study habit is not satisfactory and technique of studying used is not adequate. Psychologists have looked into the study techniques of students and have made suggestions to improve learning. One of the widely used methods and set of rules is known as Q3R method of Robinson (1961). The programme was designed to analyse and treat students' academic problems at the Ohio State University, U.S.A., and prescribes the following methods :

The first step is survey, which implies taking an overview of the entire topic or chapter and noting down the headings and sub-headings of that chapter. The use of headings is important as the organisation of materials is reflected through that. This gives the information how the headings and sub-headings relate to each other and to the main subject. This exercise is recommended to be gone through before the student starts the actual reading of the topic.

The second phase of this study routine is that since the student has completed his survey, he should survey it again and ask questions to himself; the questions or points that may be raised in the text. This is like searching for the answer by means of looking for the question. Some of the books provide questions at the end of the chapter(s) pertaining to the topic. They are of great help. In most books questions are not provided and therefore the student should ask his own questions. Questions have benefits, for one, they maintain the interest in what is being read, thus getting you actively participating in the learning process.

Reading is the next step in this routine, which means attentive and careful reading and scanning. While reading look for the answers which you have posed relating to the topic. For this you will have to challenge yourself at intervals in order to make sure what you are reading is understood by you. Besides, read to remember as well. Further, read everything carefully and do not do it haphazardly. The diagrams, tables, illustrations etc. and things written in italics you must read.

Recitation while reading is quite effective technique in study. To make certain what you are reading you should stop periodically and take stock of and remember what you have done so far. You try to recall the principal ideas under headings without consulting the book and see for yourself how far have you covered the points. If any errors or omissions are made, take note of them immediately. Repeat the process again after sometime. This process is described as recitation. This can be either oral or written. Recitation is useful for some and less for other subjects, but it is never useless.

Review is very important for preventing the reading from being lost over time. The learning can be retained if the same is reviewed. From the students' point of view, review of the reading immediately at the end of the first study and again before the examination bears good fruit. Besides, one or two reviews in between also pay. To leave the review to the last moment of examination is never very helpful.

Programmed Instruction

The programmed instruction is based on the principles of operant conditioning learning. It consists of a carefully prepared sequence of materials presented by means of a machine. The prepared material, are described as programme in the technical language. The presentation device although named as a teaching machine, does not have to be a machine. The same can be done without the use of the machine as well, but the use of a machine has its own advantage. The primary aim of the programmed instruction, however, is to make the learner learn independently at a suitable speed and gain satisfaction from his own effort. Skinner first built a machine to help children learn arithmetic. Many experiments have been conducted since then on this line and researches are still under way.

The programmed instruction and text-books have advantages as : (1) students motivation by their active participation is secured; (2) students work at their own pace irrespective of other students; (3) learning is organized step by step with not too high a demand at one time ; (4) the reinforcement in the form of knowledge of result is immediate but the programmed learning, can not make up for the personal touch of the teacher etc.

11 Remembering

We have discussed the principles, processes, conditions and methods of learning up till now and next come the question, what happens when we learn anything or how do we know that some thing has been learned? Unless we bring back the learned experience in some form or another, or in part or in full, we have no means to justify the learned experience. Thus bringing back or remembering presupposes some kind of storage and the retrieval of learned experience. In other words, learning presumes retention and recall of experience. Besides we use in our life-situations experiences to deal with problems of living and preserve the continuity of our memories.

Another speculative area in remembering is the nature of retention, which is retrieved later. The science has not been able to demonstrate the physical, neuro-chemical and organic changes, structural or functional, in the process of mental recording. One descriptive term used, however, is 'neural trace' or 'memory engram' like molecular changes occurring in a magnetic recording tape. We shall examine the neurophysiological explanation of memory function later; first, the process involved in transforming the outside energy into neural trace is being discussed.

When we try to memorise something, we form a mental picture of that. Psychologists call this imagery. We form visual images of materials or anything we want to memorise. The visual images used in sensory images are described as 'Iconic memory'. Icon is Greek word for image. In this sensory memory we include acoustic coding as well based on auditory experience. Both aspects of encoding will be dealt with under sensory memory. Further, verbal materials are translated to objects and maintain their order by locating them against a known background. This technique is called a 'method of Loci' and has been found to be used in memorizing a large number of items (Luria, 1968).

In this context of imagery a note of caution needs to be sounded about the inclusion of eidetic imagery in the general category of visual imagery. Though the process involves visual images, it is significantly different from the rest. The eidetic imagery is a literal projection of detail before the eyes not commonly found in adults and does not have to be ordered against an organised frame. Children show evidence of eidetic imagery in great proportion. Some evidence suggests that this feature is associated with retarded as well as gifted children.

In the light of the above we can formulate dual encoding system involving two separate processes. The information from the environment can be encoded in (1) pictorial form, or (2) as verbal statement. Paivio (1971) describes the two as non-verbal imagery and verbal symbolic imagery respectively. The former represents concrete spatial objects and events, and the latter, abstract verbal information. The assumption of two separate encoding processes is in accord with the study of split-brain function when the right cerebral hemisphere seems to affect the imagery process of non-verbal type and the left predominates the verbal symbolic imagery.

The imagery, sensory encoding and neural traces referred to above, definitely indicate physiochemical bearing and neural functions. Even if the physiological explanations are far from perfect, yet some of the theories put forth in support, are very plausible and encouraging. The human brain is considered to be composed of about 10 billion nerve cells. These cells interact with each other in various ways. Each of the nerve cells is capable of discharging electrical energy and firing impulses. These firings may not occur all at the same time; some do, others don't. Some do in sequence of time and with spatial patterns (Gerrad, 1953).

Experiment with planarians (a kind of flat worm) will be quoted here to demonstrate the significance of neurological function in retention and memory. Planarians were trained to respond to simple light or task and then divided into two parts. The parts were allowed to grow new heads or tails whichever necessary to the parts. The regenerated animals learned the task more rapidly than the controlled group of planarians with no previous training. Surprisingly, it did not matter which of the two halves was subjected to training. The point made of this investigation is that the learned experiences are shared by the whole organism and is retained by the divided parts.

Again, in cannibalistic experiment, the trained planarians were fed to the group of untrained planarians and their performance was compared with that of the controlled group. The result was significantly in favour of the cannibalistic group showing rapid learning. Consequently, some researchers think that memory is diffused throughout the organism's body. However, this has not been confirmed by other investigators (Halas *et al.*, 1962, Hantry *et al.*, 1964).

Studies of the sort mentioned above make strong suggestion for hypothesizing physiological bases for memory functions and have brought into lime-light the significance of RNA .(Ribonucleic Acid). According to Hyden (1969), memory is a result of changes in the RNA components of the nerve. When learning occurs some kind of changes or alterations in RNA molecules occur as well. Further, it is also suggested that RNA influences the synaptic transmission process by generating some kind of transmitter substance. However, without discrediting the role of RNA a question is not clearly answered as to whether the molecules become the repository of experiences or get altered and reflect experiences like other parts of the nervous system. The RNA theory is forceful and strong, but not yet indubitable.

Similar to RNA theory DNA (Deoxyribonucleic Acid) has also gained considerable grounds. The DNA is recognised as a substance responsible for genetic inheritance. The genes, as we know, carry everything about our physical and mental structures and functions. These genes are virtually composed of DNA. These DNA molecules, therefore, are genetic code. It is believed that DNA never leaves the cell's molecules, but directs the cell's activity by manufacturing its own assistants. The assistants are delegated responsibilities and constitute various forms of RNA and move out to the cytoplasm where they control cellular functions. Theorists like Hyden hold the view that DNA is stable and encodes 'racial memories' and RNA, on the other hand, view that DNA is stable and encodes 'racial memories', and RNA on the other hand, is modifiable and encodes individuals' memories.

The physiological basis of memory function is established even if theoretical explanation is not. Investigations with neurological cases of brain-in-jury, epileptic seizures and senile dementia have provided considerable evidence to support the neurological basis of memory functions. The brain-injury to hippocampus region in the brain affects the registration and retention of immediate and short-term materials (Milner, 1964-,1966). This point will be expanded later in the context of short-term memory function.

Now before we go on to discuss the psychological theories of memory functions, we must give you some idea about the retrieval or recall process of the stored material. In any recall or recollection, cues are employed. The cues help to put together associated traces of experiences. For example, if we recall a famous political leader who has influenced us, we get the cue of the man's attire, the platform he was speaking from, the voice he produced, the fracas that his speech aroused etc. and all these will be pieced together to re-establish the memory of whole experience. Psychologists name this as red-integration. Any part experience of some previously experienced situation can lead to the recall of a whole experience.

However, red-integration means reduced cues. Sometimes, the reduced cues do not facilitate recall and lead to wrong recall. Reduced cues can best be illustrated by the 'tip of tongue' phenomenon. Something you know very well, but can't recall it at the time you need to do so. This happens because the material gets insufficient cues to be retrieved.

There is another kind of retrieval known as recognition. Recognition is certainly different from recall because in the former the material to be brought back is present and has got to be recognised. The material has already been known before. In other words, previous familiarity with the material or experience is to be used to differentiate it from the new or unfamiliar one. Thus recognition is easier than recall. In a typical laboratory experiment the subject is first shown words, drawings or symbols of some sort and then again shown mixed together with other items not shown before. The original items picked out of the mixed lot will be the recognition score.

In our life we depend upon both, recall and recognition. Recognition is also influenced by reduced cues as recall. Responses to reduced cues are very relevant in recognition too, as we make false recognition of something or somebody due to the absence of insufficient cues. Some similarity with a friend can lead us to misrecognise some one unknown as our friend. A very interesting feature of recognition is described here which is experienced uncommonly. This is named as 'de ja vu' experience. This is a kind of feeling one gets that he has been in that place before, or met somebody or done something before. 'De ja vu' is French word meaning "already". This is also described as 'twilight experience'. Something in the present makes a person recall the original experience. However, this experience of having had it already is not a false recognition as such. The individual having 'de ja vu' gets a feeling of familiarity and not a definite incorrect identification.

Apart from recall and recognition psychologists use relearning as well to determine the degree of retention. In a learning experiment if a task is learned in 20 trials and later after a lapse of time the same is relearned in 5 trials, this will indicate a saving of 15 trials or 75 per cent or the trials. The saving in trial suggests that the retention of first learned experience was not completely lost, but partly retained. The savings method was developed as a measure of verbal learning and retention by Ebbinghous along with his other methods. He formulated it as:

$$\text{Saving} = \frac{\text{Original trials} - \text{Relearning trials}}{\text{Original trials}}$$

With the involvement of the concepts of neural traces, retention and retrieval, the examination of memory function has extensively been carried out by the psychologists and some of the studies will be dealt with here. When we attend to the sensory stimulation we encode the input, visual or verbal, and immediately take them into the short-term memory (STM). The STM is named because the message does not stay there for long. It stores messages for a very short duration. From there if processed and rehearsed, it is transferred to the long-term memory (LTM), if not, it is lost and forgotten. Here the STM and LTM, two terms, are used to denote the nature of storage, short duration and long duration. Although the dichotomy is arbitrary, it signifies that in the STM the retention of information is only for few seconds and in the LTM, the storage is for days, weeks or years. If the message or material cannot be retained for a few seconds, it cannot be retrieved later.

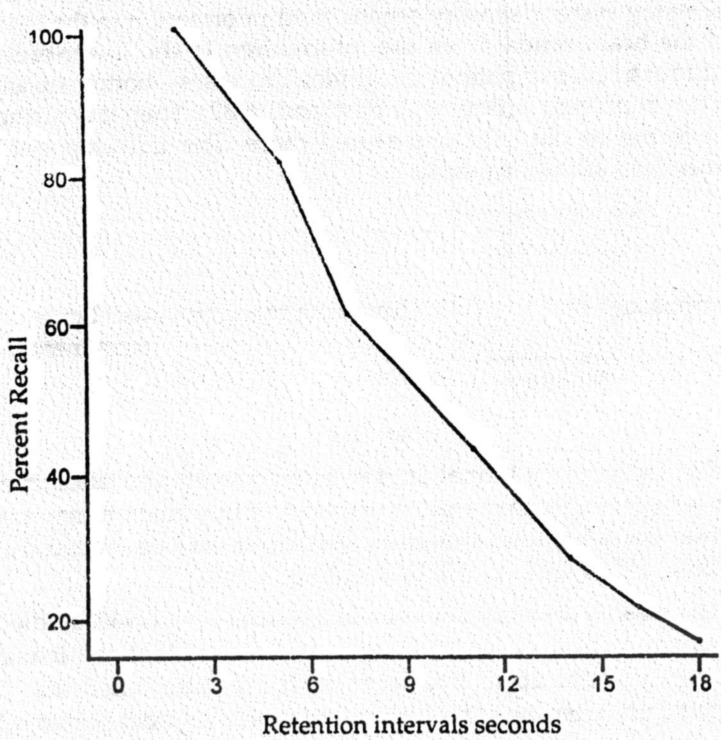

Fig. 11.1. Retention curve for short-term memory taken from Peterson and Peterson, 1959.

The short-term memory suggests a limited storage capacity as well. We see the results of memory span study where it is found that seven items can be retained by us at a time. If we learn to recode the information into chunks, with a symbol, seven such chunk-symbols can be retained (Miller, 1956).

The input of information from the environment is like sensory memory. The sensory memory holds the information for not more than one second. From sensory memory selected and attended information is transferred to the STM. The STM starts losing information between 10 and 15 seconds, unless the item of information is rehearsed by the subject. The processing of information selected from sensory memory is known as 'pattern recognition', which makes contact with the LTM. Pattern recognition involves two-way flow of information in the processing system; sensory organs send information to the brain and the brain sends down the information to the lower-order, feature extraction or pattern recognition processes—bottom up and top down process—(Bourne & Ekstrand, 1982). Then it is further transferred to the LTM and stored there. The LTM has got a tremendous storage capacity.

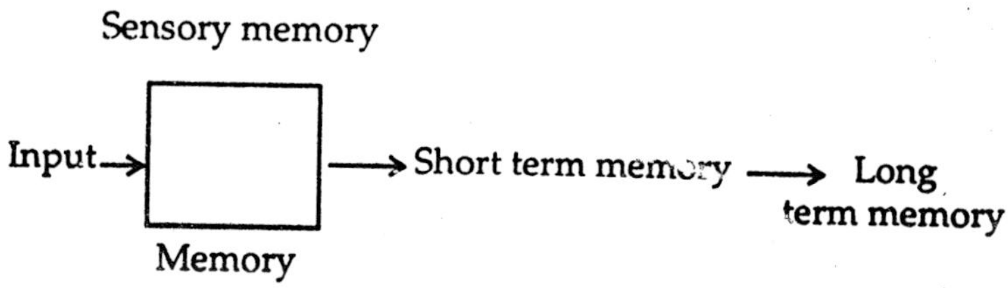

Fig. 11.2

The analysis of information is an active process and takes time. It is quite possible that a particular unit of information may not get into the perceptual system as the system may be occupied at the time and, therefore, will be lost if not stored.

The sensory memory draws on images. Sperling (1960) studied the phenomenon of iconic images and found that the iconic memory persists up to five seconds. It was also noted that if immediately after the stimulus presentation a random pattern of broken-up letters were shown to the subjects, the iconic memories were wiped out. The iconic memory is very important as it determines the item of information to be retained in the iconic store. A characteristic feature of the iconic storage is that it represents spatial location of the items. Other researchers have added that size, shape and colour of the item of information are also represented along with the loci in the iconic store.

Auditory memory is another area of sensory memory that has been studied by Broadbent (1958). His findings suggest that auditory store can contain much larger amount of information compared with iconic store. Besides, the temporal order of item of information is better retained in auditory store than anywhere else. However, these short-term memories need to be processed to be transferred to the LTM. The diagram above shows the operation of memory process :

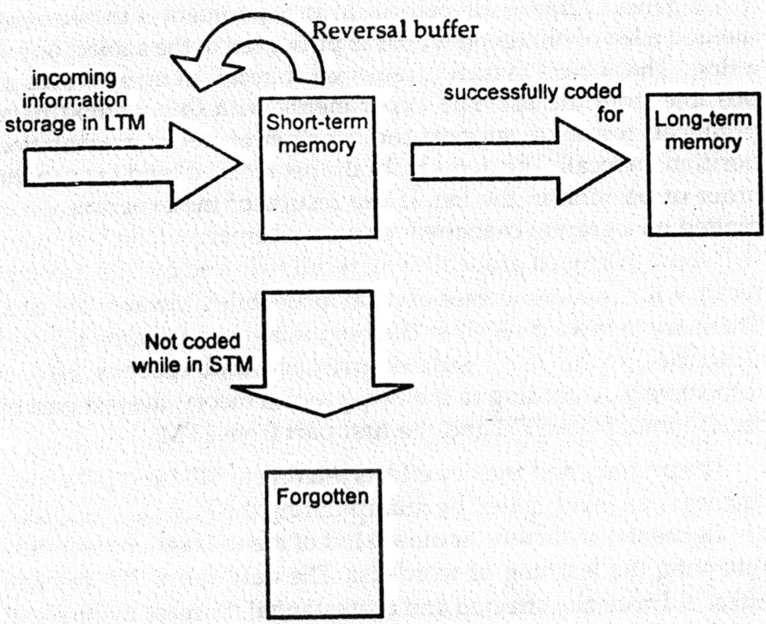

Fig. 11.3

The STM and LTM interact with each other. The STM is recognised as trace dependent and the LTM, on the other hand, is described as cue-dependent. Trace decays rapidly in the STM (Atkinson & Shifferin,1971) and retrieval of individual material fails because input of other items have caused the decay of previous inputs. Recall from the LTM fails because the item of information was not transferred to the LTM in the first place and because there are insufficient cues to help recall at the time.

Although we have evidence to show that deficiency occurs in immediate memory due to surgical intervention in the brain, it is argued that the brain does not negate all short-term retention in the patient (Milner,1966). Brain-damaged persons can concentrate and hold a series of digits and can carry out mental arithmetic, if they rehearse or repeat the items. Their difficulty becomes pronounced when they try to transfer the information from the STM to the LTM. When they stop rehearsing, they forget quickly. The material can circulate in the short-term memory-buffer and fails to get into the LTM.

Postulations about the two-process memory function are

investigated by free recall method. In an experiment with free recall method a list of unrelated words is presented to the subject one at a time. The subject in turn is required to recall as many words as possible from the list. The experiments with this method have produced results to support the function of 'serial presentation position' in recall. The items from the list recalled tend to be in the order of position in the list. If the results of the experiment are plotted on a graph, 'U-shaped' curve will emerge. First few items will show increased probability of recall followed by a decrease in recall, with greater increase of recall probability towards the end. There are increased recall in the beginning and towards the end described to be the result of primacy and recency effects respectively. According to the two-process theory, the last part of recall comes from STM and the first part from LTM.

The primacy and recency effects relating to STM and LTM have further been investigated by manipulating the memory task, like, giving mental arithmetic or other kind of mental task immediately following the learning of word-list. The data show that recency effect is drastically affected and a substantial decrease in the recall of last words of the list occurs. In other words, the trace decay in short-term memory is supported by this sort of finding (Peterson and Peterson, 1959) of the primacy effect. The hypotheses of primacy effect is also strengthened from the same findings when the recall of words from the first part of the list does not go down that much. The LTM retrieves the earlier past. Similarly, if the variables affecting LTM are studied in this manner, the recency effect in retrieval is unaffected .

Studies with serial position curve and function of primacy and recency effects have yielded the fact that immediate and delayed recalls can present different results. In immediate recall the recency effect is significant, but with delayed recall, the same is eliminated. The primacy effect, first learned, remains unaffected by delayed recall. However, there is some evidence of retrieval from the STM and LTM, both, in the recency region, but prior to recency region, the retrieval from LTM alone is found.

As we have stated earlier, the transfer of information from the STM to the LTM requires rehearsal and, therefore, is dependent upon the length of time it stays in the rehearsal buffer. The longer the time allowed, more rehearsed the item will be. In consequence, greater is the chance of its transfer to LTM. Since the first part of the list enters first into the empty rehearsal buffer it gets a longer period of treatment in comparison with the items entering towards the end. Thus, primacy effect gets stronger and pushes it into the LTM.

The STM and the LTM have been differentiated in respect of encoding information too. Experimental studies demonstrate that and acoustic code is used generally in the STM for storing items of information. Baddeley and his colleagues compared the effects of acoustic similarity and semantic similarity in items of information to be stored. The subjects were required to learn five acoustically similar words in sequence, like, mad, man, mat etc. and in other, words similar in meaning such as, big, long, great etc. A control condition was used with dissimilar words. The results supported that semantically similar words were recalled better than acoustically similar ones. Besides, acoustically dissimilar words were recalled better than acoustically similar words. For the LTM, however, the story was different. Semantic similarity impaired long-term recall and acoustic similarity had no effect at all. It has been argued that all memory differences are the result of differing degrees of processing with large number of depths (Craik & Lockhart, 1972).

As we have mentioned earlier, the LTM stores a vast number of information and experiences. The storage is fundamental as sometimes we need to recall very remote memories which have never been used before. At other times we frequently retrieve information of common use. Imagining the magnitude of complexities involved in storage and retrieval of all kinds of information and experiences, it is not easy to postulate a perfect storage system in the LTM. Nonetheless the organization of materials in the storage system must be extremely efficient to render subsequent recall. However, psychologists have attempted to discover some of the principles behind the organization of such materials.

One of the rules of organization of materials is to pattern the items after a hierarchical tree. In an experiment subjects were required to memorize four lists of words. One group of subjects was presented the list in the form of a hierarchical order and other was given the list in ordinary way with words distributed in a random order. Both groups were allowed the same amount of time to study the list. The result was that the group which learned with hierarchical arrangement retrieved significantly more than the other without such an arrangement. Sixty per cent of the hierarchical materials were recalled against nineteen per cent of the random materials. The first group's hierarchical arrangement was used as a retrieval scheme.

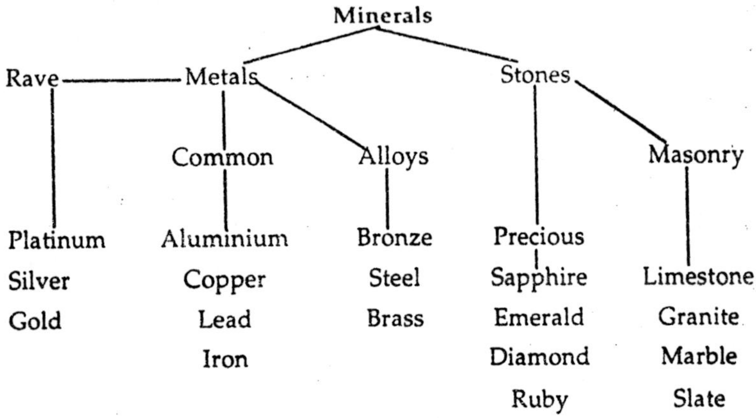

Fig. 11.4. Hierarchy for minerals from the list of Bower *et al.*

The organization of materials is also done on the basis of meaning of words. We have seen before how the meaning of words helps the STM. We have also known how confusion is created over meaning of different words in the LTM.

It is extremely difficult to say how the meanings of sentences are abstracted and stored. Measures can be devised to store words and kinds of sounds but to organize meanings of sentences seems impossible. However, in recent years attempts have been made to propose structures for such an organization. We shall quote one of the models of semantic structures developed by Collins & Quillian (1972). The model postulates a hierarchy of levels for storing information in the LTM. The scheme is given in Fig. 11.5 :

At each level of hierarchy in semantic network the words are connected to more general and more specific words. With each word are associated the properties relevant to that word. Properties common to all members of the lower level is stored in the higher level of the hierarchy.

The effect of meaning in learning has always fascinated psychologists and has been researched at as long back as 1932 when Bartlett did interesting experiments in this area. He gave

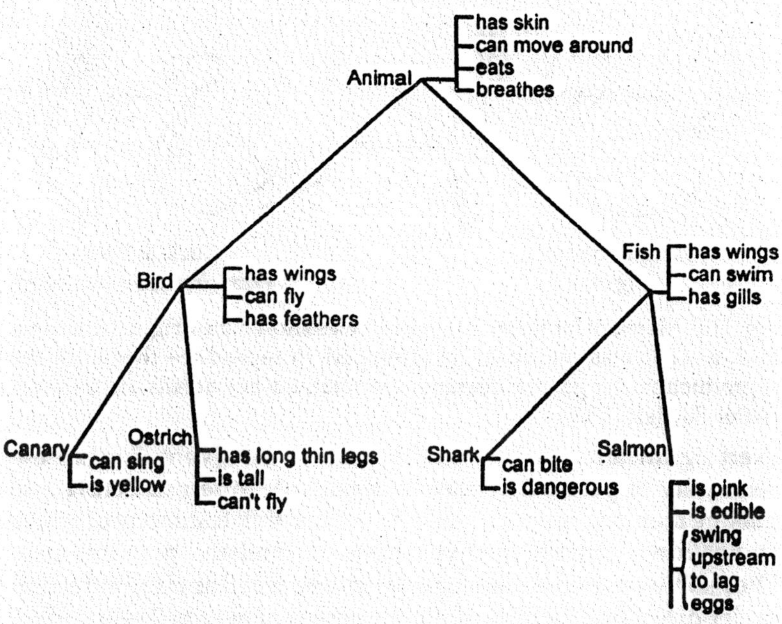

Fig. 11.5. Illustration of the hypothetical memory structure to three-level hierarchy in Quillian's semantic memory model.

his subjects meaningful stories and found that later in recall most of his subject remembered the outline of what were said or read. Details, which were not clear, were dropped out and the style of the story was changed. Subjects made their own stories for the vague points. Bartlett certainly brought about a change in the perspective of study of remembering from the quantity of retention to the quality of retention. The reproduction included characteristics of simplification, elaboration and conventionalisation. In simplification, it was shown that the parts of original story were lost in reproduction. Elaboration emphasized certain details and conventionalisation or assimilation converted features that were unfamiliar into familiar ones.

Other investigators also reported similar results (Wulf, 1935) although they employed different terms like leveling and sharpening. The role of assimilation in which experience is reported in a familiar form is supported by Allport & Postman (1947) with their study of rumour and social memory. These investigations suggest strongly that the circumstances in which the event occurs

Cock & Swan
Original

Cock & Swan
Drawing from memory

Fig. 11.6. Memory for form. The subject was shown the original drawing, and, after it was removed, he attemped to reproduce theme. In the reproduction the general features are retained but details are omitted. (After Barflett, 1932).

exert significant influence on the recall of that event. Further, the selectivity of perception plays a major role in remembering and making memory selective. Several studies with testimony of adults and children confirm the hypothesis of unreliability in this area. They show a range of inaccuracies in free recall and reproduction under direct questioning of the witnesses of events (Weld, 1954).

12 Forgetting

In preceding chapter we have discussed retention and recall or remembering learned experiences. Remembering and forgetting are like two sides of the same coin. What is retained is left over by forgetting and the same thing can be put as, what has not been forgotten, is retained or stored. Forgetting, therefore, is negative retention. It can also be said that by studying one, we can know the other. The salient features of remembering that are examined in the previous chapter are applicable to forgetting as well. Here we shall like to sum up briefly these features in terms of principles of forgetting.

Forgetting like its counter-part is a very active process and functions over time. As the time passes after learning, the onset of forgetting occurs. Forgetting, therefore, is a function of time lapse. The following graph curves will present the nature of forgetting in terms of time.

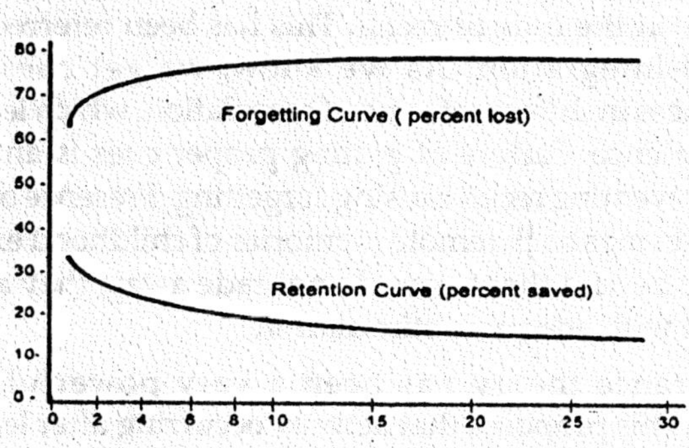

Fig 12.1. Retention and forgetting curves for non-sense syllabus. The curves illustrate that retention is the diverse of forgetting (Data from Ebbinghous).

The curves show the factor of time lapse influencing retention and forgetting. However, we must point out that the amount of forgetting we find in these studies is related to the types of methods used to test it. Investigations (Hart, 1965) have indicated that the recall yields lower retention than the recognition and relearning.

One of the theories of forgetting is the decay theory, which assumes that the neural traces decay with the passage of time. The decay is deterioration due to reasons discussed under the STM functions; limited storage capacity and no rehearsal. This theory draws on physiological hypothesis postulating the fading away of memory traces with the lapse of time. One thing needs to be emphasized that rehearsal does not mean repeating something over and over again, it means keeping the matter alive.

Akin to decay hypothesis is the theory of obliteration of sensory traces. Experimental evidence suggests that certain conditions can obliterate or erase the memory trace. Electro-convulsive shock treatments with mental patients furnish the data to support this theory. Electric current is passed through the brain using electrodes on the skull of the patient that introduces convulsion followed by unconsciousness. Later, when he regains consciousness, he does not remember things of recent origin. Experiments on mice with ECS showed poorer retention as compared with control groups (Hertz *et al.*,1966). Further evidence can be found from the people who forget everything due to emotional shock. Cases of complete amnesia of events occurring after emotional upset are reported.

Another theory goes by the name of lack of adequate stimulation at the time of recall. This has been referred to earlier under red-integration. As we know, we get cues from the circumstances in different forms of association, which lead to recall of an experience. Failure of getting proper cues is an important factor in preventing recall causing forgetting. Presence of such cues sometimes brings back remote memories of childhood experiences. Thus it can be said that traces do not fade away, they are there to be recalled with adequate stimulation.

Interference theory has been a very powerful theory of forgetting. This proposes that activity occurring after learning and before recall is crucial. Forgetting is caused by the interference of the activities between learning and recall. The experience learned does not get consolidated as other experience or activity starts unsettling it. In other words, previous learning is interfered with by the subsequent learning during the time space of learning and recall. Broadly, interference works both ways. The previous learning can interfere with subsequent learning as well. Interference proposed, therefore, is of two types; retroactive and proactive.

When interpolated activity interferes with the previously learned experience, it is described as retroactive inhibition and when the antecedent activity interferes with what is going to be learned next, is treated as proactive inhibition. The retroactive inhibition acts backwardly and proactive forwardly. For example, if a task is learned and then another task is learned, the recall of the first learned task will be interfered with retroactively due to the learning of the second. In the second situation, the first task learned will interfere with the learning and recall of the second one. The essential difference between retroactive and proactive is the time at which the interference occurs. Let us give you an example of the two from the life situation. You go to large gathering where you are introduced to a large number of new people. By the time you complete meeting so many people, you have forgotten the names of people you learned early at the start. This forgetting was due to retroactive inhibition caused by the names learned toward the end of the meeting. On the other hand, if you experience difficulty in learning the names of those people you are introduced towards the end, because you have learnt so many new names that you can't remember any more, will serve the example of proactive inhibition.

The experimental design to study retroactive inhabitation is as follows :

Table 12.1

	Learning	*Intervening Activity*	*Recall*
Experimental group	Task 1	Task 2	Task 1
Control group	Task 1	Rest	Task 1

The recall score for the experimental group will be much lower than the control group due to interpolated activity or retroactive interference. In this context it will be helpful to point out that sleep and other forms of relative inactivity after learning slow down the forgetting process. (Robinson, 1927)

Proactive inhibition is generally studied under the following study design :

Table 12.2

	Original Activity	*Learning*	*Recall*
Experimental group	Task A	Task B	Task B
Control group	Rest	Task B	Task B

With this design we try to study that earlier learning interferes with the recall of later learning. The learning of Task A by the experimental group interferes not only with the learning of Task B, but also with its retention. The poorer retention of Task B by the group, which learned Task A, is due to the intrusion of material from A into B. The interference is particularly effective when the tasks have similarity of a high degree.

The importance of proactive inhibition has been emphasized repeatedly and studies show that the amount of recall of verbal materials is directly related to the number of lists previously learned. The more lists learned before, the poorer was the recall (Underwood, 1957).

Before we go on to another theory of forgetting, a reference to Hull's theory of 'reactive inhibition' can be made here, which also contributes to the understanding of forgetting of learned response. This concept has been dealt with earlier under the chapter learning and will not be repeated here.

Repressed forgetting is the fifth viewpoint, which needs mention here. According to psychoanalysts, primarily Freud, it is a motivated forgetting. Repression is the key concept of psychoanalytic theory, which expounds that people tend to avoid and forget unpleasant, threatening and painful experiences and memories. The repression is done unconsciously, so the memories go into unconscious and become inaccessible. Many trivial example of forgetting in daily life of a person can be interpreted as due to repression. For example, forgetting the name of the person you do not like, and so on. The theorists explain that serious emotional conflicts and anxieties repressed and forgotten apparently get associated with personality disorders. Although there is prolific literature available in this area, experimental evidence to justify this construct is few and far between.

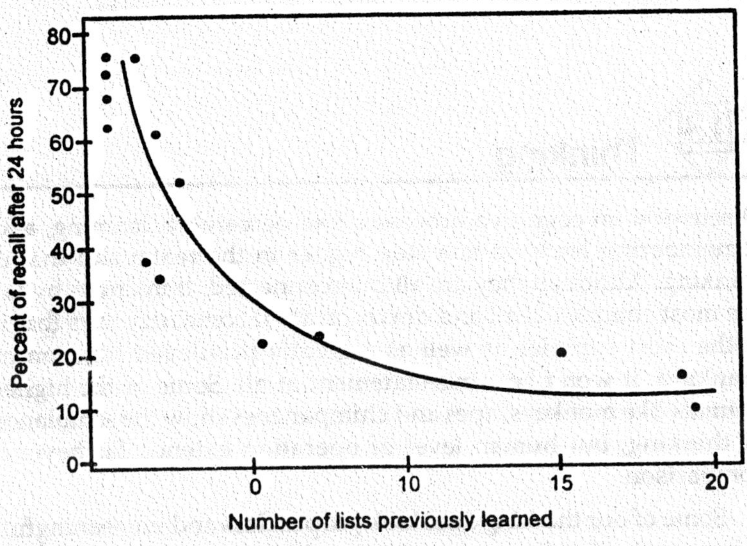

Fig.12.2. Move lists previously learned, poorer the recall (After Underwood, 1957).

Another type of motivated forgetting is based on the study of Zeigarnik (1927). This was done by comparing the forgetting of completed and incompleted tasks. The uncompleted task is not forgotten as rapidly as the completed one. The tendency to remember unfinished task is described as 'Zeigarnik effect' in the literature. This relates to the general theory of tension in motivation and when the task is completed, the tension is reduced and the task is forgotten.

As we have seen, there is not one theory but several to say why we lose what we learn and therefore, forgetting is not the result of single cause rather plural causes.

13 Thinking

Discussion on cognitive processes like perceiving, learning, and remembering leads us to a step higher in the realm and that is thinking. Although they are all interconnected, thinking is by far the most complex of all and draws on all. If somebody says that it is the most superior as well as a greatly privileged function of mankind, it won't be a mis-statement at all. Some of the higher animals like monkeys, apes and chimpanzees show the semblance of thinking, but human level of operation extends far beyond comparison.

Some of our thinking does look purposeless and unmeaningful. It is uncontrolled free-association in which we go on getting idea one after another with no direction. There is no external stimulation cue in this case, which can knowingly be accounted for. One thought stimulates the other and the chain follows. However, this may not seem purposeless to psychoanalysts as it may do to others. The psychoanalysts attach significance to this technique of free-association in exploring inner experiences of the individuals.

Similar to that of the above is day-dreaming, where again the external stimulation is missing. This is called autistic thinking by means of which we fulfill our wishes. Individuals use unrealistic means of getting satisfaction and pleasure; they imagine and fantasize and protect themselves from frustrating experiences.

Another kind of unrealistic thinking is delusional thinking. This is a distorted mode of thinking by which the individual perceives himself and the world outside differently from the ordinary people. Facts and events are associated as well as interpreted by the individual in a bizarre way. The reasoning used by him is purely personal and inflexible. This kind of thinking is considered abnormal and we hear delusion of grandeur or persecution etc.

Psychologists main interest has been in the study of intentional and purposive thinking. This is a goal-directed thinking and is used in (1) reasoning and (2) creative thinking. We shall talk about reasoning first. Reasoning is the process in which we use past experience to solve present problem. In other words, the solution of a problem is not just the repetition or reproduction of learned response(s), but has got to be the new coming out of the old. Reasoning, therefore, is to discover a principle, which can be used to solve a problem or achieve a goal. The examples of perceptual learning, insightful learning and latent learning discussed earlier will fit into the reasoning framework. In every reasoning or problem-solving behaviour we have to start with a 'set'. Correct set is vitally important in directed thinking. It is a direction in itself. In the event of incorrect set, the result will be a failure.

We give the example of a nine-dot problem in which the importance of set is illustrated. The subject is required to connect all the dots by drawing four straight lines. Further, the subject is not allowed to retrace the line nor lift up the pencil at any time.

Try to connect these dots by drawing four straight lines without taking off the pencil from the paper and without retracing any lines.

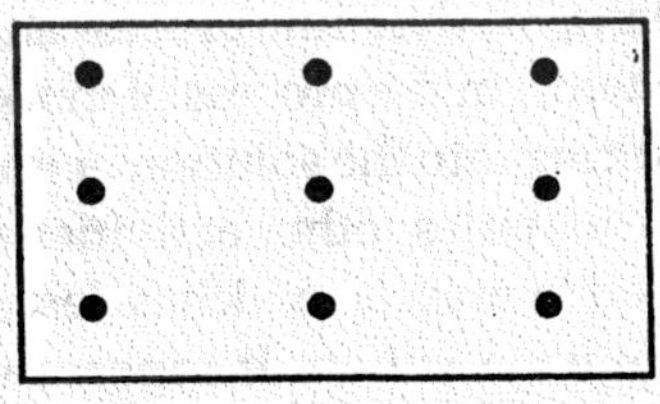

Fig. 13.1. The nine-dot problem.

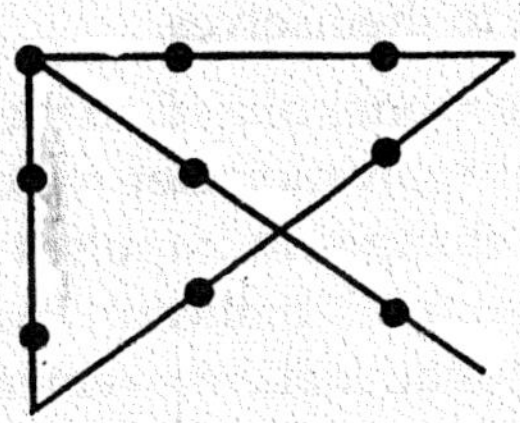

Fig. 13.2

If the wrong set is used to connect the dots with the lines, that is, to connect the dots within the borders of dots, it cannot be done. If you start with a set of connecting the dots by going out of the boundaries, the solution is reached.

Experiments with animals present some interesting features of problem-solving behaviour. We will cite a few examples here. In a maze experiment with double-alternation problem the rats were required to turn right and left while travelling down the alleys in order to reach the goal. The arrangement of these turnings was such that the subjects could not get any external cues. They had to learn precisely the order of turning, that is, the temporal arrangement and not the space-sequence. The series of alternation was right, right, left and left (rrll) and further variations of this. The results of experiments suggested that the rats could not learn the problem of temporal maze even with repeated trials. Further investigations with racoons showed that they could learn the sequence quickly which the rats did not. Monkeys, on the other hand, did better than racoons (Gellermann, 1931). These investigations certainly show one thing that higher animals have the capacity to discover principles on the basis of their past experiences and use them in finding new solutions.

The preceding argument about the capacity of higher animals leads us to brain functions and other physiological concomitants in thinking. Thinking brings about structural and functional modifications. Thinking is a dynamic process and always involves many interacting systems. In the process of thinking these systems are manipulated resulting into the solution of problems. However, along with the brain activities, other activities are also involved. First, activity is noticed in muscle, which is described as sub-vocal talking or implicit language activity. It appears as if we are talking to ourselves. Children do think aloud but later learn that grown-ups keep their thinking to themselves.

Experiments with electrodes placed on the tongue or lower lips and attached to a sensitive galvanometer, which recorded electrical impulses showed, that changes in impulses under thinking and non-thinking states were quite significant. The speech mechanism, especially tongue and throat, make movements when one thinks. Studies with deaf-mutes support this finding as well. However, there are situations when non-linguistic thinking is also possible. Under these conditions,visual images or some other experiéntial cues, auditory or olfactory or kinesthetic, are used in the same symbolic form.

Eye movement, constriction and dilation of pupils have also been noted (Hess,1965) in mental activity. Besides, there have been attempts to relate movements of other parts like, skeletal muscles of the body, etc. with thinking. The findings suggest that the body and brain, both, are involved in thinking, but do not confirm that motor activities are thought processes themselves. Some medical experiments (Smith *et al.*, 1947) reveal that thinking can occur even when other body muscles are paralysed by drugs which leave the nervous system unaffected. However, in the light of evidence available, it can be said that motor activities could be incidental or secondary to thinking process.

The importance of brain-activity cannot be undermined in the area of cognitive functioning. Still, a lot remains to be known in the area. Now we shall talk about some of the psychological explanations, other than the cognitive theory already dealt with, of our thinking process.

Traditional S-R psychologists, behaviourists and neo-behaviourists, consider thinking as an extension of the simple principle of learning. Consequently the stimulus-response-connection and habits formation are considered basic. Moreover, where the behaviourists stick to S-R association theory strongly, the neo-behaviourists add a mediation theory. In mediation theory the recognition of S-R sequence is not denied, rather added to it is the stimulus arousing receptor functions, which can activate symbolic process, and also activate one another. The internal response (r) caused by stimulus (s) may act as a stimulus to another internal response, which in turn will stimulate another internal response and so on. The mediators are the intervening links (sr) between the stimulus and overt response. Neurologically again it is postulated that one set of neural process activates the other set of neural process and so on in mediating thinking.

Stimulus		Mediation		Response
S	⟶	r o o o o o o o o o > S	⟶	R

Fig. 13.3

Mediating response has been explained by Hull as the short-circuiting of instrumental behaviour, which results into a kind of anticipating behaviour. The reaction in the behaviour sequence appears to move forward in the sequence and become anticipatory.

In other words, one act serves as stimulus to further act. Such sequences form the basis of symbolic behaviour. Osgood (1953) elaborated Hull's motion of mediation with a clear distinction between 'stimulus objects' and 'signs'. Stimulus objects are those, which he stressed, elicit particular sequence of behaviour without mediation. On the other hand, stimuli that elicit mediation process are described as signs.

Certain stimulus patterns act as signs and are associated with the systems of mediating reactions. For example, in a simple learning situation a sound of the buzzer may be a sign of food arrival, which mediates appropriate response sequences to the sign. The same mechanism operates at different levels of complexities from simple learned (S-R) reactions to the problem-solving behaviour. The mediation employs symbols and signs. Symbols and signs represent object, event, situation, activity, time, word, figure and even symbol itself. The problems are seen in symbols and solutions are reached in symbols. By handling and manipulating these symbols, we handle these concrete and abstract things in our minds.

The use of language is a highly sophisticated use of symbols and we are aware that the utilization of language in our thinking is extremely significant. These symbols are of two types : denotative and connotative. Denotative symbol implies the symbol of specific objects and things such as, names etc. and refers to specific action like stop, no cycling etc. The fundamental aspect of denotative symbol is that it stands for things, which have the same meaning for every one. Connotative symbols, on the other hand, stand for more than one thing and do not mean the same to every one. We know how different connotations of the same word generate different reactions in different people. Connotations are emotional and express preferences and judgement of some sort. Researches have shown that the connotative meaning can have three dimensions; evaluative, potency and activity (Osgood,1964). The evaluative professes good bad, potency implies strong weak, and activity expresses fast-slow dimensions.

Symbol stands for not only individual items and events, but also for a group of things and situations. It represents common properties of more than one thing. The symbolic representation of common property is called 'concept'. The concept refers to a class of things. This can be based on common elements, *viz.*, vegetables or cow, or can be based on equality of relation, such as longer and faster. Most words except proper nouns form concepts representing a class of things. Concepts are formed on the basis of discrimination learning and generalization. We abstract the essential feature of the object or event through learning and experience and derive a principle from that. When we use language we employ these concepts at a much wider scale than the examples of discrimination learning and generalization mentioned earlier. With the use of language we deal with concrete as well as abstract concepts like, beauty, honesty and normality. The formation of abstract concept is hard as compared with concrete concepts (Heidbreder,1947). Studies support that the abstract concepts are formed with growth and maturity of children. The order of difficulty for concept formation goes as follows, concrete, spatial and then number-quantity. The concepts have got to be obtained in the process of development, which later can be used by adults to learn new concepts and principles. There has been theorization in this field based on experimental evidence of Bruner (1956), and empirical findings of Piaget *et al.* (1958). Bruner propounded strategies on sequential patterning inferred on discriminable attributes and Piaget formulated developmental model by means of operation and grouping. We wont go into the details of these theories here, but must emphasize that although a wide range of conceptual activities has been covered in these studies, still we know very little about the whole process. Of course, this marks the beginning of our understanding of the complex phenomenon of thinking.

Abstracting function, therefore, plays an immensely important part in our thinking process. Psychologists have studied the abstracting level of brain-injured people and believe that it is a unique function level. They make a distinction between concrete and abstract level thinking (Goldstein & Scheerer, 1941). Normal people can do both, but the brain-damaged individuals find themselves unable to do the second one, that is, abstract level operation. Due to this, normal people can detach themselves from the environment and from their own moods and feelings, but the brain-damaged can't. For example, a brain-damaged patient was asked to repeat a false statement, 'snow is black' and he responded by saying, 'no, it is white'. Such examples of inflexibility in thinking are often found with the brain-damaged individual. The impairment is gross in the area of abstracting ability. Patients find it difficult to do simple arithmetical problems. Analogies and metaphors are not understood and interpreted by them. However, they understand language at the concrete level. They follow command and instructions given to them.

As we have stated earlier thinking without involving language is possible and examples of insightful learning in animals can support this statement. But in many thinking situations language is used and manipulation of language in finding the answer is important. Words play a very significant part in communicating ideas and thoughts. This communication is affected if there is any speech disorder with the individuals. In aphasia or dysphasia caused by the brain-damage, patients cannot find the names of objects or things, they cannot describe the events they see and cannot interpret the sentences, written or oral, given to them. Yet, interestingly enough, some of them can play the game of chess or sing a song.

In our daily living we cannot manage without the use of language. We have to learn to use complex signs and symbols, which are culturally determined. Our educational acquisitions are the result of such conditioning and great deal of our communication with each other is dependent on the use of language. But these standardized signs do not represent the same thing or mean the same thing to some people as they mean to normal individuals. These groups of people who think differently from normal people are described as thought-disordered schizophrenics. The words bring bizarre associations and carry special meanings to them. Their uncommon phraseologies, different grammar and syntax are the results of their personal world of communication and are meaningful to them above.

Language and thinking have attracted communication theorists and psycho-linguists and their investigations have added to our knowledge, but still a lot remains to be known. Now, we shall talk about a different approach in thinking, which is known as 'information-processing model' of thinking.

Information-processing model as usual denies the significance of the traditional theory of S-R connection. The model attempts to demonstrate thinking by means of a high-speed computer. The nature of problem-solving thinking can be explained in terms of programming and organizing computer system. We recognize a great deal of information by following different kinds of rules. Few draw on the LTM store or immediate environment and process the data like a computer. There is no denying now a days that computers do a lot of jobs for us. They balance our bank accounts, plan and control manufacturing process, forecast weather, play chess and translate foreign languages etc.

The computer itself cannot find out the answer, however. It has got to be programmed to do something. In other words, it has to be given a set of instructions. These instructions are given in computer language and are technically called programming. The programmes are written after making an analysis of the problem into component parts. These component parts are organized in flow-chart. The component part can also be broken into details of specific operation on its own as well as in relation to other parts. When the programme is written on these bases, it is fed into the computer and the computer does the rest. The information process model, according to some psychologists, is the hypothesis of complex cognitive processes we know.

The computer model draws on the feed-back mechanism. The analogue is TOTE system. TOTE stands for Test Operate Test Exit (Miller *et al.* 1960). This represents the sequence of events for a single behaviour unit. The example of hammering a nail into the wall is a simple unit and can be used to explain TOTE sequence.

The individual finds the head of the nail sticking up (tests), and then hammers (operates). He tests again and finding the head

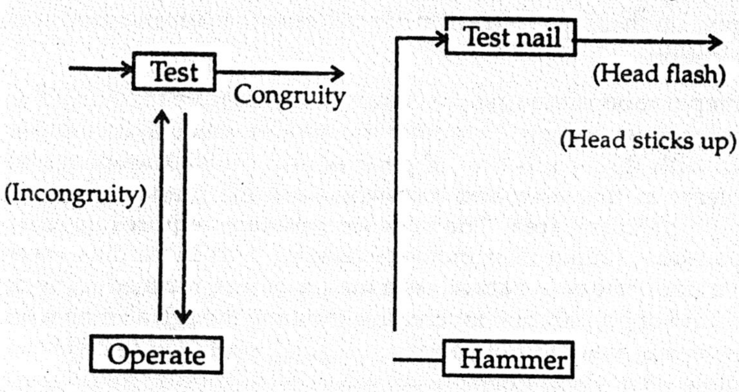

Fig. 13.4

sticking up hammers again. He continues doing so till his test indicates that the head of the nail has gone to the surface. This point acts as a signal for exit. This simplistic TOTE is the basic pattern of learned behaviour and can be extended to explain high-level thinking. It certainly rules out automatic chaining of behaviour.

A TOTE unit describes the activity of feedback loop. If control shows the activity of test to operate correctly, the goal-seeking activity is continued. In sequences again if the control is passed from test to exit phase, the goal is achieved. The advantage of the TOTE units is that it can form the basis of hierarchies of behaviour.

The programmers of the 'Logic Theorist' have shown that the computer can prove 73 per cent of the theorems of 'Principla Mathematica' without utilizing laborious 'algorithms' the method used by them is heuristic strategy, selectively searching for the best approach in terms of established categories. The result has been extraordinary. Things are done by the computers in minutes which would have taken hundreds of years (Newell *et al.* 1958) if done by man. In recent years, a General Problem Solver (Simon & Newell, 1964) has been developed which stimulates human thinking and problem-solving behaviour more than the logic theorist.

Now we shall discuss the aspect of creative thinking or original thinking which has not been covered so far. Creative thinking though looks like imagination is also problem orientated. It is linked to a theme, but the same is dealt with in an original and novel way. The process of creative thinking involves different stages, such as preparation, incubation, illumination and verification.

Preparation is the first pre-requisite for creative thinking. The inventor must prepare himself in the area he wants to invent. He starts with the acquisition of general and broad knowledge of problems in that area and narrows down his preparation to a specific problem area. The specific problem requires specific preparation. Preparation includes relating facts in various ways and is exploratory in nature. As a matter of fact, most educations are a kind of preparation for creative thinking though all men who prepare that way do not produce original work. Let us take the example of medical doctor who succeeds in producing original work in his field; he starts by preparing about the whole physical organism generally and then goes to the specific problem in medicine particularly for his creative work.

Incubation phase follows by the pursuit of a specific problem in which thinking is not active; rather, overt activity relating to that thinking is absent. Some psychologists argue that the idea is treated unconsciously during this period. The idea smolders in the mind until completed.

When the idea or thought suddenly pops up in the mind, it is characterized as illumination stage. It comes out of the incubation period like a flash. The sudden and abrupt appearance of the solution is parallel to the insight as referred to earlier under cognitive learning. Besides, it is also true that in some cases a new idea or new insight occurs even if it is not looked for. Several inventions and discoveries have happened accidentally that way.

The last stage of creative thinking has got to be a verification of what has been discovered or found as a solution. The finding has to be tested and verified in order to establish its validity. Most scientists test their theories by putting them into practice. This is applicable in the case of creative artists as well.

Without denying the phases and stages of creative thinking, Psychologists like Crutchfield and Covington (1965) emphasize the ingredients of creative thinking more than the stages of its occurrence. The first ingredient, according to them, is the variety of specific thinking skill, that is, capacity to generate original ideas, the ability to test the ideas successfully, and the skill in formulating the ideas into workable models.

Another ingredient they lay stress on is the attitudinal and motivational factor of the thinker. The creative thinker is not required to try self-induced premature criticism of his ideas. In the early stages efforts are allowed to flow uninterrupted with no criticism and evaluation. The last ingredient concerns the ability of the thinker to co-ordinate these specific skills and attitudes.

14 Motivation

We shall discuss here why do we do anything or what makes us do anything? This 'why' behind our activities has been looked into in all ages, scientifically or intuitively. Philosophers, writers and scientists have always found themselves fascinated by this problem and tried to seek answers as to why the organism performs activity. The question may sound simple and straightforward, but the answer is certainly complex and complicated.

The 'why' behind human behaviour was explained in terms of instincts by early psychologists. McDougall (1908) propounded a list of ten instincts first an later enlarged to include eighteen. According to him, it is the instinct which makes us do something like exploring, belonging to a group, caring for the young, running away from the danger, to assert, etc. Every instinct is an innate propensity to do something and is universally present in the species.

The construct of instinct, however, could not explain numerous behaviour patterns that the human beings produce as a result of learning and experiences. According to instinct theory human behaviour is dependent on and tormented by the inherited forces. A person cannot choose his goals and do something, which is outside the range of inherited instincts. Anthropologists, on the other hand, have found in their studies of other cultures and societies that some of the instincts enumerated for the western societies are not to be observed in other cultural groups. For example, the instinct of pugnacity was not observed in some peaceful societies like Arapesh of New Guinea, and members of the group never fought with the outsiders (Mead, 1939).

In recent years a revival of interest in instinctive behaviour is found with some ethologists. Their observational study of natural behaviour particularly species-specific behaviour has shown that the concept of instinct cannot be totally discarded. 'Imprinting' is one of the concepts introduced by ethologists which refers to early learning that forms the basis for the young animal's attachment to something, especially the parents (Lorenz, 1966). The ne ly hatched duckling, which is artificially, incubated follows any moving object that it first sees. It follows human beings or wooden decoy and so on. Imprinting has been observed also in dogs, sheep, guinea pigs, but found very much developed in birds.

The inadequacy of instinct theory gave rise to the concept of drive. Drive is supposed to activate the organism to do something. It results from the bodily conditions and tissue needs of the organism. The tissue conditions drive the organism to act to satisfy its needs. Drive and need are interchangeably used to denote the condition of tension within the organism. It is argued that all needs are tension states and tension leads to tension reduction by activity. In this context, thirst etc. are bodily conditions causing tension or arousal and eating food or drinking water is to satisfy those needs and reduce tension. However, although needs and drives are used interchangeably, some psychologists emphasise the distinction between the two. Some refer to needs as tissue conditions and deprivations, and to drives as the psychological aspects of those needs. Needs and drives, therefore, are parallel to each other, but not identical. The need can get stronger due to a prolonged deprivation, but may not result into stronger drive. The organism does not try to get food after a very long starvation.

The state of tension within the organism is a condition of imbalance. The process of restoring balance to maintain a constant internal environment is called 'homeostasis'. There are various mechanisms and systems, like, concentration of sugar in the blood, water balance in the body cells, oxygen and carbon dioxide levels in the blood etc. in our body. These are self-regulatory mechanisms to a large extent. If there is an extra heat in the body, it sweats out and gets cool. Exposure to cold constricts the blood vessels, the body shivers to generate heat and so on. The imbalance activates the organism to restore balance automatically.

The self-regulatory mechanism does not extend over all bodily needs in most cases it provides coverage for a brief-period and the organism has to make voluntary efforts to restore balance to last long and maintain stability. For short or long and part or full restoration of balance, the principle is the same as that of homeostasis. The organism is motivated to establish the equilibrium. The dis-equilibrium in the organism is created either by shortage and deficit or by surplus. The deficit will drive the organism to perform certain activities to make it up. The surplus on the other hand, will drive the organism to expel out the refuge by defecating or urinating and restore the equilibrium. We shall examine some of the biological needs later to elaborate on the homeostatic mechanism.

We have discussed the nature of biological conditions becoming needs and drives, but these alone do not explain fully our motivational system. Motivation is not solely tension arousal and does not end with the reduction of tension. These needs have to be related to goals or incentives to characterise motives. The goal or incentive is extremely important in this context, because it satisfies needs. The cessation of arousal is dependent upon the nature and function of goal. The goal or incentive influences, controls and directs the organism's activities. If the incentive is positive, the organism will approach it; if it is negative or deterrent, the organism will avoid it. The goal can also be primary and directly satisfy the need, like food and water, or can be secondary and act indirectly. The role of secondary goal has been dealt with under secondary reinforcement. There are socially acquired goals in our lives, which control and influence our behaviour considerably. Even at animal levels behaviour can be influenced by the outside bodily conditions. A well-fed dog will eat more if it sees another dog eating at the same time. Within human spheres the effect is remarkable. Suppose, you have appeased your hunger fully and someone offers you a very scrumptious dish of sweet or savoury, which is your favourite, you will still eat the delicious food on top of what you have eaten. Further, our different kinds of goals make us choose from amongst them the one we like. Thus the place of incentive and goals is more than just reducing the tension-drive. In modern times, the role of incentive is highly emphasised. Psychologists, therefore, believe that the study of human motivation is the study of interaction between his needs and incentives. Human beings in particular are driven by both.

Let us talk about some of the motives. Motives can be biogenetic as well as psychogenic. Biogenic motives are primary and unlearned. We are born with those motives. Psychogenic motives, on the other hand, are secondary and acquired, which we learn by interacting with other people in our society. Some of the biogenic motives are discussed first.

Hunger is a very powerful motive. The body needs certain nutrients, proteins and minerals etc. and the supply of these things has to be maintained regularly. The organism performs a series of activities to procure food and eat it to maintain a supply. When the food is needed, a state of hunger is experienced. This is an aching sensation and happens in the stomach with the contraction of smooth muscle in the abdominal wall. It is again dependent on the level of blood sugar in the blood stream. When the level goes down, the effect of hunger is experienced. Current studies have located the homeostatic control of hunger in the hypothalamus. The hypothalamus is a constellation of cell nuclei situated at the base of the brain. This is connected with the pituitary gland and other parts of the body. Furthermore, the hypothalamus has a great concentration of blood vessels, comparatively more than any other part of the brain, and is easily influenced by the change in blood chemistry. The lateral hypothalamus controls the start of the eating activity, and the ventral medial part inhibits that activity. If this hypothalamic region in the brain is affected by injury or an unnatural growth like a tumour, the consequences will be seen in the abnormal eating behaviour. The lateral damage will cause anorexia or refusal to eat, and the ventral-medial damage will result in obesity or overeating.

The food-intake is influenced by other variables as well. The preference for food is made by humans and animals alike and taste and smell contribute a great deal to this choice of food. Sometimes, the selection of food is related to a specific kind of hunger. If the organism needs protein or salt or fat or vitamin etc., it will select the property by selecting the food that will contain the property (Rozin & Kalat, 1971).

Learning also plays a significant role in developing food habits. If the rat vomits after eating a particular kind of food offered by the experimenter, it will avoid any food that would taste like the one, which gave it sickness initially. Food habits are so divergent with human beings due to cultural variations that one group's liking cannot be suited to another. Apart from cultural differences in food habits, there is a wide variation in tastes and likings of members of the same group. In a nutshell, it can be said that the hunger motive, though biologically determined, is considerably influenced by the environmental and social variables.

Thirst is another biogenic need. We lose water through evaporation from the skin and mouth and through the formation of urine. The thirst is experienced by the dryness of mouth and throat. What would happen if the water is put directly into our stomach by passing the throat, the thirst will not seem quenched immediately, although the water will be there to satisfy the bodily needs. It will take a while to absorb the water in order to moisten the throat.

The hypothalamus is again involved in the satisfaction of thirst, like hunger. Some cells in the hypothalamus are especially sensitive to the loss of water. The hypothalamus regulates the thirst mechanism with whatever water is available in the body. The existence of such a function has been demostrated in experiments with salt-solution being injected to the hypothalamus causing hyper-tonic solution and subsequent drinking behaviour of the animal (Anderson, 1953). The cells of this region appear sensitive to the concentration of blood plasm which stimulates and controls the secretion of the antidiuretic hormone from the pituitary gland and regulates the loss of water through the kidneys. We can summarise the findings to say that the thirst drive is caused due to the concentration of the blood-plasma bathing special parts of the hypothalamus and when the same is diluted, drinking is not needed. Further evidence support that the loss of blood-volume also produces thirst in the absence of cellular dehydration. An injured person incurring a heavy loss of blood feels intensely thirsty. Thus volumetric receptors trigger mechanism in the hypothalamus to cause and control thrist. Two diagrams showing the operation of thirst mechanism are given which show how the hypothalamus is involved in controlling and regulating thrist mechanism and drinking behaviour.

Control mechanisms for regulation of water intake. After Hilgard and Atkinso (1975).

Among the biogenic motives sex is quite significant. However, sexual motivation is different from hunger and thirst in as much as it is not a survival need. On the other hand, it is powerful and

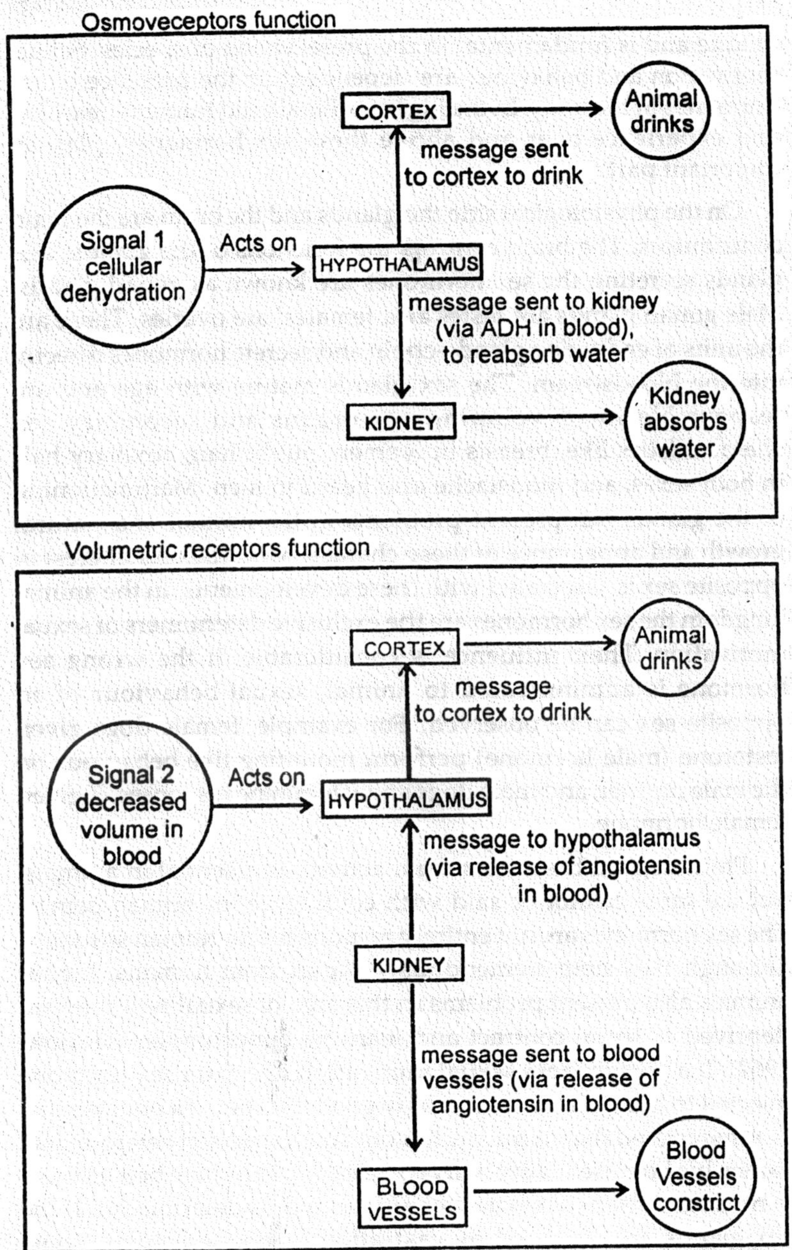

Fig. 14.1. Control mechanisms for regulation of water intake. (After Hilgard and Atkinson, 1975

unique and is fundamental to the preservation of species. Sexual motivation and behaviour are dependent on the presence of sex hormones in the body. In the higher animals and humans, learning and experience over and above these sex hormones, play an important part.

On the physiological side the glands and the brain are the main contributors. The brain controls the functions of the glands. The glands secreting the sex hormones are known as gonad glands. Male gonad glands are testes and females' are ovaries. These are the units of endocrine glands-chain and secrete hormones directly into the bloodstream. The sex glands mature with age and are responsible for developing sex organs and secondary sex characteristics like, breasts in women, public hair, auxiliary hair in both sexes, and moustache and beard in men. Malfunctioning of the glands can present problems in the normal and natural growth and appearance of these characteristics. Sexual interest in opposite sex is associated with these developments. In the animal kingdom the sex hormones are the exclusive determiners of sexual motivation. Their influence is considerable. If the wrong sex hormone is administrated to animal, sexual behaviour of an opposite sex can be observed. For example, female dogs given testorone (male hormone) perform mounting like behaviour on the male partner, and male dogs show feminine responses, if given female hormone.

Physiological basis for sexual activity is essential in animals, but the same cannot be said with confidence for human beings, The sex hormones are not entirely responsible for human sexuality, although they help tremendously. Apart from humans, higher animals also present problems in this area of sexuality if they are deprived of social contract and learning opportunities (Harlow, 1962). If a person lacks sexual motivation, the extra sex-hormone injected to him will not do him any good. Further, if a homosexual is administered that hormone, it wont lake the person heterosexual, rather, his homosexuality will be increased. In human beings there is no clear pattern of sexual behaviour and its determinant. If the sex-glands are removed by castration or oopherectomy, some people will show disappearance of sexual motivation and others will be unaffected.

In humans and higher animals sexual motivation is more a matter of learning, experience, interest and habit than anything else. There is a wide variation in this area of sexual motivation and activities as a result of conditioning by cultural and social forces. In some societies sex is treated liberally and in others it is a taboo and all sorts of notions are associated with it. Learning opportunities are again restricted and regulated strictly in some groups. Inappropriate and inadequate sexual acts, inhibitions and disorders are all related to these learning opportunities and sexual practices in different cultural groups. Thus, we can say that sex, although biogenic, is heavily conditioned culturally.

Sleep is another biogenic motive, which exerts homeostatic control. It is an unlearned motive and its universality cannot be denied. The organism needs rest and sleep to regulate its energy to meet the demands of living. In sleep, hormone balance appears important. There is not much known about the chemical changes causing sleep. However, the brain mechanisms seem to be involved in the activity of the articular system, which in turn contributes to our awakefulness. There is an antagonistic sleep-inducing system involving the lower brain stem and certain cortical areas. Impulses from the receptors travel into the central nervous system via the lower brain-centres before they reach the upper centres. The reticular formation being the part of the lower brain centres, discharges diffusely impulses that cause alertness and ascending impulses take these alerting signals to the cerebral cortex. Therefore, the reticular formation plays an important part in being alert and awake. If the reticular formation is not aroused and activated, the organism is relaxed or asleep (Murray, 1965).

Now we shall mention maternal drive which, although is a unisex behaviour, is a very strong force behind the organism's activities. The caring of young or offspring is noticed in many species. It appears naturally when the species give birth to young and is considered in most quarters as an instinctive behaviour, innate and unlearned. Apart from observations, evidence from the experimental studies also supports the reaction pattern to be very strong and powerful. In the laboratory situation the experimenter separated a mother rat from its litter and also deprived it of water and food for the same period. At the end of deprivation the mother rat was offered three goals, food, water and the litter to choose from. In approaching any of the three goals, the mother rat had to undergo a very painful experience of electric shock. The mother rat invariably ran to the litter in preference to food and water (Warden, 1931).

The physiological basis for the maternal behaviour is attributed to the influence of prolactin, a hormone secreted by the anterior of the pituitary gland in the mother. The secretion begins from the time of conception through to birth and after. This is gain responsible for the production of milk in the mother. If prolactin is injected to a virgin female rat, she will start showing signs of caring for the young. The effect of this hormone is true for many animals and most of the human beings. However, this hormone becomes ineffective with some mothers, primates and human species, whose emotional development has not been normal. The consequences of emotional instability and abnormality of mothers have been found in their 'baby bashing' or 'child battering' behaviour. Some of the mothers who have emotional disorders develop hatred for their own newborn babies and cannot stand them unless treated psychiatrically.

Maternal drive and mothering are again subject to cultural and social conditioning. In most societies the importance of maternal drive is properly realised and taken congnizance of, but there are some societies where the role of mother is taken over by a member other than the proginator herself due to cultural practices (Mead, 1939).

The biogenic motives that we have discussed explain the relevance of behaviour in serving survival needs of the organism and fits the model of drive-reduction theory of motivation. In addition, there is evidence to suggest that some of the activities are performed due to other than survival and bodily needs such as stimulation and emotional needs. The need for stimulation has been found to be quite significant with some organisms (Hall, 1956). The organism desires various kinds of stimulation. Some of the stimulation motives are dealt with here.

Affectional stimulation—a need for loving attention and affection from mother is very strong in the baby and infant. The infants with deprived homes and brought up within institutions show physical and emotional retardation, although their bodily needs are met. Experimental studies of Harlow (1958) with the mother machine reveal very valuable information regarding the effect of mothering contract with babies. In Harlow's studies the infant monkeys were provided with two mechanical mother substitutes; one made of a piece of wood but covered with sponge rubber and terry cloth, and the other covered with wire mesh. Both were similar in shape and size and could provide nourishment through a nipple. The difference was noticeable in the fact that one could give soft touch and cuddliness and the other lacked that quality. The baby monkeys made clear preference in favour of the cuddly mother substitute. In times of stress, they ran to their surrogate mothers and clung to them much the same way as the monkeys do to their real mothers. Further, in situations when novel and strange stimuli were introduced, the baby monkeys looked calmer in the presence of the cloth mother. The interesting feature observed was that these monkeys could explore the environment and keep contact with the cloth mother at the same time. The findings certainly support the concept of "contact comfort" advocated by the experimenter. There were several related studies with the primates in respect of rocking, hugging etc. which confirm directly or indirectly the affectional stimulation of the organism.

Exploratory and manipulatory motives—animals tend to run about and explore. When a dog or a rat is placed in a new situation or house, they go on inspecting, testing and sniffing etc. Some investigators call this behaviour of the organism as perceptual curiosity (Berlyne, 1955), and others describe it as motivation to know one's environment (Festinger, 1954). Animals engage in exploratory activity because they get satiated with an object or thing after sometime, and new objects and variation in situations serve as an inducement to explore (Van Lawick-Goodall, 1967). This set of activities is performed in two stages; exploration and manipulation, respectively. At the first stage the curiosity leads them to investigate, orientate and approach the object or event, and at the second stage the action takes place and the object or event is handled and manipulated. Higher animals like primates are very curious and exploratory, but human beings are much more. So this motive plays extremely important part in human learning.

Need for sensory stimulation—exploratory and manipulative drive bring new and changing sensory input and experience. The need of sensory stimulation is important for the organism. If it does not receive sensory stimulation and gets deprived, its adjustment to the environment becomes difficult. Sensory constancy is another form of sensory deprivation. Experimental studies with sensory deprivation show that the lack of external stimulation as well as no change in stimulation create undesirable reactions. In a study with college students when each one of them layed on a bed in a small cubical with no visual, auditory and tactile stimulations, and more important still with no change in the condition over a period of time, the result was that the subjects got extremely bored and wanted stimulation. They made random movements, displayed restlessness and talked to themselves etc. First they slept a great deal, because as stimulation variation is important in maintaining alertness they had none. They also had hallucinations and poor performance on the intelligence test (Bexton *et al.*, 1974).

Several studies have been conducted in this area of sensory stimulation. In some studies the subject had to keep immersed up to the neck in warm water for days together to reduce sensory stimulation. Results of these studies, however, have produced one thing in common and that is the aversive role of sensory deprivation, as the subjects got bored, irritable and emotionally upset. The studies highlight the need of change in stimulation (Zubek, 1969).

The constancy of environment often leads the person into the world of day-dreaming for want of stimulation. Fliers at the same speed on long flights or solo voyagers do report experiences of this kind. Lately, severely reduced stimulation and its effect has been studied (Petrie, 1967). With the use of perceptual tests of adaptation and figural after-effects, two types of perceivers have been identified : (1) augmenters, who tend to increase and (2) reducers, who tend to decrease their perceptual and subjective experiences. On further tests, the reducers proved to be more tolerant of pain and less tolerant of sensory constancy and would tend to reduce the minimal stimulation even more. In the light of these studies we can say that in exploring and manipulating its environment the organism engages in activity, which brings sensory stimulation and sensory variation when things are constant and invariant.

The concept of stimulation motivation has raised a few theoretical issues. The evidence discussed strongly support the construct of such a motive and its relationship with sensory reactions reflect the physiological involvement. However a definite physiological explanation as we have seen in hunger and thirst is still a far cry. According to one group of psychologists theses exploratory and manipulatory activities of the organism are the ways of becoming effective with their surroundings and environment. Stimulation, contact, novelty and variety do not directly serve the biological necessities, but develop organisms competence to adapt to the environment. It is further argued that competence increases as a result of motivated activity. It is not random but selective with a direction (White, 1959).

Another point of view suggests that the motive for novel stimuli may be regarded as a desire to avoid sensory stagnation and lack of stimulus change. The organism, according to this theory, directs its activity to relieve boredom, anxiety or similar aversive conditions (Brown, 1961). It seems that both views have their bearing on the stimulation motive. The organism gets bored with the lack of sensory change and does something new, exploration and manipulation, to learn to adapt.

Along with these stimulation motives we find emotional needs which activate the organism to perform activities. These emotional motivations have physiological origin and can come under the biogenic group. These are innate and have a share in evolutionary history and animal inheritance. However, there are some emotional arousals, which cannot be explained in terms of drives or motivations. They assume complex affective states and rise above the conditions of drives. There are disintegrating functions of emotions as well. See "Emotion" for further discussion. We concentrate here on the emotional needs and examine a few emotional needs like fear and aggression.

Fear—It is one such emotional drive, which can activate the organism to escape or avoid the danger or fear-generating stimulus. Fear is a survival need (Darwin, 1872). It is very powerful and activities and reactions to avert painful and unpleasant experience are consequences of this drive in any organism. Protection of life (self) is at the base of this, which is shared by all living creatures alike. Animals do react with fear to strange object or stimulus, loud noise and sudden loss of support and so do human babies. The fear of danger from physical stimuli extends into the psychological fear with higher animals and humans. Human beings in particular are most vulnerable to the psychological loss and threat and, therefore, their need for emotional security is very strong. Even frustration of basic needs leads to feeling of insecurity and lack of confidence in a person. Deprivation and unfulfillment of this need of emotional security has been found to cause emotional instability, fear and anxiety in person. Harlow's example of affectional stimulation discussed earlier can be used to support the hypothesis of security need in the higher animal and human beings.

Aggression—It is a very forceful drive, which makes the organism or person expresses destructively. The organism injures or harms another organism. At the human level aggressive behaviour can be expressed by harming another member physically or verbally or by destroying property. Some psychologists like Freud believe that it is an innate drive and some postulate it as a frustration–produced drive (Dollard *et al.*, 1939). The frustration-aggression hypothesis assumes that the aggressive drive is caused becuase the organism's effort to reach the goal has been thwarted. Frustration, therefore, causes aggression.

Support for the biological basis of the aggressive drive can be found in the results of some experiments with chaimpanzees in recent years. Electrodes were implanted in the specific region of hypothalamus of the chimpanzees, which could be activated through a remote control. The animal was then introduced to a group of its kind. The animal, when activated, produced rage and violent reactions to another member for no special reason. Aggression as an emotional reaction will be discussed later. Here we would like to say that the drive value of jealousy and rivalry, which stem from frustration-aggression, cannot be underestimated. Aggressive drive can be used constructively, and its expression can found in the acquisition of power, leadership, wealth and status.

In addition to the motives, which we have discussed so far, human beings have a conglomerate of complex motives that are not inborn and universal. These are motives, which human beings learn and acquire by living and interacting with other members of the society. In other words, these motives are psychogenic or sociogenic. These are acquired as personal-social motives. The individuals in a society or culture develop them in their own way.

These motives are also described as secondary motives in contrast with the primary ones discussed earlier. Secondary drives can relate to secondary goals or incentives. We have discussed the role of secondary goal and secondary re-enforcement under "Learning". In every society there are culturally created goals.

Gregariousness—This is a motive which brings human beings together and makes them maintain contact. Even in animals we find this herd instinct. However, human being depends on other human beings for survival, as he is born helpless and has to be cared for. Perhaps, the highest living organism in the evolutionary hierarchy is the most helpless and weakest of all. It cannot survive on its own. Thus dependency and growth of a human baby is very much related. Eventually this need to depend on another member grows into affiliation with others in the family, friends, relatives, neighbour, clubs, organised institutions etc. People become sociable and share and contribute to all kinds of social values and norms. The motive drives people to identify and conform to certain social, political or spiritual demands etc. Belonging to a group or organisation is termed as reference group which exerts considerable influence on human lives. In this day and age one can belong to any particular group thousands of miles apart by subscribing to the ideas and ideals of that group. However, the consequences of this motive being frustrated are seen in the behaviour of those who are out-cast in the group or are loners and deviants.

Recognition and approval—Another secondary motive is to get recognition and social approval for the things we do. We know how much praise and punishment play an important part in our behaviour. Recognition becomes a need in itself. We are strongly motivated to do something, which would bring us name and fame and the appreciation of others.

Achievement—This is the motive to acquire and accomplish something. It ranges from the acquisition of material and wealth to the success in examination, job, profession, power and status etc. Success in any form and area is a highly prized possession of the modern society. Many cultural goals are created to satisfy this need. The whole drive behind the western or eastern competitive society is to achieve, excel and exceed more than others. The more the individual has, the more he wants to have.

Dominance and ascendance—Among the cultural motives, dominance is found in some and submission in others. Some members of a group or society assert themselves naturally over their fellow members. In any social situation this motive is expressed. Even in animal groups a head or a leader is formed who orders and commands behaviour of other members of the species. The leader of any group, animal or human, has got a dominance or ascendance need.

There are some motives that are more personal than others. In choosing goals, individuals different widely. Every individual has his own level of aspiration. His ambition and expectation of achievement are his own. Experimental studies of level of aspiration suggest that some individuals set a high level of accomplishment for themselves and some set a lower level and achieve less. The level of aspiration of a person is modified by his success and failure. It has been found that the failure lowers and the success raises the level of aspiration.

At this stage it seems important to point out that there are some motives that can be explained in personal terms only. For example, the motives behind drug addiction or the deviated behaviour of criminals or sexual perversion etc. are definitely the abnegation of socio-cultural influences that we talked about so far. Thus, these can be called purely personal motives.

In the fore-going discussion we have dealt with the motivation, which we are aware of. Human motivation is sometimes unconscious. By unconscious motivation is meant that the person does not know what his real need or goal is: the person performs certain activities or behaves in certain ways without realising that he is doing so. Freud was the first to expound the theory of unconscious motivation at the turn of the country. The repressed desires and impulses, conflicts and hostilities determine our behaviour and that's why we do not know them. The concept of unconscious motivation is widely recognised, although the demonstration of such phenomena has been very difficult.

The support for unconscious motivation is drawn from 'parapraxis' meaning faulty functions or minor lapses like 'slip of tongue' , forgetting of unpleasant experiences (refer 'Motivated forgetting') etc. Freud (1914) in his book 'Psychopathology of Everyday Life' illustrated his contention. Further, a series of experimental studies have demonstrated this phenomenon.

Evidence for unconscious motivation is also drawn from the experimental studies of hypnosis (Stacey & DeMartino, 1963). The subject under hypnotic trance is given some experience and when he wakes up, he has no awareness whatsoever of what he has gone through. If the experience of hypnotic state influences behaviour, the behaviour proves the point of unconscious motivation. Studies with post-hypnotic suggestion also demonstrate the effectiveness of such a motivation. The subject under the state of hypnosis is given suggestion to perform a certain act after a specified period of time on receiving a signal. The instructions also include not remembering any suggestion made to him after he wakes up. Consequently the subject does precisely what he was told to do without knowing the reason.

Psychoanalysts posit their entire theory of human behaviour on unconscious motivation and ways of seeking satisfaction for these motives. Psychoanalytic theory will be discussed later.

Whatever the qualifications of motives, they are inter-related. In operational terms they fuse and diffuse. One motive can express through several different behaviour patterns and several motives can be met by one form of behaviour pattern. These motives arrange in an hierarchy and are flexible to change places to meet the demand of urgency and strength of a motive. They also have functional autonomy (Allport, 1937), that is, can operate independently of each other. Formation of habits, attitudes, and development of self-concept of the individual are initiated and fostered by his motives.

Measurement of Motives

In our discussion we have tried to establish 'motive' as a construct that can be inferred on the basis of behaviour observed and measured. We have found the importance of motives in controlling organism's behaviour. However, individual differences among human beings are so wide that we can't make any prediction about their motivations with full confidence. Some individuals never get so hungry or sexually motivated as others do, nor do they have the same degree of curiosity or affectional drive.

Much of the inf[illegible]t needs and drives etc. that we know of have come from the studies of rats and other animals including primates. Significant data from the studies of human subjects are comparatively less. In animal experiments Warden's Obstruction Method has generally been used. In this procedure the subject must cross the electrified grid in order to satisfy its need. The strength of shock tolerance will indicate the strength of motivation. The stronger the need, the more will be the endurance of shock. The need is created by depriving the animal of food, water or young etc. Warden (1931) investigating the relative strength of needs found them in the following order; maternal drive, thirst, hunger, sex and exploration in female animals and all except the maternal drive in male animals.

The measurement of need and drive of the rats has also been made by using 'activity wheel' device. The activity wheel records the speed and distance travelled by the rat through a revolving drum. The animal is deprived of food etc. and is placed in the activity wheel. In a study by Moskowitz (1959) the activity was found highly correlated with the loss of body weight, which was caused by deprivation.

Learning experiments are used to study the strength and type of animals' needs as well. Maze learning or Skinner box performance provides evidence to support animals' motivation. If the animal is motivated properly, its learning will be fast.

As stated earlier, the same kind of experiment cannot be performed with human subjects. However, some example of semi-starvation and its effects on human perception and thinking are mentioned before. Human motives, being more complex than animals', cannot be studied so simply. The investigations into their nature and functions are done mostly indirectly and inferentially. The methods of investigation used in this area are generally the ones that are employed in personality study and measurement, like observation and interview, questionnaire and inventory and projective tests. These techniques will be dealt with later under "Personality". However, this does not mean to say that physiological and experimental studies are not done at all in the area of human motivation.

Theories of Motivation

Human motivation has been interpreted in several theoret:

motivation, however, are not independent, rather, form parts of the general personality theories. Psychoanalytic theory is one among those and will be dealt with in detail under "Personality". None-the-less, it is pointed out here that Freud's psychoanalytic theory postulates that human behaviour is determined by unconscious instincts as referred to under unconscious motivation. His instincts are biologically determined.

Murray (1938) is another exponent of need theory in personality. He proposed a scheme for grouping these needs into Viscerogenic and Psychogenic with sub-divisions in each category. The viscerogenic needs are physiological primary needs. These gain have directions, positive and negative. Positive ones attract towards and negative ones distract away from the goals or objects. Those related to body needs like oxygen, water, food, sex, lactation and sentience come under positive needs. Expiration, expulsion of waste products from the body and harm-avoidance constitute the negative needs. The psychogenic needs category includes acquisition, order, construction, achievement, recognition, infa-voidance, counteraction, dominance, deference, autonomy, aggression, abasement, affiliation, nurturance, cognizance and exposition. These psychogenic needs are good descriptive measures of human behaviour, but the construct of these needs are not established.

Maslow (1954, 1970) a leader of a group of psychologists calling themselves humanistic psychologists has proposed ans hierarchy of motives. He organises his structure of need hierarchy originating from the biological basis of bodily needs through to the self-regard and to the self-actualisation motive in a person. The physiological needs lead to safety needs, and advances to social needs of belonging and love. Above this stratum develops egoistic needs like self-esteem, respect for others, achievement, knowledge and responsibility etc. At the top in the hierarchy is the self-actualisation motive, that is, the realisation of full potential in a person. A diagrammatic presentation of the hierarchy is shown here.

In Maslow's scheme the self-actualisation motive is the highest of all human motives. The relationships between these motives are interacting, but objective evidence to support such a hypothesis fully is still awaited.

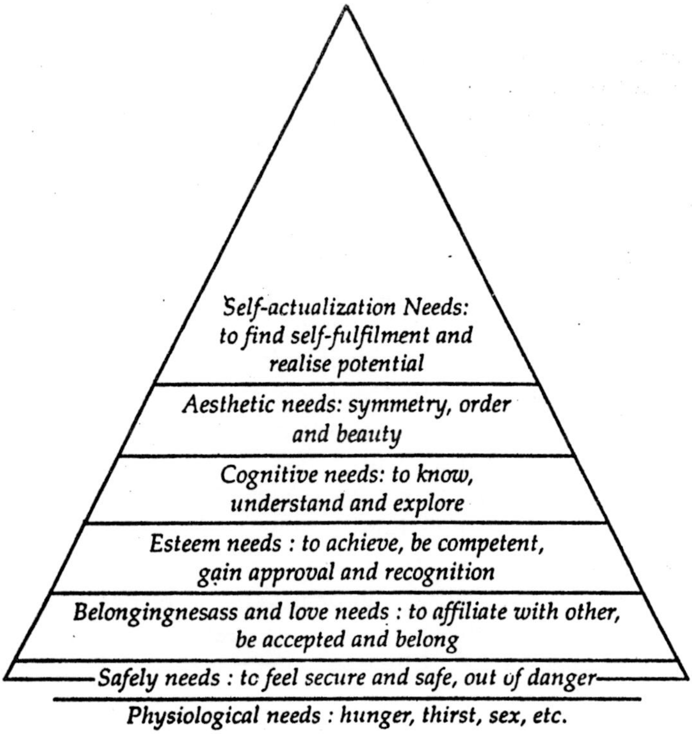

Fig. 14.2. Showing the hierarchy of human motives.

Social learning theory of motivation is another important approach to explain human motivation. This theory focuses on the behaviour and reaction patterns resulting from learning and interaction with the environment. The drives in human beings are not instinctual, rather they are the product of adaptation with the environment. They are learned drives in the society. In such learning, the role of reinforcement, discrimination learning and generalisation are emphasised. The social learning theorists, however, differ from the general behaviourists and stress the significance of cognitive learning in their approach too. They consider the anticipatory behaviour of the individual important in their own model of social learning (Bandura, 1971).

The social learning theorists also recognise the valuc of vicarious learning. The vicarious learning is affected by observing what other people do or how they behave. Many patterns of behaviour are learned by imitating other persons with whom the individual identifies. Further, in the social learning theory, motivation is considered self-regulatory. Self-reinforcement and self-punishment can control the behaviour of individuals and regulate them.

No single theory explains the complexities of human notivation. Each tells a part of the story and all, even if collated, fall short of the objecjtive of prefect explanation.

15 Emotion

We mentioned emotional drives like affection, fear and anger under motivation equating them with any other physiological or psychological motives that have activating, regulating and controlling influence on the organism's behaviour. Now we shall examine the hypothetical construct of emotion and its place in psychology. The concept of emotion has aroused more controversies than it has solved. Emotional drive is one part of the total story. The construct is represented by different points of view. As we know, there is no agreement amongst psychologists as to what the nature and function of emotion are. Some use feelings and emotions interchangeably. Some draw a distinction between the two. Some believe that emotion is a driving force (Leeper, 1948), others consider it as rooted in instincts (Darwin, 1873 & McDougall, 1923) and is associated with organism's activities. Psychoanalysts recognize emotion as a part of libidinal force, but some of them regard it as a result of conflict (Rapaport, 1950). Thee are several views, but most of them can be broadly grouped under two categories; One that recognises emotion as an organising and integrating force, and the other, that accept emotion as a disorganising and disruptive function.

Plutchick argues for the evolutionary basis of emotional behaviour. This means that emotion can be related to the basic adaptive process, such as maintenance, development, reproduction and expression. Emotion, therefore, is the reaction of the total organism and not of a particular part or parts of the body. It cannot be pinned down to the neural structure of a particular kind, though it involves integrative action of certain neural mechanism. Further, he goes on to elaborate that emotion does not confine itself to subjective experience only, rather expresses itself in behavioural form. In other words, it is an integration of neural and physiochemical reactions, subjective experiences and behavioural manifestations. He expounds eight basic primary dimensions of emotion applicable to all organisms, from the lowest to the highest level. These dimensions are bipolar and present extremes and can be grouped along bipolarity, such as, incorporation-rejection, destruction-protection, reproduction-deprivation, and orientation-exploration. Further, there is a variation of intensity with each primary emotion. He has constructed a multi-dimensional structural model for these emotional dimensions, showing joy-sorrow, anger-fear, anticipation-surprise, disgust-acceptance etc.

Young (1961), on the other hand, propounds, on the basis of experimental studies, that affective processes can be defined in terms of three attributes, sign, intensity and duration. He holds that affective process can be justified if the animal develops patterns of approach and avoidance behaviour. He describes approach and avoidance as positive and negative signs, respectively. 'Adient' (approach) or 'abient' (avoidance), according to him, has affective significance and is responsible for developing behaviour pattern. Later where behaviour becomes habitual then affective significance is lost.

He argues that intensity is another criterion to justify affective process. The affective process is related to the arousal intensity. It varies from the extreme positive to the extreme negative. He draws this conclusion from the animal's behaviour in food-choice experiments. The animals develop preference for one or the other food presented in the experimental situation. The preferred food arouses the higher intensity of positive affectivity over the non-preferred one. He emphasises that the development of a preference in naive animals indicates relative hedonic intensity rather than just preference.

Duration and temporal course have also been noted to justify affective process in these experimental studies. The number of seconds that the animal spends in contact with the preferred food and the frequency with which it makes contract with it has been found to be significantly associated with the affective process. The negative affectivity also has been tested by creating conflicts and frustration in the animal subjects.

There is also a suggestion of hedonic (pleasure principle) continuum in affective process, which varies according to the sign, intensity and temporal changes. The continuum extends from the extreme negative affectivity (distress) to the extreme of positive affectivity (delight). In the middle of the continuum, indifference, neutrality and other weak affectivity are located.

Young's writing make a case for the affective process from these experimental results, which lead to the motivational role of emotion, although he does not reject its disorganising function. He accepts the activation of neuro-behavioural patterns to regulate and direct behaviour. The direction of behaviour is geared to the principle of maximizing positive and minimizing negative signs. The affective process helps the development of motives and evaluative dispositions that become relatively stable determinants of behaviour, according to Young.

Thus, it can be said that affective processes have activating, energizing or driving function. They lead the organism to action. The activation can come from the proprioceptive (internal) tension or is aroused by the stimulus situation and the goal. It has a sensory and an affective basis.

Further, affective processes sustain and terminate activities. If the arousal is hedonically positive, the patterns of behaviour produced are repeatedly performed and sustained. For example, the sexual excitement or the appetitive state produced by honey could be repeated by the animals over and over again. In the event of hedonically negative arousal like electric shock, cold, etc. the termination of behaviour pattern is shown.

Affective processes have regulative functions, too. They determine whether positive or negative pattern of behaviour will develop. In other words, they control appetitive or aversive behaviour. In this context, the organising function of the affective processes is significantly emphasized because that fosters learning of the neuro-behavioural patterns. The positive arousal facilitates and the negative arousal inhibits activities that are necessary for the organism to learn to adapt with the environment.

Psychologists who advocate the disorganising and disorganised role of emotion, stress the arousal as a disturbed state. Some psychologists like Munn and Woodworth characterise emotion as 'an acute disturbance' or 'a stirred up state'. Accordingly, even the mildest form of emotion can upset the activities of the organism. The intensity of emotional arousal engrosses the whole organism and brings about widespread changes. Physiological and neurological processes are altered, thinking and actions are disorganised. We find the example of extraordinary behaviour under such a state. A person gets unusual energy, as if he gets wings to his feet when he runs a long distance so fast out of fright. He exhibits incredible strength in destroying things when he gets wild with anger and so on. Not only things are noticed at the behavioural and bodily levels, but also at the mental level. The person does not know what he is doing in the heat of emotional excitation. He forgets what he knows perfectly well. He can't think rationally when he panics, and so on. There are numerous sayings like 'when the lust gets in the wit goes out' to describe the state or emotional arousal.

The emotional arousal, experience and behaviour happen concurrently but in unusual proportion which individuals or organisms do not get when they are in non-emotional states. The advocates of disorganisation under emotional state capitalise on this unusual condition of body and mind. We shall discuss later the physiological changes that occur out of the ordinary functions of the organism in the state of emotional arousal. The physiological processes get so pronounced that one experiences them differently from the normal conditions, like palpitation of heart, acceleration in breathing, rise in body temperature and blood pressure, sinking feeling in the stomach, sweating and trembling, loss of bowel and bladder control, vomiting and fainting etc. These states are certainly not the usual state and can be seen as and when the individual is emotionally upset.

Sometimes, these emotional states do not remain acutely episodic in some people and take a chronic form. The emotion provoking situations may last longer and render a person victim to a state of constant emotional disturbance or illness. The thinking of the person further complicates the affective process and the results are found in his suffering from prolonged anxiety or depression or elation, etc. Often we anticipate and react emotionally in the light of our previous emotional provocations. We fear things, which never happen and also fear the fear of things and get disorganised.

Physiological Basis of Emotion

The genetic inheritance of paleomammalian brain is our

heritage from the lower mammals. This part of the brain evolved after the simple structured reptilian brain, which was responsible for mediating sleep, awakefulness, respiration, circulation and reflexive activities. The paleomammlian brain, onma the other hand, is that part of the brain structure, which mediates survival and reproduction. It is involved in struggle for survival, searching and hunting for food as well as in self-protection from danger and procreation. This brain structure is described as a limbic system (Rosenthal, 1970). The limbic system generates feeling and expression of the states of sociability. It also has been formed to produce preparatory behaviour for mating. In some of the experimental studies, the electrical stimulation of some parts of this system produced behaviour in male cats, like grooming, courtship and penile erection (Rosenthal, 1970) and comparative results were found in the monkeys, too.

The limbic system being sub-cortical organs, that is, below the cerebral cortex is primarily responsible for primitive emotional reactions. However, of special interest is that fact that the various parts of the system have a close neural relationship, as much as that the electrical stimulation of one part overflows into another. The system includes the functioning of three main organs, hypothalamus, septal region, and amygdala. The hypothalamus despite its small size has been found to be involved in the control of hunger, thirst etc. and general emotional states. It has also got close connections with the pituitary gland and influences its secretion into the blood stream. Further, it integrates the neural activity (McCleary & Moore, 1965). The impulses from receptors pass through the reticular formation of the lower brain stem and ascend through the hypothalamus. Other impulses come down from the cerebral cortex to the hypothalamus. These are initiated by emotion provoking thinking and memory. The hypothalamus also sends impulses to activate the viscera and its smooth muscles.

Some part of the hypothalamus seems to be responsible for pleasurable experience, which can be described as a pleasure centre. If that part is electrically stimulated, the rats enjoy that stimulation and seek the same at the cost of food sometimes. With some human subjects (small number of cases) similar studies have also shown 'glowing feeling' as well as negative experiences (Sem-Jacobsen and Torklisden, 1960).

Although the hypothalamus is supposed to integrate impulses, there is nothing conclusive to confirm that it activates full emotional reactions. Septal region is another important part of the limbic system involved in emotional reaction. It is situated near the hypothalamus and generates reaction in an organised or patterned manner. The researchers designate such cluster of

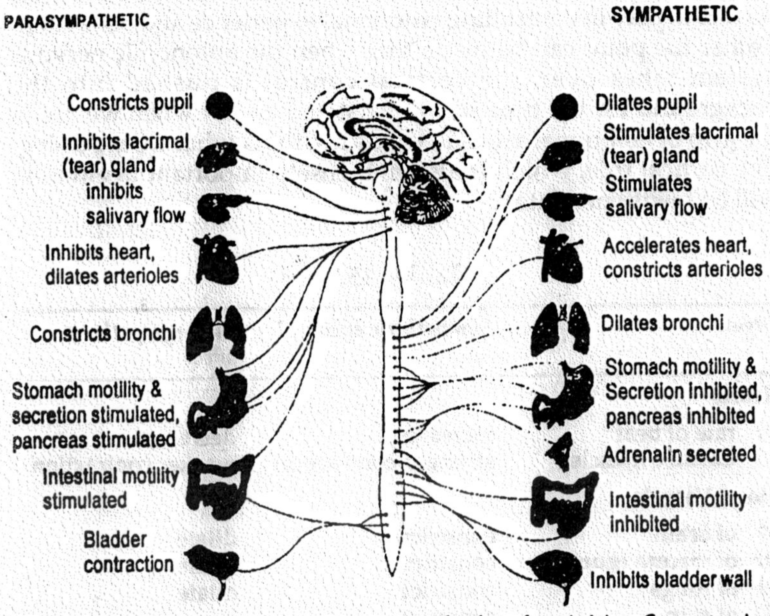

Fig. 15.1. Autonomic nervous system and related activities. Some typical relations are shown between body organs and the two major divisions of the autonomic nervous system. Connections with the sympathetic system are represented in black, those with the parasympathetic in brown; the functions of each system are indicated. While most of the internal organs have dual connections with the autonomic system, an apparent exception is the adrenal gland, for which the only known autonomic connections are with the sympathetic division, which accelerates adrenal functions. (Adapted from W.H. Johnson, R.A. Laubengayer, L.E. Dellanney, and T.A. Cole, Biology).

reactions as the septal rage syndrome. A lesion in this area among rats has produced aggressive behaviour pattern. The animals have shown attacking behaviour, disorganized activity even at the slightest stimulation. Amygdala has also been experimented upon with implanted electrodes and the results support the effectiveness of this structure in controlling aggressiveness. The evidence from amygdalectomy in animals point towards the significance of Amygdala in emotional reactions like aggressiveness and depressiveness.

In addition, physiological changes in emotion are affected by the functioning of the autonomic nervous system (ANS). As the name suggests the system works relatively independent of the cortical control. This, however, does not mean that the cortex has no role to play in controlling emotional experience and behaviour. Rather the point can be made that when the autonomic nervous system takes over, the cortical control is pushed into the background for the time being. As stated earlier when we are in the grip of emotional arousal, we do not think what we are doing. The cortical role, which is also immensely important in emotion will be mentioned later.

Table : 15.1

Organ	*Sympathetic effect*	*Para-sympathetic effect*
Hearts		
(a) rate of beat	increases	decreases
(b) Cardiac muscles	stronger contraction	weaker contraction
Blood Vessels		
(a) of brain	constrict	dilate
(b) of viscera (guts)	constrict	dilate
(c) of lungs	constrict	dilate
(d) of skin	constrict	—
(e) of heart (coronary)	dilate	constrict
Lungs		
bronchial muscles	relax	contract
Viscera		
(a) muscles of oesophagus stomach & intestine	relax	contract
(b) sphincters	contract	relax
(c) gastric glands	—	secrete
(d) pancreas	—	secrete
(e) liver	Glycogenolysis	bile flows
(f) bladders muscles	relax	contract
(g) bladder sphincter	contracts	relaxes
(h) uterus (non-pregnant)	relaxes	—
(i) uterus (pregnant)	contracts	—
Adrenal gland	secretes	—

The ANS is connected directly to specific target organs and glands in the body such as the heart, lungs, sweat glands, blood vessels, pupil of the eye etc. It has two divisions; the sympathetic nervous system and the para-sympathetic nervous system.

The sympathetic and para-sympathetic divisions have opposite functions on the target organs. The sympathetic division increases the activity or glandular secretions, whereas the para-sympathetic system decreases those functions. The following are the list of functions of the two divisions of the ANS.

During emergencies or threats, the sympathetic division is activated in preparing the individual for action; in calmer states the balance is tipped in favour of the para-sympathetic system, enabling the body to build up reserves, The table shows that some of the organs do not have innervations by both the systems. In other words, some have sympathetic system alone to innervate with and some para-sympathetic. These are the glands. In peaceful states the para-sympathetic system innervates the gastric glands to facilitate digestions. The sympathetic system innervates the adrenal glands to discharge adrenaline into the bloodstream of the person to do the extra work or meet the emergencies. Further, this system also controls the innervations of the sweat glands.

The brain areas of the limbic system and autonomic nervous mechanism though, act to a degree uncontrolled by the upper brain, are influenced by the cortical activities. Individuals' thoughts and actions, past experiences and learning generate and sustain emotion in many ways. Even after the emergency and threat have been past over, the individual may continue to remain in the same state of arousal. Besides, he can create fear and anxiety out of his imagination and memory, even if there is no real threat, and so on.

The emotional arousal in the organism, therefore, is a state of experience and reactions that involves the total organism and not a particular part of the whole. The interactions of all systems; receptors, muscles, internal organs, nervous mechanism, blood-chemistry and brain waves and so on occur concurrently.

Physiological Changes, Affective States and Emotional Behaviour

The physiological conditions have the psychological counterparts known as the affective states. The affective states are feelings and subjective experiences brought about by the physio-chemical changes within the organism. However, physiological upheaval in itself is no emotion. It has to have feeling state. Emotion without feelings is inconceivable. Fear, anger and love, which we usually name as emotions, have physiological correlates. Researchers have been interested in establishing the characteristic physiological conditions for these emotions for a long time. The general mobilisation of internal resources to fight or flight, to freeze and become motionless and to perform vigorously has been confirmed, but still, evidence is not conclusive to delimit the form of physiochemical changes in characterising emotional arousal of fear, anger and love differentially. The changes in the state of emotional arousal are so mixed up that they become indiscernible. The example we see when we get the tears of joy. We get so much overwhelmed with happiness that we start crying. At most one can say that the neuro-physiological changes provide an excitation to maximum degree (or disorganisation), and the rest happens as a result of learning and past experiences.

It is believed that fear, love and anger are the primary emotions which are biologically determined and their expression in man and animal is basic. The instinct and drive theories holding such a view are challenged by those who consider that these experiences and behaviours are learned and acquired in the context of a culture. The latter group draws on the fact that the excitation referred to above has to develop depending on the maturation of the infant and its learning. Fear, for example, can be acquired in a newborn baby. A neonate will not be frightened of a snake, because it would not be able to perceive snake as a snake as a snake and the danger associated with it. Further we know how many of the fears of parents and peers are learnt by the child as it identifies with and imitates them. These examples support the views of those who regard learning as a basis for developing emotional experience and expression.

The same explanation can be given for anxiety and anger etc. there is sufficient evidence available from the field of clinical psychology to support that anxiety is a kind of fear response learned in the process of development. Similarly, anger and aggressive behaviour are very much learned. Frustration does not always lead to naked aggression. Expression of aggression can be displaced, inhibited, or channelised in different ways. The expression of love is culturally conditioned as well. The socio-cultural variation in emotional experience and expression, therefore, is of striking significance.

The controversy, never the less, can be resolved if we accept the view that the affective or emotional states do have innate mechanism to trigger off with appropriate stimuli and act as a drive, but are modifiable by learning. The intense arousal is sheer excitation, and we would not know how to experience and express and excitation unless it is assigned meaning and interpretation, which in turn, is based on learning and past experience.

The learning creates so much variation and shades of feelings that human vocabulary is full of expressions like, joy, devotion, ecstasy, admiration, kindness, sympathy, faithfulness, jealousy, sadness, agony, hatred, disgust, surprise etc. It is not easy to delineate the boundaries of these feelings, at the same time it is not hard to admit that these feeling states have emotional connotation of some degree and have their roots in the primary emotions.

In considering emotion as a state, it is important to judge its persistence in time and its intensity of arousal. In some context, it is limited to a particular type of response lasting as long as the behaviour does. In others, it endures for a longer period of time, which we describe as mood, and keeps the individual disposed to respond in particular (emotional) ways. Besides, it can have excitation in a mild degree rising through to a maximum intensity causing disruption.

After making you familiar with the experimental studies of animals' emotional behaviour and physiological changes in human beings, we mention here some of the measures that are used in the assessment of emotional states particularly with humans.

The psycho-galvanic skin reflex, popularly termed as GSR, is one of the measures employed in studying emotional arousal. The GSR records the skin conductivity. When the individual gets emotionally aroused, he generally perspires and this leads to the lowering down of his electrical resistance in skin. In other words, conductivity of electrical energy of his skin increases. The galvanometer is connected to the skin by means of two electrodes tied to his palm and when operative, registers the electrical resistance under emotional state or tension.

The electro-encephalogram abbreviated, as EEG, is a device used to measure the brain waves generated inside the brain. These waves, again, are electrical discharges and can be registered by the aforesaid instrument. The EEG machine is connected to the different parts of the brain. The brain waves present a rhythmic pattern, which is recorded graphically. The variation in amplitude of the curve suggests the nature of rhythm inside the brain. The difference in amplitude shows diagnostic significance, for example, when a person is relaxed he produces a longer alpha wave and when apprehensive or anxious, this wave turns out to be shorter.

The electro-cardiogram referred as ECG provides the measure for the changes in heartbeat rate. When a person is emotionally aroused, the increase in heart rate can be measured. Similarly, the blood pressure, which is another correlate of emotional arousal, can be measured by the instrument called 'Sphygmomanometer'. There are other electronic amplifying systems available for assessing breathing rate and muscular tension.

In this area of emotional measurement we hear much about the polygraph or lie detector. The subject is exposed to the relevant and irrelevant stimuli in the course of investigation while his physiological changes are monitored and recorded by these devices. His answers are keyed to the physiological records marking the emotional state of arousal, and suspicion is either substantiated or rejected. The results, however, are not fool proof and still not admissible in the court of law. None-the-less, it has its advantages in narrowing down the field of criminal investigation from a long shot to a plausible one.

Apart from electronic measures of emotional arousal, bio-chemical tests can also be used. The level of adrenalin, a secretion of the adrenal gland is measured to differentiate emotional arousal from non-arousal. The increase in the adrenaline level will support the state of arousal. Further under emotional stress another hormone, ACTH (Adrenocorticotrophic hormone), a secretion of the anterior of pituitary gland, has been found to increase. In addition in cortisone, a hormone from the adrenal-cortex, is also found which can be measured independently.

The recent researches show that the WBC (white blood cells-leucocytes) tends to change towards increase immediately following the involvement of a person in a stress-situation. The bio-chemical measure of steroid content in the urine further suggests the state of arousal in the organism. The substance increases with the stress.

The foregoing measures showing changes in physio-chemical state do differentiate the conditions of arousal from non-arousal, but run into difficulties when the arousal is to be distinguished from the emotional to non-emotional state. Because arousal or tension under non-emotional stimulation brings sbout similar changes as well.

The tests and measurements that we have mentioned so far are primarily concerned with the physiological aspects of emotion. Emotion as we have stated before, has a psychological counterpart of subjective experience. The assessment of this part is extremely difficult. We either infer from the expression of emotion or emotional behaviour or depend on the self-report of the individual. We have discussed some of the experimental studies of such behaviour previously and some we will mention later under reaction to stress or frustration. Here we shall touch briefly the investigations that draw on facial expression, gestures and other expressive cues. The judgement about individuals' feeling states on the basis of photograph has not been found to be reliable. However, when the context becomes clear and the stimulus situation known, the observations of judges about such affective states form the facial expressions of the subject become more consistent. At least two main affects, positive and negative or pleasant and unpleasant have been evaluated successfully (Izard and Nunnally, 1965).

Another-technique will be further enlarged under topic personality.

Theories of Emotion

In the late nineteenth century two psychologists independently fromulated that the subjective experiences of fear, anger or sandness were the results of physiological and bodily changes. This theory was known as James-Lange theory of emotion. Certainly this was in contrast with the common belief that the subjective states were responsible for producing behaviour changes. The theorists argued that we feel sorry, because we cry; we become angry, because we strike, and so on. Feeling was the consequence of behaviour. There is some justification for holding this belief, as when we retract from the danger in ordinary life that the feeling of danger is realised, not at the time of doing something to escape it. When we step back from the front of a racing car, our heartbeat goes up and tremor starts. The experimental support for this theory, however, is not available.

The second theory widely known in this field is Cannon-Bard theory, alternatively called thalamic theory Again, they were two independent investigators, who arrived at the similar conclusions. They were twentieth century researchers and were making neurological investigation with scientific technology. These theorists proposed that the lower-brain centres, namely, thalamus and hypothalamus initiated the subjective experience and bodily changes at the same time. They brought in the cerebral cortex too, as it involved experience of the past and emotional expression. But they went too far to assert that the seat of emotion is localized in the brain, particularly involving those parts named above, which has not been established in later researches.

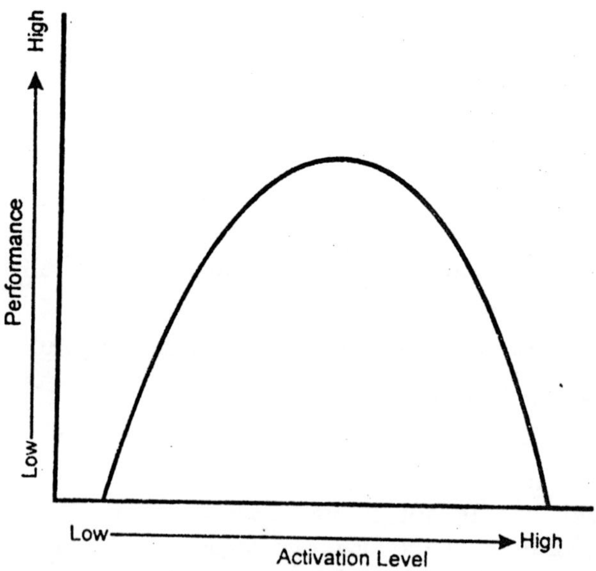

Fig 15.2

In modern times we find that the activation theory of emotion which is significantly related to the thalamic theory in as far as the level of arousal is concerned, involves brain activity. The level of arousal or energy mobilisation is immensely important and has been found to produce adaptive as well as disruptive effects in this activation theory. The positive and negative effects in performance are dependent on the level of arousal and the nature of task involved in it. The experimental studies with moderate drive level, and easy task, have shown the increased performance and quicker learning in animals. On the other hand, high drive and difficult or complex task have produced failure and frustration in them. Reaction to frustration will be discussed later. Here we would like to say that the anxiety increases the drive to a point and facilitates appropriate behaviour, but when it crosses the optimal point and becomes extreme, it produces disruptive results (Duffy, 1957; Malmo, 1959).

The relationship between arousal and performance is postulated by means of Yerkes-Dodson Law (Broadbent, 1965). A graphic presentation of Yerkes-Dodson Law is given above. According to this law, the optimal level of arousal decreases with the complexity of the task. If the task is complex, the high level of arousal is not helpful. The easy task and high arousal go well together and produce optimal performance. But if the task is complex and arousal is of a lower level the achievement will be good.

16 Frustration, Conflict and Stress Reaction

When our needs are thwarted, we feel frustrated. When we find a barrier in our way of achieving a goal we have the same feeling. Any such situation that blocks the way of satisfaction creates a kind of reaction in the organism which is known as stress-reaction or threat-reaction. Sometimes, the term conflict is employed to denote the same phenomenon. The psychological state and reaction are the same for stress, threat, frustration and conflict, and the conditions are caused by obstacles in the way of satisfaction.

Conflict can be caused by physical as well as psychological factors. The physical factor for example, the physical disability of a person comes in the way of his cherished ambition to becomes a first rate athlete makes him feel thwarted. Similarly, the impassable geographical condition like a mountain coming in the way of a person' meeting his bosom buddy, etc. can cause that reaction. On the other hand, the same can be caused by the sociological reason, like, a Hindu girl wishing to marry a Muslim boy, and so on. Furthermore, there can be psychological factors which can create conflict of different kinds and intensities.

Psychological conflict may result if a motive is strong and ways to achieve the goal are more than one. It may, again, happen if the motive is one and goals are more that one of the same desirability. Further, the psychological conflict is often caused by the conflicting motives; two motives equally strong seeking satisfaction at one time. Moreover, when we want to do something and also do not want to do that thing, we get into the situation of conflict and the choice becomes difficult. We can't easily pick out one at the cost of the other.

Psychologists have attempted to understand and explain this state of conflict and reaction to it. One of the theorists was Lewin

(1935) who developed the theory of vector psychology to deal with such a construct. He and his followers explained the phenomenon in terms of approach to the goal. The goal has a positive valence (+) or a negative valence (-). The positive valence indicates that the goal is attractive one and the individual will approach it to attain. On the contrary, the negative valance is repellant and the individual will avoid or eliminate it. A striking feature of this theory is that the barrier or obstacle in the way of achieving goal can also assume a valence particularly negative valence. The impervious barrier can be a strong deterrent. The individual however, can perceive the valence in varying degrees and his behaviour can be the resultant of attractive and repellant forces in the field.

We shall discuss some of the conflicts in their proper perspective. When the individual is faced with two alternatives it can be conflict of two approaches (approach-approach) or two avoidances (avoidance-avoidance) or (approach-avoidance at the same time. In approach-approach conflict, the individual is placed between the two equality attractive goals or positive valence; + ← Ind → +. Both valences pull the individual towards themselves. The resolution of the conflict can be found by choosing one of the two. So long as the choice is not made or decision is not taken, the conflict will continue. We often find ourselves in a situation like this; for example, a student who applied for a place in two famous colleges finds that both of them have offered him a place. Now he ponders, hesitates, considers and re-considers various pros and cons before he finally makes up his mind to join one and not the other.

In avoidance-avoidance conflict, the two valences are negative. The alternatives are equally repellant; → Ind. ←. In a situation like this the individual wants to avoid both. We use popular sayings to denote this state like 'between scylla and charybdis'; or 'between the devil and the deep blue sea'. One has to choose the lesser of the two evils, otherwise the state of conflict will continue. For example, a victim may have to make a painful choice of getting his leg cut off or to die later with gangrene if this is not done. It is also possible that the conflict can be too strong to allow any solution; consequently the person uses imaginary escape and runs away from the situation.

The conflict of approach-avoidance provides both valences, positive as well as negative in the same situation. It is a typical example of ambivalence: Ind ⇄ ±, the individual is in the state 'to do and not to do'. We hear reports about loving and hating the same person. Some psychologists use this situation of ambivalent attitude to explain the relationship of human behaviour with social unrest and conflicts.

These valences operate in multiple forms, too. Consequently, we find double or multiple approach-avoidance conflicts ± ⇄ Ind ⇆ ±. We, in our complex social living, come across a conflicting situation or situations with desirable and undesirable valences. The resolution in such situations with desirable and undesirable valences. The resolution in such situations depends on the relative strength of valence in the circumstances. For example, you need a transport to go to work. You are thinking whether to buy a motorbike or save the money for a motorcar. The bike is cheaper, but traveling by it is very strenuous in the rotten weather. A motor car will be helpful in transportation of the whole family. It is very expensive to run a motor car and you can't afford it at this income, and so on. You will resolve the conflict only after findings the acceptable alternative.

The approach-avoidance conflict has been studied with animals under experimental conditions and the results are interesting. We will cite here Miller's (1959) studies on rats. The rats were taught to run an alley to procure food in a goal-box (approach reaction). When they got there and started eating the food, a mild electric shock was given. The shock caused avoidance reaction. The situation turned out to be approach-avoidance conflict for the rats. Later, when the rats were put in the alley of the goal-box, they started running towards the food. There have been several variations in assessing the intensity of shock and the results have lent support to the approach-avoidance conflict generally.

Further studies conducted to estimate the gradients of approach and avoidance behaviour and have found that the avoidance gradient is steeper than the approach one. The rat was harnessed in the experiment so that it could be restrained when approaching or avoiding the goal-box. The rat's pull of the harness could be recorded indicating the amount of strength used. Rats under, both, approach condition and avoidance condition, had to pull the harness. It was found that nearer the subject to the positive incentive, the approach tendency increased and became stronger, but nearer to the negative incentive, the avoidance tendency got stronger. The avoidance behaviour got far more strong and rapid than the approach one when negative incentive was closer. At a distance the positive incentive appears more attractive in relation to the inhibiting effect of the negative incentive.

Frustration and conflict lead to immediate emotional response. Some of the reactions are being examined here. Experiments with children (Barker, Dembo and Lewin, 1941) showed signs of emotional disturbance in them when frustrated. A group of children were allowed one at a time in a room where they found toys with missing parts. While playing with those toys, the children made up those missing parts by imagining them and played along happily. Second day, when the same group of children came into the room, they found a different situation on the other side of the room after a glass partition were the attractive toys, some of those quite elaborate. The children had no access to that part of the room, but were left with the half toys. The frustration reactions caused by this barrier, were significant in them. They would not play with the incomplete toys; played roughly with some, occasionally jumped on them and tried to break them. One of the children would not play at all, he laid on the floor and stared at the ceiling.

Reaction to stress or frustration are generally summarized under tension, aggression, apathy, fantasy, stereotype, and regression. Tension and restlessness are the immediate reaction of any frustration. We see children or adults presenting the unhappy state too often under stress situation. They fidget, tremble, wring fingers, clench fists, pace up and down and so on. Besides, other features of tension can be monitored by electronic devices as well.

Aggression is another reaction to frustration. The example of experiment with children cited earlier lends support to this conclusion. Aggression can be directly expressed and acted out by way of hitting, destroying things etc., or it can be expressed verbally, like abusing, criticizing, making snide remarks etc. The target of aggression can be objects, individuals and institutions. In a situation where the source of frustration is powerful and formidable the anger is displaced on others. A good example of displacement can be given in the wife's behaviour who cannot take it out on her strong husband, does it on her poor child.

Nót all of us react with aggression to the same frustrating situation. Some become apathetic or indifferent to it some even withdraw. Although these differences in reactions are noticeable but why do they happen in that manner is not known fully. One of the reasons put forth by the psychologists is that the individual's reaction to frustration is a learned behaviour in the process of upbringing. The socio-cultural variation affects and shapes individual members reaction to frustration.

However, the evidence to support apathy or 'learned helplessness' can be cited here from animals' experimentation. Seligman (1975) experimented with dogs under two conditions. In one condition these dogs were subjected to unavoidable electric-shock. In the second condition the option was there and the dogs could avoid shock by learning to jump across to the safe area. The escape situation was made relatively simpler; even then the dogs would not learn to avoid it. They had accepted the shocking situation; learned helplessness is akin to rigidity, a response as shown with rats in a discrimination learning experiment (Bijou, 1943). The rats became motionless even when they were taken out of the shock-generating apparatus. Perhaps, catatonic's (a kind of schizophrenic illness), postural rigidity can be explained in the same way.

Stereotpye in behaviour as a result of stress has been characterized as repetitive behaviour of the old pattern. When the individual is frustrated repeatedly, he loses his adaptability to a new situation. He finds himself unable to adopt a new direction to tackle a problem. Again, the support can be drawn from the animal experiments. Rats in a discrimination learning experiment, which was designed to induce frustration, presented stereotyped behaviour after continual failures. They did the same thing (jumped to the right only) as if they got fixated to this reaction, although the escape from the shock or availability of food was easy by jumping to the left. The alternatives were not accepted at all by them (Maier, 1949). We notice the repetitive behaviour like stammering or stuttering etc. in some of us as a result of repeated failure and continual frustration.

Regression is another kind of reaction to the stress or conflict. As the term suggests, the individual returns to or slips back to the primitive mode of reactions. The explanation is that the person wants to go back to the state when he felt more protected and secure; what could be more safe and secure than the protection of the childhood? The behaviour like crying, screaming and needing comfort is associated with the behaviour of the safe old days of children. Thus a return to the past behaviour is described as retrogressive or regressive behaviour. However, there is another interpretation of regression, when suggests that this reaction to frustration is primitivation. It is a kind of primitive or untamed mode of reaction, which does not have to be a child-like behaviour.

Support for the concept of regression can be drawn from the experimental studies of rats by Mowrer (1940). One group of rats (experimental group) learned a habit 1 to avoid shock by sitting on the two hind legs in an apparatus. The other group (control group) was not given similar opportunity to acquire that habit 1. Both groups of rats were then put in an apparatus similar to the first one except that they had to learn to press a bar (habit 2) to end the electric shock in this. Both groups learned habit 2. Afterwards a strong conflict was created by electrifying the bar itself. The bar still, if pressed, ended the shock in the apparatus, but generated shock of higher intensity when touched. Under these conditions, the experimental group reverted to habit 1, but the control group persisted with habit 2.

Frustration reactions in human beings go much further and deeper than these simple ones of animals, and operate in very complex ways at the unconscious level. When we try to shun the frustrating experience or resolve the conflict or alleviate the anxiety without being aware of it, we are described to use defense mechanism or defense reaction. That is the way we cope with our anxiety according to the psychoanalysts, particularly Freud. We all use these mechanisms or reaction in some degree to adjust with our environment, only when their use gets exaggerated and takes a disproportionate form, then the mode becomes maladaptive. Some of the defense mechanism is as follows :

Rationalisation—This is a mechanism we often use to cope with our failure and frustration. The term does not imply to act rationally, rather is used to denote the process of discovering a reason to justify that act so that it can be acceptable. The famous saying "grapes are sour" is very apt to describe the function. When the fox could not reach the grapes after numerous attempts, it gave up trying and coped with its disappointment by making the excuse that the grapes were sour.

The reason 'used in this defensive reaction is not the right reason, but is seemingly good reason which can be socially acceptable. We make use of this mechanism too often and too many times in our lives. We find an excuse for doing something, which is not fair; we blame others easily for our failures. Sometimes we use rationalisation to convince ourselves to do an act in contravention of our own values. We grow doing it and continue to do so even in the worst state of our mental health and in psychotic illness.

Fantasy—When frustrated in action we take recourse to make that up in imagination. In other words, we fantasize. We get the satisfaction or solve the problem through wishful thinking or day-dreaming. There is no experience of painful frustration, where we can get anything we want through fantasy. However, this process of fantasization becomes a sickness when we indulge too much in it and run away from facing the harsh reality. Constructive fantasy is fruitful and yields valuable results, like scientific invention and creative art etc., but the escape from reality is never helpful. If one lives in the imaginary world of one's own, one fails to adapt to the environment and becomes a mental patient.

Projection—This reaction has two implications, general and specific. In a general sense when a person projects his feelings, he ascribes his own to others outside. If he is happy or sad, he sees other people happy or sad accordingly. He attributes his own characteristics to other persons. It involves wish fulfilment of the perceiver. In specific sense a person uses this defensive reaction to reduce his frustration. By this he does not acknowledge his underlying undesirable wishes and desires, and projects them outside to someone else. He denies his own impulses and attributes them to others and through others satisfies his own. For instance a person hates someone but cannot accept the idea of hating that person consciously, he projects his feeling of hatred to other person who has got some meaningful association for him and thinks that he (other person) hates him.

A study is cited here to support the concept of projection, which was done on fraternity brothers. The were required to rate each other and themselves on four personally traits; stinginess, obstinacy, disorderliness and bashfulness. These traits were socially unacceptable traits. Some of the brothers who were aware of their traits rated themselves high on them, but the majority was not aware at all of their undesirable traits and their ratings were quite interesting. Those who received high ratings on these traits, rated themselves low on these characteristics and others high. These brothers projected their own traits on to others (Sears, 1936).

Reaction Formation—The reaction is named to denote an opposite of what the real motive is. The actual motive is denied and repressed and the action at the surface appears in an exaggerated from of the opposite motive. For example, a mother who does not like here baby deep down in her unconscious mind shows it up in over-indulgence and overprotection of the baby in order to think that she is a good mother. In an example reported by White (1964) a pilot, who flew aircraft to drop bombs on the enemies fainted twice in his mission after a narrow escape each time. When he was interviewed after the incidents, he ridiculed the idea of fear in that situation and boasted loudly. He offered himself avidly to go on the mission again. Later when he was administered Sodium Pentathol to release his unconscious material associated with the bombing incidents, it was revealed that he was scared to death in the face of his dangerous job.

Repression—The mechanism of repression is considered by the psychologists as the most basic and fundamental in all unconscious defensive reactions. This represses or crushes down the impulses and thoughts that are unacceptable to the conscious mind. Those wishes are not allowed to come to awareness. In other words, the anxiety provoking impulses are checked or nipped in the bud successfully. We must draw a distinction here between the use of repression and suppression in our phraseology. The latter is the conscious and deliberate pushing out of the idea or impulse from the conscious mind.

When the repression is successful, the whole thing is forgotten. It causes no more anxiety or conflict. When the repression is unsuccessful and incomplete, we find the expression of impulses in indirect forms. The studies on motivated forgetting as post-hypnotic suggestion etc. referred to earlier, illustrate the significance of this mechanism.

We have discussed so far the major defensive reactions, but

there are other names also which a student can come across in the literature. These are the mechanisms of over compensation when the individual overdoes things to make up for the deficiency; sublimation, when he substitutes goals and does in a socially approved way; identification, when he identifies with a hero or character of a film or book and fulfils wishes through that character; undoing, when he does certain acts to cancel out the threatening one; isolation, when he severs the link between cognitive and emotional components of wishes; symbolisation when he seeks satisfaction through indirect representation of the goal object in symbol; somatisation; when he gets the wishes or fantasies converted into bodily symptoms etc. They all are examples of frustration-reaction and conflict resolution.

When we talk about the defense mechanism, it is usually related to the negative aspect of adjustment. However, the adaptive reactions are not generally emphasized. We shall give here the examples of adaptive aspects of defense mechanism formulated by Kroeber (1963). These mechanisms have coping methods as well as defensive reactions and are given as below.

Discrimination is such mechanism, which provides adaptive method of objectivity, that is, to separate idea from feeling, to make a rational approach to the problem. When the same is used as a defensive measure it becomes intellectualization and ideas are detached from their emotions.

Means-end symbolisation is another mechanism which gives rise to the coping method of logical analysis. The individual examines carefully the situation and explores the causation of the situation. When it becomes defensive, rationalisation occurs as plausible explanation of behaviour concealing the true nature of impulse.

Selective awareness is a mechanism adopted to focus attention on the problem situation. The adaptive means is to concentrate on the task at hand and set aside painful thoughts. When the mechanism is used as a defense, it forms into denial of the existing painful feelings or thoughts.

Sensitivity is used as a mechanism to apprehend other individual's feelings or ideas. The coping method is empathy by which one puts oneself in the position of others and realizes how the other person feels or thinks. Projection is the defense reaction to this mechanism. One attributes one's own undesirable feelings to the other person instead or recognizing them as one's own.

Impulse diversion is a mechanism used to modify and correct impulses and feeling. The adaptive reaction is found in the substitution of means to attain satisfaction. These alternative means must be socially acceptable. The defensive reaction to this mechanism is displacement where impulses are placed on an inappropriate object. It may even repress the impulse unsuccessfully for a short time.

Impulse restraint is a mechanism adopted to control and inhibit the impulses seeking expression. The coping reaction is suppression which suspends the impulses till the correct time, place and object are found the defensive reaction is repression which inhibits the impulses and ideas completely. The repressed impulses can be expressed symbolically only.

The authors believe that a person's mental health will depend upon how he uses those mechanisms, adaptively or defensively?

17 Personality

Personality as a subject of study has fascinated students from the time man became inquisitive and interested in another member of his species. Whether he was a patriarch or as head of the tribe or a preacher, or a reformer, or a philosopher, or a sociologist or a teacher or a psychologist or a head of the family, the attempt on his part was to understand the other person in relation to himself in order to adjust with him. However, all interests had different angles of approach in understanding personality and each approach influenced the other approach. When psychologists endeavoured to study personality, they made it very controversial, because the more they tried to collect information about it, the more they found it in abundance.

Personality as a term derived from the Greek word 'persona' meaning mask. In olden days when people played roles in the drama, they used to put on masks of various kinds on their faces to characterise the role. Thus personality has been in common parlance to characterise the individual one way or the other, like, good, bad, charming, magnetic, strong etc. But these descriptions are highly imperfect and do not convey much except one or a few facets of personality and that, too, unreliably. In addition to these loose expressions denoting personality, there have been systematic attempts also to identify it. Some do it by emphasising the temperamental or emotional characteristics of individuals and others stress the moral values of individuals' character. In this wrangle over the meanings and description of personality, psychologists have their own share which has been discussed in detail (Verma, 1985).

Personality has been defined by the behaviourist psychologists as the sum total of activities that can be discovered by actual observation over long enough period of time to give reliable information (Watson, 1924). Another group of psychologists hold that personality is the sum total of all the biological innate dispositions, impulses, tendencies, appetites, and instincts, as well as the acquired dispositions tendencies (Prince, 1924). The two viewpoints do not seem to explain the construct and function of personality on their own. According to the first approach, the observable behaviour or activities do not say anything about what can dispose or determine these activities. The second approach, on the other hand, capitalises on the impulse and dispositions etc. which occur internally, but cannot be observed directly. We need both, internal organisation and external manifestation of behaviour, to provide a structure of personality.

Further, personality is not the sum total of, rather is the integration of characteristics. These characteristics are physique and bodily configurations, cognitive and intellective abilities, emotion and affective behaviour, motives, interests and attitudes,, skills and achievements of a person. The integration of characteristics is such that it makes him unique, a person different from another. In other words, the uniqueness of integration gives him individuality. Personality, therefore, is a unique organisation of individual's physical, mental, emotional, social or moral characteristics that determine his reactions to the external environment.

The organisation of personality presupposes a state of enduringness in personality structure. One group of psychologists considers this enduringness of crucial importance. It is the relative stability of personality over a period of time that makes it amenable to assessment and appraisal. However, the stability does not imply constancy or permanence, rather it is regarded as dynamic and can change with experiences as well as conditions of growth, internal and external, in the process of living. It can also undergo a dramatic change due to traumatic experience, accident and disease.

Personality develops in a society and culture. The genetic and hereditary contribution to personality is important, but the socio-cultural effect on the development is immense. We have dealt with the evidence of physical and hereditary factors of personality under biological bases of behaviour; here, we shall mention the results of socio-cultural conditioning like habits, learning, motives and attitudes. In order to understand an individual's personality one will have to consider the individual's background. It is for this reason that Kluckhohn *et al.* (1949) state that every man is in certain aspects *(a)* like all other men, *(b)* like some other men, and *(c)* like no other man. The individual is like all other men because he shares biological endowments and physical environment with other members of his species. The physiological functions are the same and so are the effects of physical environment. But societies and cultures vary on this earth, and making shares ways and practices, values and judgment of the cultural group he belongs to and not to all groups. In other words, individual's reactions like some other men means that his reactions are the product of socio-cultural group, in which he is born and brought up with.

And finally, the individual has characteristics of his own which is uniquely his and cannot be found in anyone else. This point is poignantly expressed by Allport (1955) that each person is an idiom into himself, an apparent violation of the syntax of the species. An idiom develops in its own peculiar context and this context must be understood in order to comprehend it. Yet, at the same time, idioms are not entirely lawless and arbitrary; indeed they can be known for what they are only by comparing them with the syntax of the species.

The nature and concept of personality described in foregoing paragraphs, have evolved due to two major approaches in personality study : (1) nomothetic and (2) idiographic. The nomothetic approach involves analysis and quantification of personality characteristics in order to formulate general principles to explain human behaviour, like Weber's law, curve of forgetting, principles of conditioning, motivational hierarchy and so on, which govern all humans. This approach is popularly known as trait approach. Trait in psychology of personality is used to denote individual's consistent pattern of behaviour for some length of time. It is this personality trait, which justifies enduringness of the personality mentioned earlier. The personality trait can be measured and assessed and can be used to differentiate one individual from the other. The rationale for the psychology of individual difference is supported by this kind of approach. An individual can find his position on different traits or dimensions, like, intelligence, sociability and emotional stability on a continuum.

The ideographic approach contends that personality cannot be split into parts and elements and governed by a general law as the nomothetists propose, rather, it is unanalysable. By breaking the whole into pieces the nomothetists simply rob away the totality or Gestalt. Further the enumeration of a person's traits or habits does not help us to develop understanding of the 'inner' person, which is essentially his personality. Each single characteristic of a person, according to the ideographic theory, has to be considered in relation to the whole person, not a generalized law. The emphasis is laid on the qualitative approach to the understanding of personality and not on the prediction of behaviour based on measurement. For example, two individuals score the same on introversion on a personality questionnaire, but one may be very confident and bold when he is with his own family, and quiet and submissive in the company of outsiders. On the other hand, the other may be quiet submissive within his own family, and bold and aggressive with outsiders. The idiographic view is strongly entrenched in clinical methodology and framework.

Generally, the present day psychologists interested in personality study require a convergence of two views. Personality has certain qualities or characteristics amenable to measurement, but they are configured within an individual in an uncommon manner assigning him individuality. This approach bridges the gap between trait approach and type approach in personality study as well. The types of personality which have reigned the domain for long, *viz.* extrovert-introvert or cyclothyme-schizothyme etc. can be described to integrate objectively delineated traits under each category.

Before we go into the details of different theories of personality, we need to point out that description of person or personality as one type or another has been dated from the Greek time or Hippocrates (460-377 D.C). He based his characterisation on the theory of humour, black bile, yellow bile, blood and phlegm; persons with an excess of black bile become melancholic showing depression, yellow bile become choleric showing aggressiveness. Having predominance of blood turned one sanguine and cheerful, and excess phlegm caused passivity and slowness. This typology has long been discarded, but the terms as such are still in vogue.

Another classification was introduced by Lombroso (1536; 1909) who described criminal types due to the structure of head, nose and jaws of the individuals. The theory did not receive much recognition although was popular at its own time. However, there were two widely famous topologies of Kretshmer (1925) and Sheldon *et al.* (1940), which attempted to relate physique, body-build with temperamental characteristics. According to Kretshmer, three main body types, pyknic, athletic and asthenic had significantly different characters. Pyknic, being short and fat was expected to be extroverted; athletic, being muscular, was thought to be aggressive and energetic; asthenic, being thin and tall, was supposed to be introverted and shut-in. Kretshmer's typology did have some impact on medical science but it was short lived and further researches did not support the association of temperamental characteristic with the body type.

Sheldon's typology of personality in terms of physique included endomorphy, suggesting a predominance of digestive viscera; mesomorphy, showing much of muscle; ectomorphy, revealing skin and neural structure. The related temperaments were viscerotonia expressing visceral comforts, relaxed state and joviality for endomorphy; somatotonia, showing aggressiveness and energy for mesomorphy; cerebrotonia, indicating thoughtfulness and restraint etc. for ectomorphy etc. These classifications were based on ratings of physical and personality characteristics of a large number of nude photographs of young men. However, the approach is not free from critique and does not stand unscathed. There are other studies also in this area, but the established evidence to support the typology of personality on the basis of physique is not available.

Now we shall deal with some of the psychological theories of personality which have made significant contribution to understanding individuals. We shall begin with the psychoanalytic theory expounded by Freud. With the concept of unconscious mind referred to earlier he developed a theory of instincts which needed gratification in harmony with the society. He named these instinctual impulses 'id', as the original and primitive energy or content of mind functioning as a part of the unconscious mind. According to Freud, these biological instincts drive the organism to reduce tension guided by pleasure principle regardless of external reality. Later he also added death instinct to his theory and with the interaction of life and death (eros and thantos) instincts built up his theory of psychoanalysis.

The other concept he introduced to regulate these primary impulses of the individual is ego. The ego develops out of 'id' in the process of growth and experience. This part of the mind is responsible for testing reality, perceiving, thinking, reasoning and solving problems and adjusting to the external environment. The other major function of ego is defensive reaction (see discussion under frustration) by which it allows the satisfaction of instincts in different forms that are not likely to lead to punishment and guilt. It also controls these impulses of the mind so that they do not become conscious. The ego, according to Freud, tries to serve three masters at a time, the id, the super-ego and the external reality of the world.

In the structure of our mind, Freud incorporated another unconscious part and christened it the super-ego'. This is differentiated from the ego and contains moral and cultural values, do's and don't's, interjected by the individual. These rights and wrongs are interpreted to the child by the parents. This super-ego orders punishment in the form of guilt and anxiety and the ego has to experience that. When some instinctual impulses threaten to produce conflict with the super-ego, defenses are used to avoid anxiety.

According to Freud, personality develops through different stages, which he described as psychosexual phases of development. The first stage is 'oral' when the baby uses mouth to seek libidinal gratification. At this stage oral means is the only means of getting satisfaction and pleasure. It is the sucking of mother's breast that becomes the initial activity. Oral phase has two aspects; oral erotic and oral sadistic, depending on an interaction with the mother and supply of milk to the baby. In the first, the baby receives in and in the other, acts out aggressively. At each phase the conflict is inevitable. When the conflict is intensified by the parents and social forces, the growth is arrested known as fixated and strong defenses are used to protect it. If stages are passed without arrest, the characteristics are retained in varying degrees later in adulthood. Feeding becomes an area of conflict in the oral phase lasting for the first year of life.

The features of oral stage can be expressed in adulthood as the oral character. The defenses employed are projection, denial, & introjection. The personality characteristics noticeable in the adult life are optimism-pessimism, gullibility-suspiciousness, manipulative-passivity and admiration-envy.

The anal phase is the second stage of psycho-sexual development and erogenous zone is the anus. This happens in the second year of life of the child and the pleasure is derived by the activities of withholding the faeces (anal retentiveness) and expelling (defaecating aggressively) and excreting. This is the stage when conflict surrounds the bowel training, discipline and authority. The anal character uses defenses like intellectualization (substituting socially acceptable reason behind the wishes), reaction formation, isolation and undoing. The typical traits noticeable as a legacy of this anal character are stinginess-overgenerosity, stubbornness-acquiescence, orderliness-messiness, and precision-vagueness.

The phallic phase is the third stage of development and extends over from this year to fifth year of life. The erogenous zone at this satge is around the genitals and activities involve hetero-sexualizing interaction. This is the stage of Oedipus complex, when the child wants to monopolise the affection of opposite-sex parent, boy for mother and girl for father. The conflict is created by the castration anxiety for the boy and penis envy for the girl.

The defense used at this stage is the most important one in the psychoanalytic theory and that is named, 'repression'. The personality traits are vanity-self-hatred, pride-humility, courage-timidity, chastity-promiscuity.

The latency stage follows after phallic and spreads over sixth year through to puberty. This is the phase when the sexuality becomes indirect and subservient. The child learns skills of all kinds which have no high sexual significance.

Puberty is marked as genital stage and characterises mature sexuality as combination of all that is learned at the previous phases of development. The person at this stage develops fully to love, make lover and work. The major defense used at this stage is sublimation and the traits noticeable are socialisability and adjustability with the society.

Freud also introduced a concept of different level of consciousness and related reactions by the individual. Those are unconscious, preconscious and conscious. Conscious, we all know, we are aware of what we are doing, but not when we are reacting at the level of preconscious and unconscious. He drew the analogy of an ice-berg whose main base and large part is under the water (unconscious) and some is under as well as over the water (preconscious) and some part is on the top of all (conscious). The unconscious we are not at all aware of, ever with conscious effort, and preconscious can be brought to the level of consciousness in part.

Psycholo-analytic theory of personality had the strongest influence on the subject so far and still holds on, though it is widely debated these days. For some, it is the only approach that can make personality meaningful. The critics, on the other hand, argue that the claims and propositions are untestable and dubious. However, the inordinate emphasis on the biological nature of instincts reduces mankind to the animal realm and therefore, the neo-Freudians modified the approach to include the sociological influences as significant in the development of personality.

Within the psycho-analytic framework of personality theory we find the name of Jung, who initially worked with Freud in agreement with his theory, but later developed his own. His theory proposes that individuals strive towards the attainment of self-hood and the self-hood represents a balance between opposing forces of personality. These forces could be both, conscious and unconscious. He propounded principle of equivalence in achieving self-hood. This means that if one aspect of personality increases or decreases, it will be compensated for by another aspect. He also added the principle of entrophy referring to the distribution of energy in personality to seek balances. The third main feature of his theory is the transcendent function by which the personality elements are integrated into a whole.

The ego, according to Jung, is in conflict with the personal unconscious (socially unacceptable contents that were once conscious has been forced out of awareness) collective or racial unconscious (communal, representing the accumulated experience of mankind). The collective unconscious comprises archetypes. The major archetypes are the shadow (animalistic possibility of man), the anima (feminine possibility of man), the animus (masculine possibility in women), the persona (the mask adopted by individuals in the face of social pressure), and the self (a union of all the opposing forces in a person).

Jung did not propose the stages of personality development. He however, emphasized that in early life sexuality and individualistic concern of the ego are dominant, but in later adulthood, spirituality and collective unconscious tilts the emphasis. He formulated principles to explain human behaviour development as causality v teleology, (influence of past versus influence of anticipated future); progression v regression and sublimation v repression.

Jung's typology is a famous contribution to psychology of personality. He postulated introversion and extraversion as types of personality with further ramification of rational and irrational categories and sub-categories. His introverted rational is oriented towards the inner world of experience and makes either thinking or feeling modes of function. The extroverted rational, is, on the other hand, oriented toward the outer world of experience. The introverted rational is oriented toward the inner world of experience but emphasizes either sensing or intuiting modes of function. They are irrational because they passively take in without evaluating experience. The extroverted irrational is similarly oriented toward the outer world of experience by sensing or intuiting.

Adler is the other name in the trilogy of psychoanalysis. His theory of personality also presented a divergent standpoint from Freud's, Like Jung he worked with Freud originally and branched off later. His theory emphasizes the striving toward superiority as the basic drive in the individual. This tendency is not limited to individual functioning as an individual, but also as a member of society as well.

He postulated three bases for this striving toward perfection. The first one is organ inferiority, actual physical incapacities or shortcomings; the second is feelings of inferiority, the psychological feelings of inferiority and inadequacy without physical conditions; and the third is compensation, the endeavour to overcome and make-up for these inferiorities. He also hypothesizes a creative self in the individual, which expresses the capabilities of exercising free will to transcend the forces operating around and upon.

Adler did not postulate developmental stages like Freud, but laid considerable emphasis on the family. Family constellation refers to the sociological conditions as they affect individual members in the family. The point of ordinal position, first, second or third child etc., presence or absence of father, emotional relationships among family members, all matter in personality development. The traits of personality that one could develop in the family atmosphere will be (1) active—constructive style, which will be described as ambitiousness or orientation toward success (2) the passive—constructive style, as charm receiving special attention for what one is rather than what one does (3) the active—destructive style, as to be a nuisance, viscous, degenerate and (4) the passive destructive style, but differing in as much as it includes laziness, stubbornness and despair even.

Similar to Freud we find the theory of personality developed by Murray. In our previous discussion on motives we referred to the needs and their structure propounded by Murray and their functions in personality. He accepted the basic tenets of id, ego and super ego, but modified them a bit. For example, he argued that not all instincts were socially deleterious and selfish. About ego he expanded the role from defensive to non-defensive reactions as rational thinking and objective perceiving. And for his the super ego values were not finally limited to the childhood experiences, rather went beyond that stage.

Murray accepted Freud's developmental stages of personality and psycho-sexual activities and added two of his own, claustral and eurethral. In the first, no defined erogenous zone was mentioned, but dependency on mother is emphasized. This stage was characterised by the interuterine period of life. In the second, the urinary apparatus was recognized as the erogenous zone and the period was marked between oral and anal stages. Activities mentioned were obviously urinary display.

Fixation and character traits were similar to Freud's except for the two additions. The major defense was denial for the claustral complex and traits were passivity and withdrawal. For the eurethral complex, however, the defenses wee similar to the anal stage of Freud and traits emphasised compitiveness and acquiescence. In Murray's theory needs were triggered by press or environmental forces, sometimes by imaginary situations, and personality was the process of meeting them.

Erikson is another personality theorist whose influence in psychology is recognised. He also accepts Freud's concept of id, ego and super-ego with modification. His modification concerns the ego. The ego, according to him, has a wider function to perform that what is proposed by Freud. It does rational thinking and realistic perception that are not related to conflict between the id and the society. The ego is considered by Erikson partly innate and has its own instincts.

He accepted psycho-sexual stages of development of Freud, but sees them as psycho-social features of conflict between child and parents. Further, he proposes development of personality on a longer basis than Freud did and extends the process throughout life span. However, fixations associated by him are similar to Freud. His conflicts stages are the following :

Trust v Mistrust, in which the amount of conflict determines the positive learning. It compares with Freud's oral stage.

Autonomy v Shame and Doubt, in this, the conflict determines whether positive or negative pole is learned. It is similar to Freud's anal phase.

Initiative and Responsibility v Guilty Functioning, in this, again, this amount of conflict determines whether the positive or negative pole is learned. This parallels Freud's phallic stage.

Industry v Inferiority, in which the amount of conflict determines whether the positive or negative pole is learned. This is similar to Freud's latency period.

Identity v Role diffusion, in which conflict is generated by the socially imposed task of becoming an independent adult, and the difficulty of adolescents. Again, the amount of conflict determines whether positive or negative pole is learned. This period extends from puberty to the end of adolescence.

Intimacy v Isolation, in this the conflict determines whether positive or negative pole is learned when the person has to face the socially imposed task of developing close relationship and the difficulty in not doing so. This is the characteristic of young adulthood.

Generativity v Stagnation, in which the conflict is produced by socially imposed task of fore-going one's own immediate needs in favour of others, particularly bringing up children, and difficulty associated with not doing so. The conflict determines, again whether positive or negative pole is learned. This is the middle adulthood period.

Ego Integrity v Despair, in this the conflict is caused due to decrease in important social and biological roles as old age approaches, and difficulty in accepting this role. The amount of conflict determines whether the positive of negative pole is learned. The period extends from middle adulthood through to death.

The eight stages of development in personality are more suggestive of stage of growth rather than character types. However, Erikson proposes that whenever a fixation occurs, the sound development through subsequent stages is marred.

Among the other modifiers of orthodox psychoanalytic theory of personality are the important names of Fromm and Sullivan, which will be briefly dealt with here. Erich Fromm proposes that human nature is different from animals and there is no conflict between the two. Human's personality attempts to express human nature. Besides, human nature has the need for relatedness. It also has the need for transcendence, that is feeling separate from them, and rootedness, having belongingness. In addition it includes the realization of identity, to know oneself, and frame of reference, to perceive the world in a positive way.

He proposes no developmental stages of personality, but describes three types of parent-child relationship affective growth of personality. The first type he calls symbiotic relatedness, in which people experience relatedness and dependence on others. The second one he names as withdrawal-destructiveness indicating thereby indifference or negative relatedness with other people. The third type is love, in which there is a mutual respect and appreciation between people. He also propounds different kinds of personality orientations as a result of these interactions in parent-child relationship.

The receptive orientation, in which the person feels that good things are outside himself and he is a passive agent. This is a masochistic pattern and the characteristics he builds up are passivity, submissiveness and cowardice, because the person remains a passive party in symbiotic relationship with parents.

The exploitative orientation is the sadistic pattern of behaviour because of his dominant role in symbiotic relationship with parents. The person thinks of good things outside himself and wants to take them by force. The characteristics expressed are aggression conceit, stubbornness and seductiveness.

The hoarding orientation is the behaviour pattern learned by the child due to destructiveness with which he reacts to his parental withdrawal. This is the result of withdrawal-destructive type of relationship with parents. In this, the security is based on hoarding and storing what one has got rather than depending on the outside source. The characteristics are suspiciousness, stinginess, possessiveness and arrogance.

The marketing orientation stems from the withdrawal pattern of behaviour learned in parent-child relationship. The child learns to react to parental destructiveness in their withdrawal-destructive type relationship with him. He thinks as if he is a commodity and has a value for the market. The traits associated are opportunism, inconsistency, lack of principle and aimlessness etc.

The productive orientation is described as the behaviour pattern learned through a love relationship with parents. The person values himself and others as well, and experiences security. The characteristics are the wholesome aspect of all other orientations, *e.g.* modesty, adaptability, trust, confidence, pride, loyalty, open-mindedness, etc., the ideal of Fromm's concept.

Sullivan is another famous theorist in the line who explained personality in terms of individual's striving for maximum satisfaction with the minimum of insecurity. He recognized pursuit of satisfaction relating to biological needs such as food, water, air, sex and to excrete and described the pursuit of security in psychological sense. The biological and psychological characteristics were taken as power motive, according to him, coupled with the desire for physical closeness. He emphasized that both were rooted in the person and frustration of these led to insecurity.

Sullivan postulated dynamisms, which are relatively enduring configuration of energy and which manifest in interpersonal relationship of the individuals. He categorized three kinds of dynamisms, oral, lust and self. In oral dynamism the pleasure is in stimulation of the mouth and lust dynamism concerns sexual needs and stimulations. The self-dynamism, which is mainly unconscious is the most important of all in his view and is composed of person's experiences of approval and disapproval of other persons. The person behaves to avoid the insecurity caused by disapproval of others.

He recognised five stages of personality development starting from infancy, when the person is basically helpless. The mode of experiencing at this stage is prototaxis in which the child cannot differentiate between oneself and the external world. The defense associated with this mode of experiencing is dissociation which is similar to Freud's repression. The conflict arises at this stage of development because of child's feeling of helplessness and the nature of parental response. Parataxis marks the end of this infancy as the child starts maturing language capacity and can clearly differentiate oneself from others. Prototaxis symbols of good mother and bad mother depending on the experiences of approval and disapproval are formed. This leads to the emergence of self-dynamism as good bad and me me.

Childhood is the next stage of development considered by Sullivan which takes the child into the need for peer affiliation. At this stage, the child learns values of culture and society at wider level although the parents are still a strong influence on the child. If the relationship between parents-child is not disturbing the child learns the defense mechanism of sublimation and becomes compatible with the society and self-dynamism. One significant feature of this stage is 'malevolent transformation' which, if becomes strong, distorts the child's response to the affectionate expression of other people.

The Juvenile era is the time when the person picks up and tries out social values like competitiveness and cooperativeness, group identification and rejection etc. he does things he likes and learns to distinguish facts from fantasies. The mature mode of experiencing is the development of 'syntaxis'. This mode is the full appreciation of logical relatedness of the various symbols.

The person goes into pre-adolescence stage after juvenile phase, which is marked by the need for and intimate relationship with a peer of the same sex. The person gets into the genital, lust dynamism. Besides a change from egocentricism to love is found. The relationship brings in the feeling of equality and reciprocity.

The final phase is the adolescence, according to Sullivan, which requires coming to terms with the lust dynamism. This happens in two stages; firstly, the development of stable patterns of satisfying genital drives takes place, and then it grows into full inter-personal maturity. If the integration at this level is not attained, the person regresses to the juvenile era and becomes egocentric and can't make intimate relationship with others.

In sequence of his theory of personality development several organised patterns are proposed which have crucial significance as well. For example, he mentions the self-absorbed person who is prone to wishful thinking like infant; the incorrigible person, who is hostile and unfriendly as a result of unsuccessful competition at juvenile stage; the negative person, who has inferiority feelings; the non-integrative or psychopathic person who is inconsistent and irresponsible for want of full development; the ambition-ridden person, who has insatiable urge of competitiveness; the asocial person, who has his own values of his personal worth and is detached and lonely; the inadequate person who is passive and dependent on others; the homosexual person, who extends love to his own sex; and the chronically adolescent person, who always runs after an ideal and never attains it.

Trait Approach

Over 50 years ago trait concept and theory was introduced by Allport (1937), which implied biophysical characteristics as structure in personality. He distinguishes trait from habit; habit according to him, is narrow response to specific stimuli and the trait is the general "form of readiness for response". He also recognizes trait as guiding the course of behaviour. According to him trait is a product of the interaction between genetic and environmental factors. However, a distinction is drawn by Allport in the application of traits to personality. He thinks of two types of traits, individual and common. The individual traits vary from person to person and, therefore, comparability of individuals on these is of no significance. Characteristics like aggression, extraversion, impulsivity etc. vary amongst individuals as to range and style. He further mentions about measurable units as the universal aspects of individual traits and calls them common traits. Although he talks about common traits, he argues that these common traits do not correspond to the neuropsychic dispositions of individuals.

Allport, though initiated the concept of trait and its function in personality organisation, he did not accept that the same could be consistent in individuals. He cited the example of contradictory traits to be present in a person, like, extreme ascendance and extreme submission. For him traits vary in communality, independence, consistency and importance. The trait theorists later, on the other hand, developed a composite approach to establish the construct of personality traits as found on the basis of large number of evidence from experimental investigations and empirical studies by means of observations and questionnaires.

As referred to earlier in connection with nomothetic framework, a trait is regarded as any characteristic along which one individual differs from another in relatively enduring and consistent manner. Further, the trait theorists with the use of sophisticated statistical methodology, *e.g.*, factor analysis and discriminant function analysis etc. have isolated universal traits, which can be described and measured to a reliable extent. We shall mention here some of the famous factor theorists who strongly advocate the use of personality traits.

Cattell is one of the leaders in this area of personality study who has made the most extensive use of the factor-analytic technique. He has attempted to define mathematically the trait composition, moods, sentiments, instinctual drives, intelligence and creativity. He has come up with 16 unitary factors which he describes as 'source traits'. These traits are named as here under.

Table 17.1

A.	Reserved, detached, critical	Vs	Outgoing, warm-hearted, easy going
B.	Less intelligent, Concrete-thinking	Vs	More intelligent, abstract thinking, bright
C.	Affected by Feelings, emotionally less stable, easily upset (lower ego strength)	Vs	Emotionally stable, faces reality, calm (higher ego strength)
E.	Submissive, mild, conforming	Vs	Dominant independent, aggressive
F.	Serious, sober, prudent (desurgency)	Vs	Happy-go-lucky, lively, impulsive (surgency)

G.	Expedient, evades rules, feels few obligations (weaker super ego strength)	Vs	Conscientious, persevering, rule bound (stronger super super ego strength)
H.	Shy, restrained, diffident timid (threctia)	Vs	Venturesome, socially bold, uninhibited (parmia)
I.	Tough-minded, self-reliant, realistic, (harria)	Vs	Tender-minded dependent, over protected, sensitive (premsia)
L.	Trusting, adaptable, free from jealousy, easy to get on with (alaxia)	Vs	Suspicious self opinionated hard to fool (pretension)
M.	Practical, conventional, proper (praxernia)	Vs	Imaginative, wrapped up in inner urgencies, careless of practical matters (autia)
N.	Forth-right, artless sentimental (artlessness)	Vs	Shrewd, calculating, worldly (shrewdness)
O.	Placid, self-assured confident (untroubled adequacy)	Vs	Apprehensive, worrying, depressive (guilt proneness)
Q1.	Conservative, respecting traditions, ideas (conservatism)	Vs	Experimenting critical, liberal, free thinking (radicalism)
Q2.	Group-dependent, a joiner, sound follower (group adherence)	Vs	Self-sufficient, prefers own decision, (self sufficiency)
Q3.	Undisciplined self conflict, careless of social demands, follows own urges (low integration)	Vs	Controlled, sociality precise, following self-images (high self-concept integration)
Q4.	Relaxed, tranquil, unfrustrated (low ergic tension)	Vs	Tense, frustrated, driven, over-wrought (high ergic tension)

Cattell obtained several second-order factors from the intercorrelations of his primary factors, like anxiety vs adjustment, introversion Vs extraversion, tenderminded emotionality Vs alert poise, and subduedness Vs independence.

His 16-personality Factor test is very popular as providing items for the assessment of these traits. A personality profile can be plotted with the scores of the test. The test has been used in the educational and vocational guidance programmes very widely.

There are several other well-known American Psychologists who contributed to the factor-analytic theory of personality but we wont discuss them here, rather we shall mention one British theorist, Eysenck, who has made a distinct contribution in the establishment of personality construct and its measurement. Basically, he is a factor-analyst, but he has expounded a dimensional approach to personality study. He has evolved a broad explanatory theory and related it to physiological functioning and socialization. A massive body of researchers has grown up across countries to support his theory. The differences of emphasis, however, have been among the factorists themselves, but the impact of Eysenck's hypotheses has been quite considerable.

Eysenck believes that most of the variances in human personality can be accounted for by three dimensions or factors of N, neuroticism (emotional instability), E, extraversion and P psychoticism. These are relatively independent of each other. Those who score high on N are anxious, worrying, mostly depressed and overly emotional. Those who score high on E, they are sociable, impulsive, excitable, easygoing, responsive, active etc. The high P score hypothesizes to show that the scores are cold, impersonal, lacking sympathy, unemotional, anti-social and subject to paranoid delusions. He has empounded his theory and constructed personality-questionnaire after a good deal of hypothesis testing by means of items on inventories and self-report, objective tests like, body sway and manual dexterity, figural after-effects, flicker fusion test etc., and other experiments on conditionability of the individuals.

In order to establish his theory of personality he draws on the biological and genetic evidence as well as the hypothesis of cortical activity, excitation and inhibition, mediated by the ascending reticular activating system (ARAS). The balance between excitation and inhibition of the cortex affect the individual's reaction.

In the dimensional frame-work one could score high on N and low on E and can be described as introverted neurotics or can be said unstable introverts. He postulates that the group of individuals scoring high on these two dimensions are dysthymic. This category includes neurotics with high anxiety, obsessive-compulsive neurotics, phobics and reactive depressives. The other combination can be of high score on N and high on E, that is, extraverted neurotics or unstable extraverts. The group of people showing high score on these dimensions is characterized as hysterics and psychopaths. Again, one could score low on N and high or low on the other dimension and thus can present reaction of stable introvert or stable extrovert. His P, psychoticism dimension can also be used in conjunction with the others to explain personality reactions. He proposed that reactive and process schizophrenia in particular of the psychotic disorder can be better understood in this dimensional framework. The use of dimensional hypothesis has found greater support for the neurotic personality and disorders than psychotic ones so far. However, Eysenck and his colleagues argue that on the basis of the dimensional theory normals and neurotics, normals and psychotics, and psychotics and neurotics can be differentiated from one another.

Eysenck's theory of personality has been very significant specially from the clinical and psychiatric standpoint. It has helped in recognizing the use of objective means to study personality disorders. Further, the treatment of some psychiatric disorders or abnormalities has been influenced by his theory too. His personality inventories and questionnaire (Eysenck personality inventory and Eysenck personality questionnaire) are used extensively in the clinical and non-clinical settings in the U.K.

In this area of personality measurement, a personality inventory which has a different emphasis and is in use in many institutions and clinics needs to be brought in here. This personality inventory is called the Minnesota Multiphasic Personality Inventory (MMPI) which is one of the oldest and has served as a mother for the production of items for several later inventories. It has specifically been devised to appraise personality characteristics which have psychiatric significance and denote abnormalities. This inventory has been developed on the empirical basis but is factorially imperfect. There are nine clinical scales and three validation ones constructed to differentiate the control group (normal group) from the criterion groups of the hospitalized patients. The clinical scales are, hypochondriasis (Hs), depression (D), hysteria (Hy), psychopatic-deviation (Pd), masculinity-femininity (Mf), paranoia

(Pa), psychoesthenia (Pt), schizophrenia (Sc), and hypomania (Ha). The non-clinical scales to check the reliability of the inventory is lie scale (L), validity (F) and K (k). In scoring and interpreting the data, the weighted score is used adding K values. The characteristics show the reaction tendencies of the individuals and does not make the psychiatric diagnosis of diseases.

Humanistic Theory

Unrelated to trait theory, there are several personality theories which employ phenomenological principles to explain personality. The phenomenological theory embraces the experience as a vital function in personality. They stress that it is not the objective stimuli that matters, but the related experience which determines behaviour. Sharing this principle there are several theories but widely known are field theory, self theory and existential theory. We shall select self theory for our discussion which is also known as humanistic approach to personality study. This approach emphasises the place of man's potential for self-direction. Within this framework we find more than one theory, but all have one common meeting ground and that is, 'self' of the individual. The humanistic school rejects psychoanalytic as well as behaviouristic conceptions of personality as the human being is seen by those theories as helpless creature either dependent on internal instincts or external conditions. The individual according to humanistic approach, behaves as he perceives himself in relation to the world on the basis of his personal experiences.

The stress in the humanistic theory is on the present rather than past events of the childhood. The individual is always growing and striving towards self-actualisation. The positive nature of humans is considered important. We shall discuss here two of the theories of the humanistic psychology; Carl Roger's and Abraham Maslow's.

Rogers' Self-Theory

Rogers considers that all behaviour is goal directed and is influenced by physical, emotional and spiritual aims. The need for love and acceptance is basic and so is a need for self-regard in a person. A person's behaviour is shaped by his interactions with others. He also develops self-concept through interaction with others around and learns to evaluate himself in terms of criteria acquired from them. He learns that certain behaviour earns positive regard for him from parents and peers, and other actions result into ostracism. Self-concept conceptualizes behaviour in terms of unified process in which all the variables are intertwined and interacting at the same time. In plain terms it may be described as the function of total accumulation of values, judgments, attitudes, and goals, which constitute an individual's self-perception and self-evaluation.

The desires and urges are sometime not in consonance with a person's self-concept and conflict ensues. The conflict may be resolved by resorting to defense mechanisms, like rigidity, intellectualization, and autistic thinking. In the event of severe conflicts, maladaptive reactions are likely too. Conflict may also occur if there is a perception of discrepancy between the real self and the ideal self. The ideal self is the image of the person he would like to be. The lesser the gap between the real and the ideal, the better it is. Self-actualisation is not possible if these two selves are at odds. Rogers also posited two learned needs in every individual, positive regard and self-regard. The positive regard refers to the need of being accepted and loved by other people and the self-regard accounts for the values approved by the society which the individual possesses. A conflict between the two results into difficulties in individual's growth.

Rogers has developed his technique of therapy, which is known as "client-centred" or "non-directive counselling". His theory assumes that every individual has the capabilities and motivation to change and grow and the therapist's function is to facilitate progress toward this change. He has also developed a measure of self-concept.

Maslow's Self-Actualisation Theory

Maslow's hierarchy of needs we have already referred to under Motivation. Here we shall explain that he postulated his theory to denote full development of individuality by means of self-actualisation. According to him all parts of personality must be in complete harmony to achieve this self-actualisation or fulfilment. Maslow studied very successful persons in their lives and found that their talents and capabilities were fully used. He derived a list of values found in such experiences of fulfilment, as. wholeness, aliveness, self-sufficiency, uniqueness and the values of beauty, goodness and truth. The person strives towards the actualisation of inherent potentialities and also to satisfy needs ensuring physical and psychological survival. The actualizing tendency leads to the enhancement of life and is named as growth motivation. Survival tendency, on the other hand, ensures maintenance of life. When there is an obstruction in the fulfilment of these needs, conflict arises and defenses are used.

Self-actualised person has a characterise of realistic orientation. He shows acceptance of self, others and the natural world. His activities are spontaneous and task orientated not self-preoccupied. There are other features of a self actualized person which include privacy, independence, spirituality, identity with mankind and creativeness and non-conformism etc.

Rogers and Maslow, both have accepted self-actualization as the realization of inner potentiality and personality function as striving to obtain this goal. The characterization in values and experiences of self-actualised person are similar in both camps. However, the differences are significant too. Maslow maintains that self-actualisation can only be realised after the basic survival needs are met. Rogers, on the other hand, does not consider this as pre-requisite for self-actualisation.

Maslow regards a higher incidence of peak-experience among self-actualising individuals. These are, according to him, transient moments of near perfection and can occur in any activity. Rogers' self-actualisers do not come across optimum experiences so often. In his views self-actualisation is related to striving and achieving congruence between self and experience. Both theorists, however, seem to make a somewhat over generalized description of the personality and still lack empirical validity.

Social Learning Theory

Social learning theory of personality is another approach which warrants discussion in this context. Learning theory, however, can be treated as an explanation to bridge the gap between stimulus-response (S-R) concepts and psychoanalytic concepts. Dollard & Miller (1950) have presented a theory which attempts to relate psycho-analytic thinking and learning theories in the process of personality development.

The Dollard and Miller theory makes use of the concept of drive, cue, response and reinforcement from the learning approach. Drive impels the organism to activity, cues enables them to discriminate among stimuli and direct behaviour, response is made as reinforced, as we have discussed under learning. The different aspects of personality that we encounter are the results of learning. We have also mentioned earlier the secondary drives and secondary reinforcers and their nature and functions. They all influence development of the individual. Along with these processes are used the concept of conflicts and stages of development from the psycho-analytic theory with emphasis on the early training situations of feeding, cleanliness, sex training and anger-anxiety conflicts. Conflicts assuming severity produce neurotic reactions.

Some psychologists think that there is nothing new as far as constructs are concerned in the learning theory of personality. According to them, traditional laws of learning are applied to the traditional theory of Freudian psycho-analysis, particularly repression and phobia. But to some the emphasis is still different in these two sets of theories, learning and psychoanalysis; the first bases the removal of symptoms on deconditioning and relearning, and the second capitalises on dealing with the unconscious processes.

There is another view of social learning theory put forward by Bandura (1973) & Mischell (1973) currently influencing the personality theory. This leaning theory viewpoint rejects the Freudian concepts outright and uses, instead, social factors and cognitive reactions as well as the role of observational model in determining human behaviour. The individual develops in the varying social conditions and learns behaviour patterns through direct experience. His behaviour is influenced by reward and punishment, but some responses are acquired by indirect processes as well. He also learns by observing the other person do something without having direct experience, and makes note of the consequences of other person's action. The individual also uses memory of experiences and coded observations made by him and by other person(s).

The social theorists assume that person's own behaviour produces reinforcement. The individual stores a large number of learned behaviour, but picks out specific one for the specific situation in order to secure reinforcement. Thus reinforcement, according to them, controls the expression of learned behaviour.

It may be direct or vicarious, that is through the observation of some one else. Further, it may be self-administered while the person praises or reproaches himself.

The social theorists believe in studying the individual's behaviour patterns and cognitive activities in relation to the specific conditions that are operating at the time. Hence, the situation evokes and also modifies the behaviour. The emphasis is not on the individual's structure of personality, like his traits or underlying motives, but on how he behaves in relationship with the conditions present.

A Brief Critique of Personality Theories

Psychoanalytic theories are generally charged with dealing in untestable hypothesis which can not be verified objectively. There is a great deal of subjectivity involved in interpreting personality in psychoanalytic terms. They lack precision and are not amenable to quantification and prediction. There is too much emphasis on urges and instinctual forces acting on the individual and excessive control of past over his present behaviour, as if childhood experiences determine personality forever. The neo-Freudians did modify the basic approach and emphasized the role of socializing process, still the methodology of studies adopted are far from objective and some of the concepts and constructs employed to explain human behaviour and personality are yet to be established.

The trait theory draws on objective methods in assessing personality and uses statistical techniques to refine the instrument or measure for use. Even then the predictive validity or power of prognostication of these tests is very low. The major criticism that this approach faces is in regard to its inefficiency of making prediction about individual's behaviour from one situation to another. It is relatively more successful in differentiating one group of individuals from another, like normal from psychotics or neurotics, than saying positively about one person when he is going to behave and in what way. Further, there is a disagreement among trait theorists about the nature and number of primary traits. Another difficulty is that the trait approach counts on inadequate interaction principle between the individual and the situational influence, for many actions may be dependent on the situation. Last but not the least, the trait theorists are criticised for the isolated traits that they come up with without showing the organisation of traits within the personality.

Humanistic theory faces criticism that there is a lack of theory in it. It is rather an approach or a framework than a theory, as considered by many psychologists. It does not stand sufficient empirical tests because the data are subjective experiences. However, interests in modern times have been directed towards the subjective aspects of life which have so far been neglected.

Social learning theory as compared with other approaches has made significant contribution to personality theory and also to clinical psychology. It has emphasised the environmental variables which evoke specific behaviour. Developed in the laboratory conditions it has an aura of objectivity and its principles and concepts can be subjected to empirical test. The conditions that control our action and reaction and the changes and modifications that can be brought about by learning principles are open to examination.

The social learning theory, on the other hand, is criticised for exaggerating the significance of situational factors at the cost of individual differences. The theorists do not show interest in innate differences and characteristics of the individual. The critics hold that the experimental methods used in the study measuring differences in behaviour in different situations are particularly sensitive to the impact of situational variables.

None of the personality theories examined here is fool-proof and fully comprehensive. Psychoanalytic and humanistic theories suffer from the lack of objectivity and scientific methodology and trait and social learning theories, although use scientific methodology, are inadequate to reveal the full picture of the individual.

Assessment of Personality

Personality assessment is done in various life situations with a view to understanding, improving and predicting behaviour of the individual. Education uses to help students to develop all round. Industry utilizes it to select the right person for the right job and to increase work and workers efficiency. So do the army, business firms etc. to serve their needs. Clinical psychologists and psychiatrists use personality assessment for diagnosing and providing help to the individuals who need it in the area of mental health. Besides, researchers are interested too in knowing personality-structure and function and so on. We shall mention here some of the methods employed in personality assessment.

Observation and interview are the oldest techniques used in this area. The observers observe and make notes of what the individual does or says or as the reacts in a specified situation. They summarize their observations on a rating scale or in a qualitative form. When they use the rating scale, they grade the behaviour from very high to very low or in certain defined order. The same gradation can be expressed in the numerical form as well, like, 1,2,3,4, etc. In the interview situation, apart from observation, the interviewer asks questions and gets answers. Through the medium of these answers and modes of answering, the interviewer infers about the personality characteristics of the interviewe. The interview situation is a face-to-face interpersonal situation and is very elastic and can be easily adjusted to the need and demand of the situation.

The interview can be classified along a continuum from the structured to the unstructured one. In the former, the kind and sequence of questions and topic are pre-determined. The nature of questions and responses is objectified to a greater degree beforehand. Whereas in the latter, the topics are picked up in the process of interviewing as they arise. Usually, the structured interview shows higher reliability than the unstructured one, but the latter is much more revealing than the former. However, the interview technique, on the whole, falls short of the two standard criteria of assessment, reliability and validity, as compared with the objective standard tests of abilities.

Situational tests are also employed in personality assessment by some agencies and institutions. The purpose of this test is to see the reactions of the individual in a specific situation. Situational tests were used by the American War Department, known as office of Strategic Services (OSS) during the World War II. This was designed to assess the group participation in problem solving and natural leadership. The men were taken in a group of four to seven to a brook, which was flowing extremely fast and could not allow anything to hold in a place at the bottom The men were required to transport some materials to the other side of the stream. In order to solve the problem the men had to cooperate effectively and some people had to emerge as leaders to see the project executed. The situational tests are used these days also with rating scales and employed by the observers to assess the personality characteristics in question. Reliability of such ratings is again a problem because different observers select different points and interpret the reactions differently in terms of their own frame of reference.

Inventories and Questionnaires popularly called as personality tests are those which contain statements, questions or adjectives that describe the way a person feels, thinks and does something. These statements describe personality characteristics and the person who takes the test checks or answers various items to show his own reactions. The statements or items have assigned values or marks according to their appropriateness of presence or absence and the score is calculated in terms of those marks obtained by the individual on the test. The item of the test are compiled, selected and thoroughly validated by means of statistical treatment. The trait or factor analytic approach discussed earlier, posits on the validation, purification and refinement of the items and the test as a whole. One obvious advantage of these personality tests and inventories is the reliability of the measures which is significantly high and shows consistency of measurement over other techniques. The validity of these tools, predictive validity in particular, is not that good, because more than one factor determine the individual's behaviour in a situation, and all those factors can not be controlled. Another criticism directed towards these inventories is that subjects can fake the responses due to social desirability or lack of co-operation etc., which vitiate the results. The names of personality inventories, such as, 16PF test or E.P.Q, or M.M.P.I. etc. stated earlier are the examples of this method.

Projective techniques are other famous methods of personality Investigation which are referred to in the psychological literature. As the name indicates the investigator is interested in finding out the individual's motives, attitudes, fantasies, apprehensions and conflicts etc. indirectly through these tests. The subject projects outside his own attributes and characteristics on other person, objects and situations. The salient feature of these projective tests is that the stimuli presented to the subject are unstructured and hazy and, therefore, evokes him to make up and structure the responses from his own personal materials. Another important feature is that the subject projects his unconscious and less conscious aspect of personality because of the indirect and vague stimulus situation. The psycho-dynamic approach banking on the unconscious conflict of individuals supports the use of this indirect means of projective tests.

There are a number of projective tests available in the field like, sentence-completion test, and word association test etc. but we shall mention here a few widely used and famous ones.

Rorschach Inkblot Test

This test was developed by a Swiss psychiatrist, Herman Rosharch, in the 1920s. This consists of 10 cards containing ink blots, some coloured and some black-white. The cards are shown to the subject one at a time in prescribed manner, and the subject is instructed to report whatever he sees on the card and everything the inkblot could look like or bring to his mind. The subjects' responses are scored and analysed under three categories : (1) location which part, small or entire blot, involved, (2) determinant, shapes, colours texture etc, involved, (3) content responses representing object, things, anatomy etc. there is an elaborate system of scoring which produces quantitative results but interpretation of those responses is done qualitatively.

Thematic Apperception Test (T.A.T)

This is another kind of projective test, developed by Murray (1930s) and whose reference we have already given under Motivation. This test consists of 20 picture cards with variation for male and female subjects, which depicts unstructured situation. The subject is required to imagine a story on each of these pictures, which should reflect the past that led to the present situation. The present describing what is happening and the future that would come out of the story. This requires apperception. That is perception based on past experience of the subject. The stories are analysed in terms of needs, press, theme and outcome. The hero of the story is significant because the subject identifies himself with that character and project own attitudes through him.

Evaluation of projective technique presents the same problem of poor reliability and validity. The Rorschach test in particular has been a victim of such evaluation by the standard criteria of reliability and validity. The clinician's judgment plays a major part in these qualitative interpretations of the test results and, therefore, reduces its scientific value. In spite of intensive researches, the Rorschach test does not enjoy the same status as it used to.

The T.A.T. on the other hand does better than the Rorschach. The scoring system has been modified and it measures a few things like achievement motive etc. with a degree of reliability. But its reliability, on the whole, compared with other inventories is very low. Validity, on the other hand, is also poor. However, the use of T.A.T. provides clues for further investigation into personal conflicts etc. and has been found very helpful by clinicians.

Bibliography

Allport, G.W. (1937). Functional Autonomy of Motives. Amer. J. Psychat., 50, 141 -145.

Allport, G.W. and Postman (1947). The psychology of rumours. New York : Holt.

Anderson, B. (1953). The effect of injections of Hypertonic Nacl-Solutions into different parts of the hypotha lamous of goat. *Acta Psychologica, Scandinavica* 28, 188-201.

Atkinson, R.A., and Shiffrin, R.M. (1971). The Control of Short Term Memory. *Scientific American* 224, 82-90.

Ausubel, D.P. (1966a). Meaningful reception learning and the acquisition of concepts. In H.J. Klausmeir and C.W. Harris (eds.) Analysis of Concept Learning. New York : Academic Press.

Ausubel, D.P., and Fitzerald, D. (1962). Organizer, general background and antecetent learning variables in sequential verbal learning. *J. Educ. Psychol.* 53, 243-249.

Bandura, A.L. (1971). Social Learning Theory. New York : General Learning Press.

Bandura, A.L. (1973). Aggression : A Social Learning Analysis. Englewood Cliffs. N.J. Prentice Hall.

Barker, R.G., Dembo, T., and Lewin, K. (1941). Frustration and regression : An experiment with young children. University of Iowa Studies in Child Welfare, 18.

Berlyne, D.E. (1955). The arousal and satiation of perceptual curiousity in the rat. *J.Comp Physiol. Psychol.* 48, 238-246.

Bexton, W. H., Heron, W., and Scott, T.H. (1954). Effects of decreased variation in the environment. *Cand.J. Psychol.* 8, 70-76.

Bijou, S. W. (1943). A study of experimental neurosis in the rat by the conditioned response technique. *J. Comp. Psychol.* 36, 1- 20

Broadbent, D.E. (1971). A reformulation of the Yerkes—Dodson Law. *British J. Math. Stat. Psychol.* 18, 145-157.

Brown, J.S. (1961). The motivation of behaviour. NewYork : McGraw Hill.

Bruner, J.S. (1956). Social Psychology and Perception. In E.E. Maccoby, T. M . Newcomb, and E.L Hartley (eds. Readings in social psychology (3rd ed.), New York : Holt.

Bruner, J.S. (1961). The act of discovery. Harvard Educational Review, 31, 21-32.

Collins, A.M. and Quillan, M.R. (1972). How to make a language user. In Tulbig, E. and Donaldson, W. (eds), Organisation of Memory, N.Y. Academic Press.

Cook, S.W. (1939). Production of experimental neurosis in the whit rat. Psychomatic Medicine 1, 293-308.

Crutchfield, R.S. and Covington M.U. (1965). Programmed instruction and creativity, No. 4, 1-2, 8-10.

Darwin, C. (1872). The expression of emotions in man and animals. University of Chicago Press, Chicago Press.

Dobelle, W. H. Mladejovsky, M.G. and Girvin, J.P. (1974). Artificial vision for the blind. Electrical stimulation of visual cortex offers hope for a functional prothessis. *Science* 183.

Dollard, J., and Miller, N.E. (1950). Personality and Psychotherapy : An analysis in terms of learning, thinking and culture. New York : McGraw Hill.

Dollard, J., Miller, N.E., Doob, L.W., Mowrer, O.H. and Sears, R.R. (1939). Frustration and aggression. New Haven, Conn : Yale University Press, 70.

Duffy, E. (1957). The Psychological significance of the concept of arousal or activation. *Psychol. Review*. See Smith and Duffy (1955). J. *Comparative as Physiological Psychology*, 48.

Ebbinghaus, H. (1913). Memory. New York : Teachers College, Columbia University.

Elwell, J.L., and Grindley, G.C. (1938). The effect of knowledge of results on learning and performance. *British J. Psychol.*

Estes, W.K. (1960). Learning theory and the new "mental chemistry". *Psychol. Rev.* 67, 207-223.

Evienenmeyer-Kimling, L. an Jarvik, L.F. (1963). Genetics and intelligence : *A review. Science*, 142.

Fechner, G. (1860). Elements of Psychophysics (trans. By H.E. Adler). New York : Holt Rinehart and Winston, 1966.

Festinger, L.A. (1954). Motivations leading to social behaviour. In M.R. Jones (Ed). Nebraska symposium on motivation. Univ. of Nebraska Press.

French, G.M. and Harlow, H.F. (1962). Variability of delayed reaction performance in normal and brain damaged rhesus monkeys. J. *Neurophysiology*, 25: 585-99.

Freud, S. (1914). Psychopathology of everyday life. New York : Macmilan.

Galanter, E. (1962). Contemporary psychophysics. In Brown R. and others (eds). New directions in psychology. N.Y. : Holt Rinehart and Winston.

Gerrad, R.W. (1953). What is memory? Scientific American, Sept. 118-126.

Goldstein, K. and Scheere, M. (1941). Abstract and concrete behaviour : An experimental study with special tests. *Psychol. Monogr*. 53, 2, Whole No. 239.

Guilford, J.P. (1967). The nature of human intelligence. N.Y. : Mcgraw Hill.

Halas, E.S., James, R.L., Knutson, C. (1962). An attempt at classical conditioning in the planarian. *J. Comp. Physiol*. 55, 969-971.

Hantry, A.L., Keith-Lee, P. and Morton, W.D. (1964). Planaria: Memory transfer through cannibalism reexamined. *Science*. 146, 274-275.

Harlow, H.F. (1949). The formation of learning sets. *Psychol. Rev*. 56, 51-65.

Harlow, H.F. (1958). The nature of love. *American Psychologist*, 13.

Harlow, H.F. and Harlow, M.K. (1962). Social deprivation in monkeys. *Scientific Americans*, 207.

Hart, J. T. (1965). Memory and the feeling-of-knowing experience. *J. Educ. Psychol*. 56, 208-216

Heidbreder, E. (1947). The attainment of concepts III. *The problem journal of Psychology*, 24, 93-138.

Helson, H., and Bevan, W. (eds) (1967). Contemporary approaches to Psychology princeton, N.J.: D. Van Nostrand.

Heron, W., Doane, B.K., and Scott, T.H. (1956). Visual disturbances after prolonged perceptual isolation. *Canadian Journal of Psychology*, 10 : 13-16.

Herz, M.J., Peeke, H.V.S and Wyers, E.J. (1966). Amnesic effects of ether and electro convulsive shock in mice. *Psychonomic Science*, 4, 375-376.

Hilgard, E.R., Atkinson, R.C., and Atkinson, R. (1975). Introduction to Psychology. Harcourt Brace, Jovanovich Inc.

Hubel, D.H., and Wiesel, T.N. (1965). Receptive fields and functional architecture in two non-striate visual areas of the cat. *Journal of Neurophysiology*.

Hull, C.L. (1943). Principles of behaviour. New York : Appliton-Century-Crofts.

Izard, C.E and Nunnaly, J.C. (1965). Evaluative responses to Affectively positive and negative facial photographs : Factor structure and content validity. *J. Educ. Psychol. Mesm.* 25, 1061-1071.

Jarvik, L.F. (1963). See Erlenmeyer-Kimling, and Jarvik, L.F. (1963).

Kohler, W. (1925). The mentality of apes. New York : Harcourt Brace Jovanovich.

Kretshmer, E. (1925). Physique and character. New York : Harcourt Brace World.

Land, E.H. (1959). Colour vision and the natural Image. *Proc. Nat. Acad.* Sci., 45 Part I, 115-124, 636-44.

Leeper, R. W. (1948). A motivational theory of emotion to replace emotion as a disorganised response. *Psychol. Rev.* 55.

Lewin, K. (1935). A dynamic theory of personality. New York : McGraw Hill.

Lorenz, K. (1966). On aggression. New York : Harcourt Brace Jovanvich.

Luria, A.R. (1968). The mind of mnemonist. New York : Basic Books.

Maier , N.R.F. (1949). Reasoning in white rats. *Comp. Pschol. Monogr.* No. 6, 23.

Malmo, R.B. (1959). Activation: A neuro-Physiological Dimension. *Psychol. Review.* 66.

Maslow, A.H. (1954,1970). Motivation & Personality. New York : Harper.

McCleary, R.A. and Moore, R.Y. (1965). Subcortical mechanisms of behaviour. New York : Basic Books

McConnell, R.A. (1969). ESP and Credibility in Science. *American Psychologist*, 24: 531-38.

McNemar, Q. (1942). The revision of Stanford - Binet Scale, Boston : Houghton Miffin.

Mead, M. (1939). Sex and temperament in from the South Seas. New York : Morrow.

Miller, G.A, Glanter, E., and Primbram, K.H. (1960). Plans and the structure of behaviour. New York : Holt.

Miller, N.E. (1959). Liberalization of basic S-R concepts : Extensions of conflict behaviour, motivation and social learning. In S. Koch (Ed.) Psychology : A study of science, Vol. 2., New York : McGraw Hill 196-292.

Miller, N.E. and Dollard, J. (1941). Social Learning and Imitation. New Haven, Conn : Yale Univ. Press.

Milner, B. (1966). Neuropsychological evidence of differing memory processes. Abst. from symposium. *Proc. 18th Int. Cong. Pschol.*, Moscow.

Milner, B. (1966). Some effects of frontal lobectomy in man. In Warren, J.M. and Akert, K. (eds) the frontal granular cortex and behaviour New York : McGraw Hill.

Mischel, W. (1973). Toward a cogtnitive social learning reconceptualization of personality. Psychlo Review, 80, 252-83.

Moskowitz, M.J. (1959). Running wheel activity of the white rat as a function of combined food and water deprivation. *J. Com. Physiol. Psychol*. 52. 621-625.

Mowrer, O.H. (1940). An experimental analogue of 'regression'with incidental observation on reaction formation. *J Abnorm. Soc. Psychol.* 35, 56-87.

Murray, H.A. (1938). Explorations in personality. New York : Oxford Univ. Press.

Newell, A., Shaw, J.C, and Simon, H.A. (1958). Elements of a theory of human problem solving. *Psychol. Rev.* 65, 151-166.

Osgood, C.E. (1967). Semantic differential technique in the comparative study of cultures. In Jakobovits, L.A and Miron, M.S. (eds) Readings in the psychology of language. Englewood Cliff, N.J. Prentice Hall.

Paivio, A. (1971). Imagery and Verbal Process. New York : Holt, Rinehart and Winston.

Paschal, F.C. (1941). The trend of theories of attention. *Psychol. Rev.* 48, 383-403.

Penfield, W. (1969). Consciousness, memory, and man's conditioned reflexes. In Pribram, K.H. (ed). On the Biology of learning. NewYork Harcourt Brace Jovanovich, 49.

Perlmuter, L.C. (1966). Effect of CS manipulations on the conditioned eyelid respose : Compounding generalization, the inter-CS-interval and pre-exposure. *Psych. Mongr. Suppl*. 1, 271-286.

Peterson, L.R and Peterson, M.J. (1959). Short-term retention of individual verbal items. *Journal of experimental Psychology*. 30, 93-113.

Petrie, A. (1967). Individuality in pain and suffering. Chicago : University of Chicago Press.

Pfaffman, C. (1964). Taste, its sensory and motivating properties. *American Scientist*, 52, 187-206.

Pieron, H. (1929). Principles of experimental psychology. NewYork : Harcourt Brace.

Pribram, K.H. (1969). The neurophysiology of remembering. Scientific American-220.SS.

Robinson, F.P. (1961). Effective study (rev. ed.), New York : Harper.

Rozin, P. and Kalat, J.W. (1971). Thirst-brain control of water balance. *American Scientist*. 59 : 408.

Sears, R.R. (1936). Experimental study of projection. I. Attribution of traits. *J. Soc. Psychol.* 7, 151-163.

Seligman, M.E.P. (1975). Helplessness. San Fransisco : Freeman.

Sheldon, W.H., Stevens, S.S., and Tucker, W.B. (1940). The varieties of human physique. New York : Harper.

Simon, H.A. and Newell, A. (1960). Information processing in computer and man. American Scientist, 52, 281-300.

Skinner, B.F. (1953). Science and Human Behaviour. New York : Macmillan.

Skodak, M., and Skeels, H.M. (1949). A final follow up of one hundred adopted children. *J. Genet. Psychol*. 75.

Smith, S.M., Brown, H.O., Tolman J.E.P., Goodman, L.S. (1947). The lack of cerebral effects of d-tubocurarine. *Anesthesiology*., 8, 1-14.

Soloman, P. and Mendelson, J. (1962). Hallucination in sensory deprivation. In L.J. West (ed.), Hallucination. Grune Stratton : New York.

Spearman, C. (1927). Abilities of man. New York : MacMillan.

Sperling, G. (1960). The information available in brief visual presentations. Psychological Monograph - 74, Whole No. 498.

Sperry, R.W. (1970). Perception in the absence of neocortical commissurisers In perception and its disorders. Res. Pub. A.R.N.M.D. Vol. 48.

Stacey, C.L. and De Martino, M.F. (eds) (1963). Understanding human motivation Cleveland : Howard Alto.

Thorndike, E. L. (1911). Animal intelligence : An experimental study of the association process in animals. In N.L. Munn, L.D. Fernand and Peter S . Fernold. Introduction to Psychology (2nd ed.) 1969, Houshton Miffin, Boston.

Thurstone, L.L. and Thurstone T.G. (1941). Factorial studies of intelligence. *Psychometric monogr*. No. 2, Chicago : Univ. Chicago Press.

Tolman, E.C. (1949). There is more than one kind of learning. *Psychol. Rev*. 56, 144-155.

Van Laurick Goodall, J. (1967). Mother -Offspring relationship in free ranging chimpanzees. In D. Morris (ed) Primate ethology. London : Werdenfeld and Nicholas.

Verma, R.M. (1985). Clinical Psychology : Theory and Practice, Motilal Banarsi Das, Delhi.

Warden , C. J. (1931). Animal motivation : Experimental studies in the albino rat. NewYork : Columbia Univ. Press.

Watson, J.B. (1930). Behaviourism. NewYork : W.W. Norton.

Weld, H.P. (1954). Legal Psychology : The psychology of testimony. In F.L. Marcuse (Ed.) Areas of Psychology. New York : Harper.

Wever, E.G. (1949). Theory of Learning, NewYork : Wiley.

White, R.W. (1964). The abnormal personality. New York : Ronald Press.

Wulf, F. (1938). Tenderness in figural variation.In W. D. Ellis (ed). *A source book of Gestalt Psychology*. New York : Harcourt Brace.

Zeigarnik, B. (1927). In Introduction to psychology, Norman L. Munn, L. Dodge Fernald and Peter S. Fernald, Houghton Miffin, Boston.

Zubek, J.P. (1969). Sensory deprivation : Fifteen years of research. New York : Appleton-Century-Croft.

Index